MORE JOEL ON SOFTWARE

Further Thoughts on
Diverse and Occasionally
Related Matters That
Will Prove of Interest
to Software Developers,
Designers, and Managers,
and to Those Who,
Whether by Good Fortune
or Ill Luck, Work with Them
in Some Capacity

Joel Spolsky

Apress®

More Joel on Software: Further Thoughts on Diverse and Occasionally Related Matters That Will Prove of Interest to Software Developers, Designers, and Managers, and to Those Who, Whether by Good Fortune or Ill Luck, Work with Them in Some Capacity

ISBN-13 (paperback): 978-1-4302-0987-4

ISBN-13 (electronic): 978-1-4302-0988-1

Printed and bound in the United States of America 9 8 7 6 5 4 3 2 1

Trademarked names may appear in this book. Rather than use a trademark symbol with every occurrence of a trademarked name, we use the names only in an editorial fashion and to the benefit of the trademark owner, with no intention of infringement of the trademark.

Lead Editor: Jeffrey Pepper
Editorial Board: Clay Andres, Steve Anglin, Ewan Buckingham, Tony Campbell, Gary Cornell, Jonathan Gennick, Matthew Moodie, Joseph Ottinger, Jeffrey Pepper, Frank Pohlmann, Ben Renow-Clarke, Dominic Shakeshaft, Matt Wade, Tom Welsh
Associate Publisher | Project Manager: Grace Wong
Senior Copy Editor: Ami Knox
Associate Production Director: Kari Brooks-Copony
Production Manager: Kelly Winquist
Compositor: Dina Quan
Proofreader: April Eddy
Indexer: Broccoli Information Management
Artist: April Milne
Cover Designer: Kurt Krames
Manufacturing Director: Tom Debolski

Distributed to the book trade worldwide by Springer-Verlag New York, Inc., 233 Spring Street, 6th Floor, New York, NY 10013. Phone 1-800-SPRINGER, fax 201-348-4505, e-mail orders-ny@springer-sbm.com, or visit http://www.springeronline.com.

For information on translations, please contact Apress directly at 2855 Telegraph Avenue, Suite 600, Berkeley, CA 94705. Phone 510-549-5930, fax 510-549-5939, e-mail info@apress.com, or visit http://www.apress.com.

Apress and friends of ED books may be purchased in bulk for academic, corporate, or promotional use. eBook versions and licenses are also available for most titles. For more information, reference our Special Bulk Sales–eBook Licensing web page at http://www.apress.com/info/bulksales.

The information in this book is distributed on an "as is" basis, without warranty. Although every precaution has been taken in the preparation of this work, neither the author(s) nor Apress shall have any liability to any person or entity with respect to any loss or damage caused or alleged to be caused directly or indirectly by the information contained in this work.

For Jared,

כי אהבת נפשו, אהבו

CONTENTS

JOEL, APRESS, BLOGS, AND BLOOKS

"A long time ago in a galaxy far, far away . . ." Well, actually it was late in 2000, during Apress's first full year of operation. We were a tiny little computer book publisher then, with little name recognition, and we planned to publish only a handful of books that year—roughly as many books for that whole year as Apress now publishes in a single month.

I was learning the hard way about how to be a publisher and probably spending way too much time looking at web sites and programming than I should have in response to that. Anyway, one day I came across this web site called *Joel on Software*, which was run by a guy with strong opinions and an unusual, clever writing style, along with a willingness to take on the conventional wisdom. In particular, he was writing this ongoing series about how bad most user interfaces were—mostly because programmers by and large knew, as Joel and I would say, using the same Yiddish-derived NYC vernacular that we both share, "bupkis" about what users really want. And I, like many, was hooked both by the series and the occasional random essay that Joel wrote.

And then I had this epiphany: I'm a publisher, I like reading his stuff, why not turn it into a book? I wrote Joel, introduced myself, and though he was initially skeptical, I somehow convinced him that if he would turn the user interface essays into a book, people would buy tons of them and he and I would make lots and lots of money. (Of course, this was long before FogBugz became the success it is and Joel started to command serious dollars as a coveted speaker—but then we were both younger and, yes, a whole lot poorer in those days.)

Anyway, Joel added some new content to make the book more appealing and, I thought, more marketable, and suddenly, Apress had to figure out how to publish its first full-color book. The result, *User Interface Design for Programmers*, officially appeared on June 21, 2001, and is now acknowledged as the first "blook" ever. Somewhat shockingly to the computer book industry and me, it became a runaway best seller by the standard of the times. By the way, it is still in print, still selling very well, and still worth reading. (Although, speaking as your publisher and not as your friend, Joel, how 'bout that revision?)

Anyway, some would (now) argue that *User Interface Design for Programmers* isn't a pure blook because the addition of "too much" new material that was not on Joel's web site makes it a hybrid—as I suppose befits its pioneering status.

But a few years later, Joel on Software was the most popular blog for programmers in the world because Joel of course had kept on writing these amazingly interesting essays—perhaps the most famous being the classic "How Microsoft Lost the API War," which I know literally turned parts of Microsoft's development upside down.

And then I had yet another epiphany: let's collect the best of these essays and publish them with no substantial new content other than an occasional foreword where Joel thought it appropriate. And even though 98 percent of the material in the book that became *Joel on Software* was available on the Web, and people thought Apress was nuts for publishing it in late 2004, the book has gone through ten printings and remains a best-selling book today.

Because, it still seems, when it comes to digesting the chocolate truffle that is the typical Joel essay, print is still more pleasurable for many than a browser.

But Joel hasn't stopped thinking hard about what it takes to program well or hire good programmers, nor has he stopped challenging the conventional wisdom with his insights. So I convinced him the time was right for a sequel that collected the "best of Joel" published since the first *Joel* came out in late 2004.

And so you have in your hands the second collection of Joel's insights, occasional random thoughts, and yes, occasional rants—all encased in the sparkling prose that Joel is known for. And even though nothing has been done to his writing save for some minor copy editing, you do have the latest "best of Joel" in a very high-contrast form compared to your screen or even your Kindle, known now as a "blook." (And Joel, I obviously hope you will enjoy them as much as you did the ones in the first collection.)

This book, like the first, has a somewhat unusual cover and subtitle. This is because Joel and I are both bibliophiles (OK, Joel is a bibliophile; I'm a bibliomaniac) and we are both very fond of the kind of thing the classic book printers of the 17th and 18th centuries did to liven up their books—and their titles. In the case of the first *Joel on Software* covers, we paid homage to Burton's *Anatomy of Melancholy*; here we pay homage to Hobbes's *The Leviathan* and the famous frontispiece where the giant is made up of lots of individuals, because both Joel and I felt this was not a bad metaphor for how programming is done: individuals building something gigantic—but individuals are the key.

Finally, on a more personal note: In spite of his now substantial fame, Joel remains a down-to-earth kind of guy, or again in our common vernacular, a true mensch and someone I am proud to have as a close friend.

Gary Cornell
Cofounder, Apress

ABOUT THE AUTHOR

Joel Spolsky is a globally recognized expert on the software development process. His web site, *Joel on Software* (www.joelonsoftware.com), is popular with software developers around the world and has been translated into over 30 languages. As the founder of Fog Creek Software in New York City, he created FogBugz, a popular project management system for software teams. Joel has worked at Microsoft, where, as a member of the Excel team, he designed VBA, and at Juno Online Services, developing an Internet client used by millions. He has written three previous books: *User Interface Design for Programmers* (Apress, 2001), *Joel on Software* (Apress, 2004), and *Smart and Gets Things Done* (Apress, 2007), and is the editor of *The Best Software Writing I* (Apress, 2005). Joel holds a BS from Yale in computer science. He served in the Israeli Defense Forces as a paratrooper, and was one of the founders of Kibbutz Hanaton.

part one

Managing People

one

MY FIRST BILLG REVIEW

Friday, June 16, 2006

In the olden days, Excel had a very awkward programming language without a name. "Excel Macros," we called it. It was a severely dysfunctional programming language without variables (you had to store values in cells on a worksheet), without locals, without subroutine calls: in short, it was almost completely unmaintainable. It had advanced features like "Goto," but the labels were actually physically invisible.

The only thing that made it appear reasonable was that it looked great compared to Lotus macros, which were nothing more than a sequence of keystrokes entered as a long string into a worksheet cell.

On June 17, 1991, I started working for Microsoft on the Excel team. My title was Program Manager. I was supposed to come up with a solution to this problem. The implication was that the solution would have something to do with the Basic programming language.

Basic? Yech!

I spent some time negotiating with various development groups. Visual Basic 1.0 had just come out, and it was pretty friggin' cool. There was a misguided effort underway with the code name MacroMan, and another effort to make Object-Oriented Basic code-named Silver. The Silver team was told that they had one client for their product: Excel. The marketing manager for Silver, Bob Wyman, yes, that Bob Wyman, had only one person he had to sell his technology to: me.

MacroMan was, as I said, misguided, and it took some persuading, but it was eventually shut down. The Excel team convinced the Basic team that what we really needed was some kind of Visual Basic for Excel. I managed to get four pet features added to Basic. I got them to add Variants, a union data type that could hold any other type, because otherwise you couldn't store the contents of a spreadsheet cell in a variable without a switch statement. I got them to add late binding, which became known as IDispatch, a.k.a. COM Automation, because the original design for Silver required a deep understanding of type systems that the kinds of people who program macros don't care about. And I got two pet syntactic features into the language: For Each, stolen from csh, and With, stolen from Pascal.

Then I sat down to write the Excel Basic spec, a huge document that grew to hundreds of pages. I think it was 500 pages by the time it was done. ("Waterfall," you snicker. Yeah, yeah, shut up.)

In those days, we used to have these things called BillG reviews. Basically, every major important feature got reviewed by Bill Gates. I was told to send a copy of my spec to his office in preparation for the review. It was basically one ream of laser-printed paper.

I rushed to get the spec printed and sent it over to his office.

Later that day, I had some time, so I started working on figuring out if Basic had enough date and time functions to do all the things you could do in Excel.

In most modern programming environments, dates are stored as real numbers. The integer part of the number is the number of days since some agreed-upon date in the past, called the epoch. In Excel, today's date, June 16, 2006, is stored as 38884, counting days where January 1, 1900, is 1.

I started working through the various date and time functions in Basic and the date and time functions in Excel, trying things out, when I noticed something strange in the Visual Basic documentation: Basic uses December 31, 1899, as the epoch instead of January 1, 1900, but for some reason, today's date was the same in Excel as it was in Basic.

Huh?

I went to find an Excel developer who was old enough to remember why. Ed Fries seemed to know the answer.

"Oh," he told me. "Check out February 28, 1900."

"It's 59," I said.

"Now try March 1."

"It's 61!"

"What happened to 60?" Ed asked.

"February 29, 1900, was a leap year! It's divisible by 4!"

"Good guess, but no cigar," Ed said, and left me wondering for a while.

Oops. I did some research. Years that are divisible by 100 are *not* leap years, unless they're also divisible by 400.

1900 wasn't a leap year.

"It's a bug in Excel!" I exclaimed.

"Well, not *really*," said Ed. "We had to do it that way because we need to be able to import Lotus 123 worksheets."

"So, it's a bug in Lotus 123?"

"Yeah, but probably an intentional one. Lotus had to fit in 640K. That's not a lot of memory. If you ignore 1900, you can figure out if a given year is a leap year just by looking to see if the rightmost two bits are zero. That's really fast and easy. The Lotus guys probably figured it didn't matter to be wrong for those two months way in the past. It looks like the Basic guys wanted to be anal about those two months, so they moved the epoch one day back."

"Aargh!" I said, and went off to study why there was a check box in the options dialog called "1904 Date System."

The next day was the big BillG review.

June 30, 1992.

In those days, Microsoft was a lot less bureaucratic. Instead of the eleven or twelve layers of management the company has today, I reported to Mike Conte, who reported to Chris Graham, who reported to Pete Higgins, who reported to Mike Maples, who reported to Bill. About six layers from top to bottom. We made fun of companies like General Motors with their eight layers of management or whatever it was.

In my BillG review meeting, the whole reporting hierarchy was there, along with their cousins, sisters, and aunts, and a person who came along from my team whose whole job during the meeting was to keep an accurate count of how many times Bill said the F word. The lower the f*** count, the better.

Bill came in.

I thought about how strange it was that he had two legs, two arms, one head, etc., almost exactly like a regular human being.

He had my spec in his hand.

He had my spec in his hand!

He sat down and exchanged witty banter with an executive I did not know that made no sense to me. A few people laughed.

Bill turned to me.

I noticed that there were comments in the margins of my spec. He had read the first page!

He had read the first page of my spec and written little notes in the margin!

Considering that we only got him the spec about 24 hours earlier, he must have read it the night before.

He was asking questions. I was answering them. They were pretty easy, but I can't for the life of me remember what they were, because I couldn't stop noticing that he was flipping through the spec . . .

He was flipping through the spec! [Calm down, what are you a little girl?]

 . . . and THERE WERE NOTES IN ALL THE MARGINS. ON EVERY PAGE OF THE SPEC. HE HAD READ THE WHOLE GOD-DAMNED THING AND WRITTEN NOTES IN THE MARGINS.

He Read The Whole Thing! [OMG SQUEEE!]

The questions got harder and more detailed.

They seemed a little bit random. By now I was used to thinking of Bill as my buddy. He's a nice guy! He read my spec! He probably just wants to ask me a few questions about the comments in the margins! I'll open a bug in the bug tracker for each of his comments and make sure it gets addressed, *pronto!*

Finally, the killer question.

"I don't know, you guys," Bill said, "Is anyone *really* looking into all the details of how to do this? Like, all those date and time functions. Excel has so many date and time functions. Is Basic going to have the same functions? Will they all work the same way?"

"Yes," I said, "except for January and February, 1900."

Silence.

The f*** counter and my boss exchanged astonished glances. *How did I know that? January and February WHAT?*

"OK. Well, good work," said Bill. He took his marked-up copy of the spec.

 . . . *wait! I wanted that* . . .

and left.

"Four," announced the f*** counter, and everyone said, "Wow, that's the lowest I can remember. Bill is getting mellow in his old age." He was, you know, 36.

Later I had it explained to me. "Bill doesn't really want to review your spec, he just wants to make sure you've got it under control. His standard M.O. is to ask harder and harder questions until you admit that you don't know, and then he can yell at you for being unprepared. Nobody was really sure what happens if you answer the hardest question he can come up with because it's never happened before."

"Can you imagine if Jim Manzi had been in that meeting?" someone asked. "'What's a date function?' Manzi would have asked."

Jim Manzi was the MBA-type running Lotus into the ground.

It was a good point. Bill Gates was amazingly technical. He understood Variants, and COM objects, and IDispatch, and why Automation is different from vtables, and why this might lead to dual interfaces. He worried about date functions. He didn't meddle in software if he trusted the people who were working on it, but you couldn't bullshit him for a minute because he was a programmer. A real, actual, programmer.

Watching nonprogrammers trying to run software companies is like watching someone who doesn't know how to surf trying to surf.

"It's OK! I have great advisors standing on the shore telling me what to do!" they say, and then fall off the board, again and again. The standard cry of the MBA who believes that management is a generic function. Is Steve Ballmer going to be another John Sculley, who nearly drove Apple into extinction because the board of directors thought that selling Pepsi was good preparation for running a computer company? The cult of the MBA likes to believe that you can run organizations that do things that you don't understand.

Over the years, Microsoft got big, Bill got overextended, and some shady ethical decisions made it necessary to devote way too much management attention to fighting the US government. Steve took over the CEO role on the theory that this would allow Bill to spend more time doing what he does best, running the software development organization, but that didn't seem to fix endemic problems caused by those eleven layers of management, a culture of perpetual, permanent meetings, a stubborn insistence on creating every possible product no matter what (how many billions of dollars has Microsoft lost, in R&D, legal fees, and damage to reputation, because they decided that not only do they have to make a web browser, but they have to give it away free?), and a couple of decades of sloppy, rapid hiring has ensured that the brainpower of the median Microsoft employee has gone way down (Douglas Coupland, in *Microserfs*: "They hired 3,100 people in 1992 alone, and you know not all of them were gems.")

Oh well. The party has moved elsewhere. Excel Basic became Microsoft Visual Basic for Applications for Microsoft Excel, with so many ™s and ®s I don't know where to put them all. I left the company in 1994, assuming Bill had completely forgotten me, until I noticed a short interview with Bill Gates in the *Wall Street Journal*, in which he mentioned, almost in passing, something along the lines of how hard it was to recruit, say, a good program manager for Excel. They don't just grow on trees, or something.

Could he have been talking about me? Naw, it was probably some-one else.

Still.

two

FINDING GREAT DEVELOPERS

Wednesday, September 6, 2006

~

Where are all those great developers?

The first time you try to fill an open position, if you're like most people, you place some ads, maybe browse around the large online boards, and get a ton of resumes.

As you go through them, you think, "Hmm, this might work," or, "No way!" or, "I wonder if this person could be convinced to move to Buffalo." What *doesn't* happen, and I guarantee this, what *never* happens, is that you say, "Wow, this person is brilliant! We must have them!" In fact, you can go through thousands of resumes, assuming you know how to read resumes, which is not easy, but you can go through thousands of job applications and quite frankly never see a great software developer. Not a one.

Here is why this happens.

The great software developers, indeed, the best people in every field, are quite simply *never on the market*.

The average great software developer will apply for, total, *maybe*, four jobs in their entire career.

The great college graduates get pulled into an internship by a professor with a connection to the industry, then they get early offers from that company and never bother applying for any other jobs. If they leave that company, it's often to go to a startup with a friend, or to follow a great boss to another company, or because they decided they really want to work on, say, Eclipse, because Eclipse is cool, so they look for an Eclipse job at BEA or IBM, and then of course they get it because they're brilliant.

If you're *lucky*, if you're *really lucky*, they show up on the open job market once, when, say, their spouse decides to accept a medical internship in Anchorage and they actually send their resume out to what they think are the few places they'd like to work at in Anchorage.

But for the most part, great developers (and this is almost a tautology) are, uh, great, (OK, it is a tautology), and, usually, prospective employers recognize their greatness quickly, which means, basically, they get to work wherever they want, so they honestly don't send out a lot of resumes or apply for a lot of jobs.

Does this sound like the kind of person you want to hire? It should.

The corollary of that rule—the rule that the great people are never on the market—is that the bad people—the seriously unqualified—are on the market *quite a lot*. They get fired all the time, because they can't do their job. Their companies fail—sometimes because any company that would hire them would probably also hire a lot of unqualified programmers, so it all adds up to failure—but sometimes because they *actually are so unqualified that they ruined the company*. Yep, it happens.

These morbidly unqualified people rarely get jobs, thankfully, but they do keep applying, and when they apply, they go to Monster.com and check off 300 or 1,000 jobs at once trying to win the lottery.

Numerically, great people are pretty rare, and they're never on the job market, while incompetent people, even though they are *just as rare*, apply to thousands of jobs throughout their career. So now, Sparky, back to that big pile of resumes you got off of Craigslist. Is it any surprise that most of them are people you don't want to hire?

Astute readers, I expect, will point out that I'm leaving out the largest group yet: the solid, competent people. They're on the market more than the great people, but less than the incompetent, and all in all they will show up in *small* numbers in your 1,000 resume pile, but for the most part, almost every hiring manager in Palo Alto right now with 1,000 resumes on their desk has the same exact set of 970 resumes from the same minority of 970 incompetent people that are applying for every job in Palo Alto, and probably will be for life, and only 30 resumes even worth considering, of which maybe, rarely, one is a great programmer.

OK, maybe not even one. And figuring out how to find those needles in a haystack, we shall see, is possible but not easy.

~

Can I get them anyway?

Yes!
Well, Maybe!
Or perhaps, It Depends!
Instead of thinking of recruiting as a "gather resumes, filter resumes" procedure, you're going to have to think of it as a "track down the winners and make them talk to you" procedure.

I have three basic methods for how to go about this:

1. Go to the mountain.

2. Internships.

3. Build your own community.*

("Build your own community" comes with a little asterisk that means "hard," like the famous math problem that George Dantzig solved because he came into class too late to hear that it was supposed to be unsolvable.)

You can probably come up with your own ideas, too. I'm just going to talk about three that worked for me.

~

To the mountain, Jeeves!

Think about where the people you want to hire are hanging out. What conferences do they go to? Where do they live? What organizations do they belong to? What websites do they read? Instead of casting a wide net with a job search on Monster.com, use the *Joel on Software* job board and limit your search to the smart people who read my site. Go to the really interesting tech conferences. Great Mac developers will be at Apple's WWDC. Great Windows programmers will be at Microsoft's PDC. There are a bunch of open source conferences, too.

Look for the hot new technology of the day. Last year it was Python; this year it's Ruby. Go to their conferences where you'll find early adopters who are curious about new things and always interested in improving.

Slink around in the hallways, talk to everyone you meet, go to the technical sessions and invite the speakers out for a beer, and when you find someone smart, BANG!—you launch into full-fledged flirt and flattery mode. "Ooooh, that's so *interesting!*" you say. "Wow, I can't believe you're so *smart*. And handsome, too. Where did you say you work? Really? *There?* Hmmmmmmm. Don't you think you could do better? I think my company might be hiring . . . "

The corollary of this rule is to *avoid* advertising on general-purpose, large job boards. One summer, I inadvertently advertised our summer internships using MonsterTRAK, which offered the option to pay a little extra to make the internship visible to students at every school in the USA. This resulted in literally hundreds of resumes, not one of which made it past the first round. We ended up spending a ton of money to get a ton of resumes that stood almost no chance at finding the kind of people we wanted to hire. After a few days of this, the very fact that MonsterTRAK was the source of a resume made me think that candidate was probably not for us. Similarly, when Craigslist first started up and was really just visited by early adopters in the Internet industry, we found great people by advertising on Craigslist, but today, virtually everyone who is moderately computer literate uses it, resulting in too many resumes with too low of a needle-to-haystack ratio.

Internships

One good way to snag the great people who are never on the job market is to get them before they even realize there *is* a job market: when they're in college.

Some hiring managers hate the idea of hiring interns. They see interns as unformed and insufficiently skilled. To some extent, that's true. Interns are not as experienced as experienced employees (no, really?!). You're going to have to invest in them a little bit more, and it's going to take some time before they're up to speed. The good news about our field is that the really great programmers often started programming when they were 10 years old. And while everyone else their age was running around playing soccer (this is a game many kids who can't program computers play that involves kicking a spherical object called a ball with their feet—I know, it sounds weird), they were in their dad's home office trying to get the Linux kernel to compile. Instead of chasing girls in the playground, they were getting into flamewars on Usenet about the utter depravity of programming languages that don't implement Haskell-style type inference. Instead of starting a band in their garage, they were implementing a cool hack so that when their neighbor stole bandwidth over their open-access Wi-Fi point, all the images on the Web appeared upside-down. BWA HA HA HA HA!

So, unlike, say, the fields of law or medicine, over here in software development, by the time these kids are in their second or third year in college they are pretty darn good programmers.

Pretty much everyone applies for *one* job: their first one, and most kids think that it's OK to wait until their last year to worry about this. And in fact, most kids are not that inventive and will really only bother applying for jobs where there is actually some kind of on-campus recruiting event. Kids at good colleges have enough choices of good jobs from the on-campus employers that they rarely bother reaching out to employers that don't bother to come to campus.

You can either participate in this madness, by recruiting on campus, which is a good thing, don't get me wrong, or you can subvert it by trying to get great kids a year or two *before* they graduate.

I've had a lot of success doing it that way at Fog Creek. The process starts every September, when I start using all my resources to track down the best computer science students in the country. I send letters to a couple of hundred Computer Science departments. I track down lists of CS majors who are, at that point, two years away from graduating (usually you have to know someone in the department, a professor or student, to find these lists). Then I write a personal letter to every single CS major that I can find. Not e-mail, a real piece of paper on Fog Creek letterhead, which I sign myself in actual ink. Apparently, this is rare enough that it gets a *lot* of attention. I tell them we have internships and personally invite them to apply. I send e-mail to CS professors and CS alumni, who usually have some kind of CS-majors mailing list that they forward it on to.

Eventually, we get a lot of applications for these internships, and we can have our pick of the crop. In the last couple of years, I've gotten 200 applications for every internship. We'll generally winnow that pile of applications down to about 10 (per opening) and then call all those people for a phone interview. Of the people getting past the phone interview, we'll probably fly two or three out to New York for an in-person interview.

By the time of the in-person interview, there's such a high probability that we're going to want to hire this person that it's time to launch into full-press *recruitment*. They're met at the airport here by a uniformed limo driver who grabs their luggage and whisks them away to their hotel, probably the coolest hotel they've ever seen in their life, right in the middle of the fashion district with models walking in and out at all hours and complicated bathroom fixtures that are probably a part of the permanent collection of the Museum of Modern Art (but good luck trying to figure out how to brush your teeth). Waiting in the hotel room, we leave a hospitality package with a T-shirt, a suggested walking tour of New York written by Fog Creek staffers, and a DVD documentary of the 2005 summer interns. There's a DVD player in the room, so a lot of them watch how much fun was had by previous interns.

After a day of interviews, we invite the students to stay in New York at our expense for a couple of days if they want to check out the city, before the limo picks them up at their hotel and takes them back to the airport for their flight home.

Even though only about one in three applicants who make it to the in-person interview stage passes all our interviews, it's really important that the ones who *do* pass have a positive experience. Even the ones who don't make it go back to campus thinking we're a classy employer and tell all their friends how much fun they had staying in a luxury hotel in the Big Apple, which makes their friends apply for an internship the next summer, if only for the chance at the trip.

During the summer of the internship itself, the students generally start out thinking, "OK, it's a nice summer job and some good experience and maybe, just *maybe,* it'll lead to a full-time job." We're a little bit ahead of them. We're going to use the summer to decide if we want them as a full-time employee, and they're going to use the summer to decide if they want to work for us.

So we give them real work. Hard work. Our interns always work on production code. Sometimes they're working on the coolest new stuff in the company, which can make the permanent employees a little jealous, but that's life. One summer we had a team of four interns build a whole new product from the ground up. That internship paid for itself in a matter of months. Even when they're not building a new product, they're working on real, shipping code, with some major area of functionality that they are totally, personally responsible for (with experienced mentors to help out, of course).

And then we make sure they have a great time. We host parties and open houses. We get them free housing in a rather nice local dorm where they can make friends from other companies and schools. We have some kind of extracurricular activity or field trip every week: Broadway musicals (this year they went crazy about *Avenue Q*), movie openings, museum tours, a boat ride around Manhattan, a Yankees game. And believe it or not, one of this year's favorite things was a trip to Top of the Rock. I mean, it's just a tall building where you go out on the roof in the middle of Manhattan. You wouldn't think it would be such an awe-inspiring experience. But it was. A few Fog Creek employees go along on each activity, too.

At the end of the summer, there are always a few interns who convinced us that they are the truly great kinds of programmers that we just have to hire. Not all of them, mind you—some are merely great programmers that we are willing to pass on, and others would be great somewhere else, but not at Fog Creek. For example, we're a fairly autonomous company without a lot of middle management, where people are expected to be completely self-driven. Historically, a couple of times a summer intern would be great in a situation where they had someone to guide them, but at Fog Creek they wouldn't get enough direction and would flounder.

Anyway, for the ones we really want to hire, there's no use in waiting. We make an early offer for a full-time job, conditional on their graduating. And it's a great offer. We want them to be able to go back to school, compare notes with their friends, and realize that they're getting a higher starting salary than anyone else.

Does this mean we're overpaying? Not at all. You see, the average first-year salary has to take into account a certain amount of risk that the person won't work out. But we've already auditioned these kids, and there's no risk that they won't be great. We know what they can do. So when we hire them, we have more information about them than any other employer who has only interviewed them. That means we can pay them more money. We have better information, so we're willing to pay more than employers without that information.

If we've done our job right, and we usually have, by this point the intern completely gives up and accepts our offer. Sometimes it takes a little more persuading. Sometimes they want to leave their options open, but the outstanding offer from Fog Creek ensures that the first time they have to wake up at 8:00 a.m. and put on a suit for an interview with Oracle, when the alarm goes off, there's a good chance that they'll say "Why the heck am I getting up at 8:00 a.m. and putting on a suit for an interview with Oracle when I already have an excellent job waiting for me at Fog Creek?" And, my hope is, they won't even bother going to that interview.

By the way, before I move on, I need to clarify something about internships in computer science and software development. In this day and age, in this country, it is totally expected that these are *paid* internships, and the salaries are usually pretty competitive. Although unpaid internships are common in other fields from publishing to music, we pay $750 a week, plus free housing, plus free lunch, plus free subway passes, not to mention relocation expenses and all the benefits. The dollar amount is a little bit lower than average, but it includes the free housing, so it works out being a little bit better than average. I thought I'd mention that because every time I've talked about internships on my website somebody inevitably gets confused and thinks I'm taking advantage of slave labor or something. You there—young whippersnapper! Get me a frosty cold orange juice, hand-squeezed, and make it snappy!

An internship program creates a pipeline for great employees, but it's a pretty long pipeline, and a lot of people get lost along the way. We basically calculate we're going to have to hire two interns for every full-time employee that we get out of it, and if you hire interns with one year left in school, there's still a two-year pipeline between when you start hiring and when they show up for their first day of full-time work. That means we hire just about as many interns as we can physically fit in our offices each summer. The first three summers, we tried to limit our internship program to students with one year left in school, but this summer we finally realized that we were missing out on some great younger students, so we opened the program to students in any year in college. Believe it or not, I'm even trying to figure out how to get high school kids in here, maybe setting up computers after school for college money, just to start to build a connection with the next generation of great programmers, even if it becomes a six-year pipeline. I have a long horizon.

~

Build the community (*hard)

The idea here is to create a large community of like-minded smart developers who cluster around your company, somehow, so you have an automatic audience to reach out to every time you have an opening.

This is, to tell the truth, how we found so many of our great Fog Creek people: through my personal web site, *Joel on Software* (joelonsoftware.com). Major articles on that site can be read by as many as a million people, most of them software developers in some capacity. With a large, self-selecting audience, whenever I mention that I'm looking for someone on the home page, I'll usually get a pretty big pile of very good resumes.

This is that category with the asterisk that means "hard," since I feel like I'm giving you advice that says, "To win a beauty pageant, (a) get beautiful, and (b) enter the pageant." That's because I'm really not sure why or how my site became so popular or why the people who read it are the best software developers.

I really wish I could help you more here. Derek Powazek wrote a good book on the subject (*Design for Community: The Art of Connecting Real People in Virtual Places*, New Riders, 2001). A lot of companies tried various blogging strategies, and unfortunately a lot of them failed to build up any kind of audience, so all I can say is that what worked for us may or may not work for you, and I'm not sure what you can do about it. I did just open a job board on the site (jobs.joelonsoftware.com) where, for $350, you can list a job that *Joel on Software* readers will see.

~

Employee referrals: may be slippery when wet

The standard bit of advice on finding great software developers is to ask your existing developers. The theory is, gosh, they're smart developers, they must know other smart developers.

And they might, but they also have very dear friends who are not very good developers, and there are about a million land mines in this field, so the truth is I generally consider the idea of employee referrals to be one of the weakest sources of new hires.

One big risk, of course, is noncompete agreements. If you didn't think these mattered, think about the case of Crossgain, which had to fire a quarter of its employees, all ex-Microsoft, when Microsoft threatened them with individual lawsuits. No programmer in their right mind should ever sign a noncompete agreement, but most of them do because they can never imagine that it would be enforced, or because they are not in the habit of reading contracts, or because they already accepted the employment offer and moved their families across the country, and the first day of work is the first time they've seen this agreement, and it's a little bit too late to try to negotiate it. So they sign, but this is one of the slimiest practices of employers, and they *are* often enforceable and enforced.

The point being noncompete agreements may mean that if you rely too heavily on referrals and end up hiring a block of people from the same ex-employer, which is where your employees know the other star programmers from in the *first* place, you're taking a pretty major risk.

Another problem is that if you have any kind of selective hiring process at all, when you ask your employees to find referrals, they're not going to even consider telling you about their real friends. Nobody wants to persuade their friends to apply for a job at their company only to get rejected. It sort of puts a damper on the friendship.

Since they won't tell you about their friends, and you may not be able to hire the people they used to work with, what's left is not very many potential referrals.

But the *real* problem with employee referrals is what happens when recruiting managers with a rudimentary understanding of economics decide to offer cash bonuses for these referrals. This is quite common. The rationale goes like this: it can cost $30,000 to $50,000 to hire someone good through a headhunter or outside recruiter. If we can pay our employees, say, a $5,000 bonus for every hire they bring in, or maybe an expensive sports car for every ten referrals, or whatever, think how much money that will save. And $5,000 sounds like a fortune to a salaried employee, because it is. So this sounds like a win-win all-around kind of situation.

The trouble is that suddenly you can see the little gears turning, and employees start dragging in everyone they can think of for interviews, and they have a real strong incentive to get these people hired, so they coach them for the interview, and Quiet Conversations are held in conference rooms with the interviewers, and suddenly your entire work-force is trying to get you to hire someone's useless college roommate.

And it doesn't work. ArsDigita got a lot of publicity for buying a Ferrari and putting it in the parking lot and announcing that anyone who got ten referrals could have it. Nobody ever got close, the quality of new hires went down, and the company fell apart, but probably not because of the Ferrari, which, it turns out, was rented, and not much more than a publicity stunt.

When a Fog Creek employee suggests someone that might be perfect to work for us, we'll be willing to skip the initial phone screen, but that's *it*. We still want them going through all the same interviews, and we maintain the same high standards.

~

A field guide to developers

What do developers look for in a job? What makes one job more appealing to them than another? How can you become the employer of choice? Read on!

three

A FIELD GUIDE TO DEVELOPERS

Thursday, September 7, 2006

Unfortunately, you can advertise in all the right places, have a fantastic internship program, and interview all you want, but if the great programmers don't want to work for you, they ain't gonna come work for you. So this section will serve as a kind of field guide to developers: what they're looking for, what they like and dislike in a workplace, and what it's going to take to be a top choice for top developers.

~

Private offices

Last year I went to a computer science conference at Yale. One of the speakers, a Silicon Valley veteran who had founded or led quite an honor roll of venture-capital funded startups, held up the book *Peopleware* by Tom DeMarco and Timothy Lister (Dorset House, 1999).

"You have to read this book," he said. "This is the bible of how to run a software company. This is the most important book out there for how to run software companies."

I had to agree with him: *Peopleware* is a great book. One of the most important, and most controversial, topics in that book is that you have to give programmers lots of quiet space, probably private offices, if you want them to be productive. The authors go on and on about that subject.

After the speech, I went up to the speaker. "I agree with you about *Peopleware*," I said. "Tell me: did you have private offices for your developers at all your startups?"

"Of course not," he said. "The VCs would never go for that."

Hmm.

"But that might be the number one most important thing in that book," I said.

"Yeah, but you gotta pick your battles. To VCs, private offices look like you're wasting their money."

There's a strong culture in Silicon Valley that requires you to jam a lot of programmers into a big open space, despite a preponderance of evidence that giving them private offices is far more productive, something which I've covered repeatedly on my site. I'm not really getting through to people, I don't think, because programmers kind of *like* being social, even if it means they are unproductive, so it's an uphill battle.

I've even heard programmers say things like, "Yeah, we all work in cubicles, but *everyone* works in a cubicle—up to and including the CEO!"

"The CEO? Does the CEO really work in a cubicle?"

"Well, he *has* a cubicle, but actually, now that you mention it, there's this one conference room that he goes to for all his important meetings . . ."

Mmmm hmmm. A fairly common Silicon Valley phenomenon is the CEO who makes a big show of working from a cubicle just like the hoi polloi, although somehow there's this one conference room that he tends to make his own ("Only when there's something private to be discussed," he'll claim, but half the time when you walk by that conference room there's your CEO, all by himself, talking on the phone to his golf buddy, with his Cole Haans up on the conference table).

Anyway, I don't want to revisit the discussion of why private offices make software developers more productive, or why just putting on headphones to drown out the ambient noise has been shown to reduce the quality of work that programmers produce, and why it doesn't really cost that much more in the scheme of things to have private offices for developers. I've talked about that already. Today I'm talking about recruiting, and private offices in recruiting.

No matter what you think about productivity, and no matter what you think about egalitarian workspaces, two things are incontrovertible:

1. Private offices have higher status.

2. Cubicles and other shared space can be socially awkward.

Given these two facts, the bottom line is that programmers are more likely to take the job that offers them a private office. Especially if there's a door that shuts, and a window, and a nice view.

Now, it's an unfortunate fact that some of these things that make recruiting easier are not really within your power. Even CEOs and founders can be prevented from establishing private offices if they're dependent on VCs. Most companies only move or rearrange their office space every five to ten years. Smaller startups may not be able to afford private offices. So my experience has been that a number of excuses all pile up until it's virtually impossible to get private offices for developers in any but the most enlightened of companies, and even in those companies, the decision of where to move and where people should work is often taken once every ten years by a committee consisting of the office manager's secretary and a junior associate from a big architecture firm, who is apt to believe architecture-school fairy tales about how open spaces mean open companies, or whatever, with close to zero input from the developers or the development team.

This is something of a scandal, and I'll keep fighting the good fight, but in the meantime, private offices are *not* impossible; we've managed to do it for all of our full-time programmers, most of the time, even in New York City, where the rents are some of the highest in the world, and there's no question that it makes people much happier about working at Fog Creek, so if you all want to keep resisting, *so be it*, I'll just let this remain a competitive advantage.

~

The physical workspace

There's more to the physical workspace than private offices. When a candidate comes to your company for the day of interviews, they're going to look around at where people are working, and try to imagine themselves working there. If the office space is pleasant, if it's bright, if it's in a nice neighborhood, if everything is new and clean, they'll have happy thoughts. If the office space is crowded, if the carpets are ratty and the walls haven't been painted and there are posters up with pictures of rowing teams and the word TEAMWORK in large print, they're going to have Dilbert thoughts.

A lot of tech people are remarkably unaware of the general condition of their office. In fact, even people who are otherwise attuned to the benefits of a nice office may be blinded to the particular weaknesses of their own office, since they're so used to them.

Put yourself in your candidate's heads, and think honestly:

- What will they think of our location? How does Buffalo sound, compared to, say, Austin? Do people really want to move to Detroit? If you're in Buffalo or Detroit, can you at least try to do most of your interviewing in September?

- When they get to the office, what is the experience like? What do they see? Do they see a clean and exciting place? Is there a nice atrium lobby with live palm trees and a fountain, or does it feel like a government dental clinic in a slum, with dying corn plants and old copies of *Newsweek*?

- What does the workspace look like? Is everything new and shiny? Or do you still have that gigantic, yellowing TEAM BANANA sign up, the one that was printed on fanfold paper on a dot matrix printer back when there used to be a thing called fanfold paper and a thing called dot matrix printers?

- What do the desks look like? Do programmers have multiple large flat screens or a single CRT? Are the chairs Aerons or Staples Specials?

Let me, for a moment, talk about the famous Aeron chair, made by Herman Miller. They cost about $900. This is about $800 more than a cheap office chair from Office Depot or Staples.

They are *much* more comfortable than cheap chairs. If you get the right size and adjust it properly, most people can sit in them all day long without feeling uncomfortable. The back and seat are made out of a kind of mesh that lets air flow so you don't get sweaty. The ergonomics, especially of the newer models with lumbar support, are excellent.

They last longer than cheap chairs. We've been in business for six years, and every Aeron is literally in mint condition: I challenge anyone to see the difference between the chairs we bought in 2000 and the chairs we bought three months ago. They easily last for ten years. The cheap chairs literally start falling apart after a matter of months. You'll need at least four $100 chairs to last as long as an Aeron.

So the bottom line is that an Aeron only really costs $500 more over ten years, or $50 a year. One dollar per week per programmer.

A nice roll of toilet paper runs about a buck. Your programmers are probably using about one roll a week, each.

So upgrading them to an Aeron chair literally costs the same amount as you're spending on their *toilet paper*, and I assure you that if you tried to bring up toilet paper in the budget committee, you would be sternly told not to mess around, there were important things to discuss.

The Aeron chair has, sadly, been tarnished with a reputation of being extravagant, especially for startups. It somehow came to stand for the symbol of all the VC money that was wasted in the dot-com boom, which is a shame, because it's not very expensive when you consider how long it lasts; indeed, when you think of the eight hours a day you spend sitting in it, even the top of the line model, with the lumbar support and the friggin' *tailfins*, is so dang cheap you practically *make* money by buying them.

Toys

Similar logic applies for other developer toys. There is simply no reason not to get your developers top-of-the-line computers, at least two large (21") LCD screens (or one 30" screen), and give them free rein on Amazon.com to order any technical book they want. These are obvious productivity gains, but more importantly to our discussion here, they're crucial recruiting tools, especially in a world where most companies treat programmers as interchangeable cogs, typists, really—why do they need such a big monitor and what's wrong with 15" CRTs? When *I* was a kid, . . .

~

The social life of developers

Software developers are not really all that different from regular people. Sure, I know, it's popular these days to think of developers as stereotypical Asperger's geeks, totally untuned to interpersonal things, but that's just not true, and even Asperger's geeks care about the social aspect of a workspace, which includes these issues:

How are programmers treated inside the organization?

Are they hotshots or typists? Is company management made up of engineers or former programmers? When developers go to a conference, do they fly first class? (I don't care if that seems like a waste of money. Stars go first class. Get used to it.) When they fly in for an interview, does a limo pick them up at the airport, or are they expected to find their own way to the office? All else being equal, developers are going to prefer an organization that treats them like stars. If your CEO is a grouchy ex-sales person who doesn't understand why these prima donna developers keep demanding things like wrist pads and big monitors and comfortable chairs, who do they think they are?, your company probably needs an attitude adjustment. You're not going to get great developers if you don't respect them.

Who are their colleagues?

One thing programmers pay close attention to in the day of interviewing is the people they meet. Are they nice? More importantly: are they smart? I did a summer internship once at Bellcore, a spinoff of Bell Labs, and everybody I met kept telling me the same thing, again and again: "The great thing about working for Bellcore is the people."

That said, if you have any grouchy developers who you just can't get rid of, at least take them off the interview schedule, and if you have cheerful, social, cruise-director types, make sure they're on it. Keep reminding yourself that when your candidate goes home and has to make a decision about where to work, if everyone they met was glum, they are not going to have such a positive memory of your company.

By the way, the original hiring rule for Fog Creek, stolen from Microsoft, was "Smart, and Gets Things Done." Even before we started the company, we realized that we should add a third rule: "Not a jerk." In retrospect, at Microsoft, not being a jerk is not a requirement to get the job; although I'm sure they would pay lip service to how important it is for people to be nice to one another, the bottom line is that they would never disqualify someone for a job just because they were a jerk, in fact, being a jerk sometimes seems like a prerequisite for getting into upper management. This doesn't really seem to hurt from a business perspective, although it does hurt from a recruiting perspective, and who wants to work at a company where jerks are tolerated?

Independence and autonomy

When I quit my job at Juno, back in 1999, before starting Fog Creek Software, HR gave me a standard exit interview, and somehow, I fell into the trap of telling the HR person everything that was wrong about the management of the company, something which I knew perfectly well could have no possible benefit to me and could only, actually, hurt, but I did it anyway, and the main thing I complained about was Juno's style of hit-and-run management. Most of the time, you see, managers would leave people alone to quietly get their work done, but occasionally, they would get themselves involved in some microscopic detail of something that they would insist be done exactly their way, no excuses, and then they'd move on to micromanage some other task, not staying around long enough to see the farcical results. For example, I remember a particularly annoying period of two or three days where everyone from my manager to the CEO got involved in telling me exactly how dates must be entered on the Juno signup questionnaire. They weren't trained as UI designers and didn't spend enough time talking to me about the issues to understand why I happened to be right in that particular case, but it didn't matter: management just would not back down on that issue and wouldn't even take the time to listen to my arguments.

Basically, if you're going to hire smart people, you're going to have to let them apply their skills to their work. Managers can advise, which they're welcome to do, but they must be extremely careful to avoid having their "advice" interpreted as a command, since on any given technical issue it's likely that management knows less than the workers in the trenches, especially, as I said, if you're hiring good people.

Developers want to be hired for their skills, and treated as experts, and allowed to make decisions within their own realm of expertise.

No politics

Actually, politics happen everywhere that more than two people congregate. It's just natural. By "no politics" I really mean "no dysfunctional politics." Programmers have very well-honed senses of justice. Code either works, or it doesn't. There's no sense in arguing whether a bug exists, since you can test the code and find out. The world of programming is very just and very strictly ordered, and a heck of a lot of people go into programming in the first place because they prefer to spend their time in a just, orderly place, a strict meritocracy where you can win any debate simply by being *right*.

And this is the kind of environment you have to create to attract programmers. When a programmer complains about "politics," they mean—very precisely—any situation in which personal considerations outweigh technical considerations. Nothing is more infuriating than when a developer is told to use a certain programming language, not the best one for the task at hand, because the boss likes it. Nothing is more maddening than when people are promoted because of their ability to network rather than being promoted strictly on merit. Nothing is more aggravating to a developer than being forced to do something that is technically inferior because someone higher than them in the organization, or someone better connected, insists on it.

Nothing is more satisfying than winning an argument on its technical merits even when you should have lost it on political merits. When I started working at Microsoft, there was a major, misguided project underway called MacroMan to create a graphical macro programming language. The programming language would have been very frustrating for real programmers, because the graphical nature didn't really give you a way to implement loops or conditionals, but would not have really helped nonprogrammers, who, I think, are just not used to thinking in algorithms and wouldn't have understood MacroMan in the first place.

When I complained about MacroMan, my boss told me, "Nothing's gonna derail *that* train. Give up." But I kept arguing, and arguing, and arguing—I was fresh out of college, about as unconnected as anyone could be at Microsoft—and eventually people listened to the meat of my arguments and the MacroMan project was shut down. It didn't matter who I was, it mattered that I was right. That's the kind of nonpolitical organization that delights programmers.

All in all, focusing on the social dynamics of your organization is crucial to making a healthy, pleasant place to work that will retain programmers and attract programmers.

~

What am I working on?

To some extent, one of the best ways you can attract developers is to let them work on something interesting. This may be the hardest thing to change: doggone it, if you're in the business of making software for the gravel and sand industry, that's the business you're in, and you can't pretend to be some cool web startup just to attract developers.

Another thing developers like is working on something simple enough or popular enough that they can explain it to Aunt Irma at Thanksgiving. Aunt Irma, of course, being a nuclear physicist, doesn't really know that much about Ruby programming in the gravel and sand industry.

Finally, many developers are going to look at the social values of the company they're working for. Jobs at social networking companies and blog companies help bring people together and don't really pollute, it seems, so they're popular, while jobs in the munitions industry or in ethically challenged accounting-fraud-ridden companies are a lot less popular.

Unfortunately, I'm not really sure if I can think of any way for the average hiring manager to do anything about this. You can try to change your product lineup to make something "cool," but that's just not going to go very far. There are a few things, though, that I've seen companies do in this area:

Let the top recruits pick their own project

For many years, Oracle Corporation had a program called MAP: the Multiple Alternatives Program. This was offered to the college graduates whom they considered the top candidates from each class. The idea was that they could come to Oracle, spend a week or two looking around, visiting all the groups with openings, and then choose any opening they wanted to work in.

I think this was a good idea, although probably someone from Oracle knows better whether this worked out.

Use cool new technologies unnecessarily

The big investment banks in New York are considered fairly tough places for programmers. The working conditions are dreadful, with long hours, noisy environments, and tyrannical bosses; programmers are very distinct third-class citizens, while the testosterone-crazed apes who actually sell and trade financial instruments are corporate royalty, with $30,000,000 bonuses and all the cheeseburgers they can eat (often delivered by a programmer who happened to be nearby). That's the stereotype, anyway, so to keep the best developers, investment banks have two strategies: paying a ton of money and allowing programmers basically free rein to keep rewriting everything over and over again in whatever hot new programming language they feel like learning. Wanna rewrite that whole trading app in Lisp? Whatever. Just get me a goddamned cheeseburger.

Some programmers couldn't care less about what programming language they're using, but most would just love to have the opportunity to work with exciting new technologies. Today that may be Python or Ruby on Rails; three years ago it was C# and before that Java.

Now, I'm not telling you not to use the best tool for the job, and I'm not telling you to rewrite in the hot *language-du-jour* every two years, but if you can find ways for developers to get experience with newer languages, frameworks, and technologies, they'll be happier. Even if you don't dare rewrite your core application, is there any reason your internal tools, or less-critical new applications, can't be written in an exciting new language as a learning project?

~

Can I identify with the company?

Most programmers aren't looking for just a gig to pay the rent. They don't want a "day job": they want to feel like their work has meaning. They want to identify with their company. Young programmers, especially, are attracted to ideological companies. A lot of companies have some connection to open source or the free software movement (these are not the same thing), and that can be attractive to idealistic developers. Other companies line up with social causes, or produce a product which, in some way, can be perceived or framed as benefitting society.

As a recruiter, your job is to identify the idealistic aspects of your company and make sure candidates are aware of them.

Some companies even strive to create their own ideological movements. Chicago-area startup 37signals has strongly aligned themselves with the idea of simplicity: simple, easy to use apps like Backpack and the simple, easy-to-use programming framework Ruby on Rails.

For 37signals, simplicity is an "-ism," practically an international political movement. Simplicity is not just simplicity, oh no, it's summertime, it's beautiful music and peace and justice and happiness and pretty girls with flowers in their hair. David Heinemeier Hansson, the creator of Rails, says that their story is "one of beauty, happiness, and motivation. Taking pride and pleasure in your work and in your tools. That story simply isn't a fad, it's a trend. A story that allows for words like passion and enthusiasm to be part of the sanctioned vocabulary of developers without the need to make excuses for yourself. Or feel embarrassed about really liking what you do" (www.loudthinking.com/arc/2006_08.html). Elevating a web programming framework to a thing of "beauty, happiness, and motivation" may seem like hubris, but it's very appealing and sure differentiates their company. In propagating the narrative of Ruby on Rails as Happiness, they're practically guaranteeing that at least some developers out there will be looking for Ruby on Rails jobs.

But 37signals is still new at this identity management campaign thing. They don't hold a *candle* to Apple Computer, which, with a single Superbowl ad in 1984, managed to cement their position *to this day* as the countercultural force of freedom against dictatorship, of liberty against oppression, of colors against black and white, of pretty women in bright red shorts against brainwashed men in suits. The implications of this, I'm afraid, are ironically Orwellian: giant corporations manipulating their public image in a way that doesn't even make sense (like, uh, they're a computer company—what the hell does that have to do with being against dictatorships?) and successfully creating a culture of identity that has computer shoppers around the world feeling like they're not just buying a computer, they're *buying into a movement*. When you buy an iPod, of course, you're supporting Gandhi against British Colonialism. Every MacBook bought takes a stand against dictatorship and hunger!

Anyway. Deep breath . . . The real point of this section is to think of what your company stands for, how it's perceived, and how it could be perceived. Managing your corporate brand is just as important for recruiting as it is for marketing.

~

One thing that programmers don't care about

They don't care about money, actually, unless you're screwing up on the other things. If you start to hear complaints about salaries where you never heard them before, that's usually a sign that people aren't really loving their job. If potential new hires just won't back down on their demands for outlandish salaries, you're probably dealing with a case of people who are thinking, "Well, if it's going to have to suck to go to work, at least I should be getting paid well."

That doesn't mean you can underpay people, because they do care about justice, and they will get infuriated if they find out that different people are getting different salaries for the same work, or that everyone in your shop is making 20% less than an otherwise identical shop down the road, and suddenly money will be a big issue. You do have to pay competitively, but all said, of all the things that programmers look at in deciding where to work, as long as the salaries are basically fair, pay will be surprisingly low on their list of considerations, and offering high salaries is a surprisingly ineffective tool in overcoming problems like the fact that programmers get 15" monitors and salespeople yell at them all the time and the job involves making nuclear weapons out of baby seals.

four

THREE MANAGEMENT METHODS (INTRODUCTION)

MONDAY, AUGUST 7, 2006

If you want to lead a team, a company, an army, or a country, the primary problem you face is getting everyone moving in the same direction, which is really just a polite way of saying "getting people to do what you want."

Think of it this way. As soon as your team consists of more than one person, you're going to have different people with different agendas. They want different things than you want. If you're a startup founder, you might want to make a lot of money quickly so you can retire early and spend the next couple of decades going to conferences for women bloggers. So you might spend most of your time driving around Sand Hill Road talking to VCs who might buy the company and flip it to Yahoo!. But Janice the Programmer, one of your employees, doesn't care about selling out to Yahoo!, because she's not going to make any money that way. What she cares about is writing code in the latest coolest new programming language, because it's fun to learn a new thing. Meanwhile, your CFO is entirely driven by the need to get out of the same cubicle he has been sharing with the system administrator, Trekkie Monster, and so he's working up a new budget proposal that shows just how much money you would save by moving to larger office space that's two minutes from his house, what a coincidence!

The problem of getting people to move in *your* direction (or, at least, *the same* direction) is not unique to startups, of course. It's the same fundamental problem that a political leader faces when they get elected after promising to eliminate waste, corruption, and fraud in government. The mayor wants to make sure that it's easy to get city approval of a new building project. The city building inspectors want to keep getting the bribes they have grown accustomed to.

And it's the same problem that a military leader faces. They might want a team of soldiers to charge at the enemy, even when every individual soldier would really just rather cower behind a rock and let the others do the charging.

Here are three common approaches you might take:

- The **Command and Control** Management Method
- The **Econ 101** Management Method
- The **Identity** Management Method

You will certainly find other methods of management in the wild (there's the exotic *Devil Wears Prada* Method, the Jihad Method, the Charismatic Cult Method, and the Lurch From One Method To Another Method), but over the next three chapters, I'm going to examine these three popular methods and explore their pros and cons.

Next in this series: The Command and Control Management Method

five

THE COMMAND AND CONTROL
MANAGEMENT METHOD

TUESDAY, AUGUST 8, 2006

> *Soldiers should fear their officers more than all the dangers to*
> *which they are exposed. . . . Good will can never induce the com-*
> *mon soldier to stand up to such dangers; he will only do so through*
> *fear.*
>
> Frederick the Great

The Command and Control form of management is based on military management. Primarily, the idea is that people do what you tell them to do, and if they don't, you yell at them until they do, and if they still don't, you throw them in the brig for a while, and if that doesn't teach them, you put them in charge of peeling onions on a submarine, sharing two cubit feet of personal space with a lad from a farm who really never quite learned about brushing his teeth.

There are a million great techniques you can use. Rent the movies *Biloxi Blues* and *An Officer and a Gentleman* for some ideas.

Some managers use this technique because they actually learned it in the military. Others grew up in authoritarian households or countries and think it's a natural way to gain compliance. Others just don't know any better. Hey, it works for the military, it should work for an Internet startup!

There are, it turns out, three drawbacks with this method in a high-tech team.

First of all, people don't really like it very much, least of all smarty-pants software developers, who are, actually, pretty smart and are used to thinking they know more than everyone else, for perfectly good reasons, because it happens to be true, and so it really, really bothers them when they're commanded to do something "because." But that's not really a good enough reason to discard this method . . . we're trying to be rational here. High-tech teams have many goals, but making everyone happy is rarely goal number one.

A more practical drawback with Command and Control is that management literally does not have enough time to micromanage at this level, because there simply aren't enough managers. In the military, it's possible to give an order simultaneously to a large team of people because it's common that everyone is doing the same thing. "Clean your guns!" you can say to a squad of 28, and then go take a brief nap and have a cool iced tea on the officer's club veranda. In software development teams, everybody is working on something else, so attempts to micromanage turn into **hit-and-run micromanagement**. That's where you micromanage one developer in a spurt of activity and then suddenly disappear from that developer's life for a couple of weeks while you run around micromanaging other developers. The problem with hit-and-run micromanagement is that you don't stick around long enough to see why your decisions are not working or to correct course. Effectively, all you accomplish is to knock your poor programmers off the train track every once in a while, so they spend the next week finding all their train cars and putting them back on the tracks and lining everything up again, a little bit battered from the experience.

The third drawback is that in a high-tech company the individual contributors always have more information than the "leaders," so they are really in the best position to make decisions. When the boss wanders into an office where two developers have been arguing for two hours about the best way to compress an image, the person with the *least* information is the boss, so that's the last person you'd want making a *technical* decision. I remember when Mike Maples was my great-grand-boss, in charge of Microsoft Applications, he was adamant about refusing to take sides on technical issues. Eventually, people learned that they shouldn't come to him to adjudicate. This forced people to debate the issue on the merits, and issues were always resolved in favor of the person who was better at arguing, er, I mean, issues were always resolved in the best possible way.

If Command and Control is such a bad way to run a team, why does the military use it?

This was explained to me in NCO school. I was in the Israeli paratroopers in 1986. Probably the worst paratrooper they ever had, now that I think back.

There are several standing orders for soldiers. Standing order number one: if you are in a mine field, *freeze*. Makes sense, right? It was drilled into you repeatedly during basic training. Every once in a while the instructor would shout out "Mine!" and everybody had to freeze just so you would get in the habit.

Standing order number two: when attacked, *run toward your attackers while shooting*. The shooting makes them take cover so they can't fire at you. Running toward them causes you to get closer to them, which makes it easier to aim at them, which makes it easier to kill them. This standing order makes a lot of sense, too.

OK, now for the Interview Question: what do you do if you're in a minefield, and people start shooting at you?

This is not such a hypothetical situation; it's a really annoying way to get caught in an ambush.

The correct answer, it turns out, is that you ignore the minefield and run toward the attackers while shooting.

The rationale behind this is that if you freeze, they'll pick you off one at a time until you're all dead, but if you charge, only some of you will die by running over mines, so for the greater good, that's what you have to do.

The trouble is that no rational soldier would charge under such circumstances. Each individual soldier has an enormous incentive to cheat: freeze in place and let the other, more macho, soldiers do the charging. It's sort of like a Prisoners' Dilemma.

In life or death situations, the military needs to make sure that they can shout orders and soldiers will obey them even if the orders are suicidal. That means soldiers need to be programmed to be obedient in a way that is not really all that important for, say, a software company.

In other words, the military uses Command and Control because it's the only way to get 18-year-olds to charge through a minefield, not because they think it's the best management method for every situation.

In particular, in software development teams where good developers can work anywhere they want, playing soldier is going to get *pretty* tedious, and you're not really going to keep anyone on your team.

Next in this series: The Econ 101 Management Method

six

THE ECON 101 MANAGEMENT METHOD

Joke: A poor Jew lived in the shtetl in nineteenth-century Russia. A Cossack comes up to him on horseback.

"What are you feeding that chicken?" asks the Cossack.

"Just some bread crumbs," replies the Jew.

"How dare you feed a fine Russian chicken such lowly food!" says the Cossack, and hits the Jew with a stick.

The next day, the Cossack comes back. "Now what are you feeding that chicken?" ask the Jew.

"Well, I give him three courses. There's freshly cut grass, fine sturgeon caviar, and a small bowl of heavy cream sprinkled with imported French chocolate truffles for dessert."

"Idiot!" says the Cossack, beating the Jew with a stick. "How dare you waste good food on a lowly chicken!"

On the third day, the Cossack again asks, "What are you feeding that chicken?"

"Nothing!" pleads the Jew. "I give him a kopeck and he buys whatever he wants."

(Pause for laughter)

(No?)

(Ba dum dum)

(Still no laughter)

(Oh well)

I use the term "Econ 101" a little bit tongue-in-cheek. For my non-American readers: most US college departments have a course numbered

"101," which is the basic introductory course for any field. Econ 101 management is the style used by people who know just enough economic theory to be dangerous.

The Econ 101 manager assumes that everyone is motivated by money, and that the best way to get people to do what you want them to do is to give them financial rewards and punishments to create incentives.

For example, AOL might pay their call-center people for every customer they persuade *not* to cancel their subscription.

A software company might give bonuses to programmers who create the fewest bugs.

It works about as well as giving your chickens money to buy their own food.

One big problem is that it replaces intrinsic motivation with extrinsic motivation.

Intrinsic motivation is your own natural desire to do things well. People usually start out with a lot of intrinsic motivation. They want to do a good job. They *want* to help people understand that it's in their best interest to keep paying AOL $24 a month. They *want* to write less buggy code.

Extrinsic motivation is a motivation that comes from outside, like when you're paid to achieve something specific.

Intrinsic motivation is much stronger than extrinsic motivation. People work much harder at things that they *actually want to do*. That's not very controversial.

But when you offer people money to do things that they wanted to do anyway, they suffer from something called the Overjustification Effect. "I must be writing bug-free code because I like the money I get for it," they think, and the extrinsic motivation *displaces* the intrinsic motivation. Since extrinsic motivation is a much weaker effect, the net result is that you've actually *reduced* their desire to do a good job. When you stop paying the bonus, or when they decide they don't care that much about the money, they no longer think that they care about bug-free code.

Another big problem with Econ 101 management is the tendency for people to find local maxima. They'll find some way to optimize for the specific thing you're paying them, without actually achieving the thing you really want.

So, for example, your customer retention specialist, in his desire to earn the bonus associated with maintaining a customer, will drive the customer so crazy that the *New York Times* will run a big front page story about how nasty your customer "service" is. Although his behavior maximizes the thing you're paying him for (customer retention), it doesn't maximize the thing you really care about (profit). And then you try to reward him for the company profit, say, by giving him 13 shares of stock, and you realize that it's not really something he controls, so it's a waste of time.

When you use Econ 101 management, you're encouraging developers to game the system.

Suppose you decide to pay a bonus to the developer with the fewest bugs. Now every time a tester tries to report a bug, it becomes a big argument, and usually the developer convinces the tester that it's not really a bug. Or the tester agrees to report the bug "informally" to the developer before writing it up in the bug tracking system. And now nobody uses the bug tracking system. The bug count goes way down, but the number of bugs stays the same.

Developers are clever this way. Whatever you try to measure, they'll find a way to maximize, and you'll never quite get what you want.

Robert D. Austin, in his book *Measuring and Managing Performance in Organizations*, says there are two phases when you introduce new performance metrics. At first, you actually get what you want, because nobody has figured out how to cheat. In the second phase, you actually get something *worse*, as everyone figures out the trick to maximizing the thing that you're measuring, even at the cost of ruining the company.

Worse, Econ 101 managers think that they can somehow avoid this situation just by tweaking the metrics. Dr. Austin's conclusion is that you just *can't*. It never works. No matter how much you try to adjust the metrics to reflect what you think you want, it always backfires.

The biggest problem with Econ 101 management, though, is that it's not management at all: it's really more of an abdication of management. A deliberate refusal to figure out how things can be made better. It's a sign that management simply doesn't know how to teach people to do better work, so they force everybody in the system to come up with their own way of doing it.

Instead of training developers on techniques of writing reliable code, you just absolve yourself of responsibility by paying them if they do. Now every developer has to figure it out on their own.

For more mundane tasks, working the counter at Starbucks or answering phone calls at AOL, it's pretty unlikely that the average worker will figure out a better way of doing things on their own. You can go into any coffee shop in the country and order a short soy caramel latte extra-hot, and you'll find that you have to keep repeating your order again and again: once to the coffee maker, again to the coffee maker when they forget what you said, and finally to the cashier so they can figure out what to charge you. That's the result of nobody telling the workers a better way. Nobody figures it out, except Starbucks, where the standard training involves a complete system of naming, writing things on cups, and calling out orders, which ensures that customers only have to specify their drink orders once. The system, invented by Starbucks HQ, works great, but workers at the other chains never, ever come up with it on their own.

Your customer service people spend most of the day talking to customers. They don't have the time, the inclination, or the training to figure out better ways to do things. Nobody in the customer retention crew is going to be able to keep statistics and measure which customer retention techniques work best while pissing off the fewest bloggers. They just don't care enough, they're not smart enough, they don't have enough information, and they are too busy with their real job.

As a manager, it's your job to figure out a system. That's Why You Get The Big Bucks.

If you read a little bit too much Ayn Rand as a kid, or if you took one semester of economics, before they explained that utility is not measured in dollars, you may think that setting up simplified bonus schemes and Pay For Performance is a pretty neat way to manage. But it doesn't work. Start doing your job managing and stop feeding your chickens kopecks.

"Joel!" you yell. "In the previous chapter, you told us that the developers should make all the decisions. Today you're telling us that the managers should make all the decisions. What's up with that?"

Mmm, not exactly. In the previous chapter, I told you that your developers, the leaves in the tree, have the most information; micromanagement, or Command and Control barking out orders, is likely to cause nonoptimal results. Here, I'm telling you that when you're creating a system, you can't abdicate your responsibility to train your people by bribing them. Management, in general, needs to set up the system so that people can get things done, it needs to avoid displacing intrinsic motivation with extrinsic motivation, and it won't get very far using fear and barking out specific orders.

Now that I've shot down Command and Control management and Econ 101 management, there's one more method managers can use to get people moving in the right direction. I call it the Identity Management Method, and I'll talk about it more in the next chapter.

Next in this series: The Identity Management Method

seven

THE IDENTITY MANAGEMENT METHOD

Thursday, August 10, 2006

When you're trying to get a team all working in the same direction, we've seen that Command and Control management and Econ 101 management both fail pretty badly in high-tech, knowledge-oriented teams.

That leaves a technique that I'm going to have to call the Identity Management Method. The goal here is to manage by making people *identify* with the goals you're trying to achieve. That's a lot trickier than the other methods, and it requires some serious interpersonal skills to pull off. But if you do it right, it works better than any other method.

The problem with Econ 101 management is that it subverts intrinsic motivation. The Identity Management Method is a way to *create* intrinsic motivation.

To follow the Identity Management Method, you have to summon all the social skills you have to make your employees identify with the goals of the organization so that they are highly motivated, and then you need to give them the information they need to steer in the right direction.

How do you make people identify with the organization?

It helps if the organizational goals are virtuous, or perceived as virtuous, in some way. Apple creates almost fanatic identification, almost entirely through a narrative that started with a single Superbowl ad in 1984: we are against totalitarianism. Doesn't seem like a particularly bold position to take, but it worked. Here at Fog Creek, we stand bravely in opposition to killing kittens. Yaaaay!

A method I'm pretty comfortable with is eating together. I've always made a point of eating lunch with my coworkers, and at Fog Creek we serve catered lunches for the whole team every day and eat together at one big table. It's hard to overstate what a big impact this has on making the company feel like a family, in the good way, I think. In six years, nobody has ever quit.

I'm probably going to freak out some of our summer interns by admitting this, but one the goals of our internship program is to make people identify as New Yorkers so they're more comfortable with the idea of moving here after college and working for us full time. We do this through a pretty exhausting list of extracurricular summer activities: two Broadway shows, a trip to the Top of the Rock, a boat ride around Manhattan, a Yankees game, an open house so they can meet more New Yorkers, and a trip to a museum. Michael and I host parties in our apartments, not only as a way of welcoming the interns, but also as a way for interns to visualize living in an apartment in New York, not just the dorm we stuck them in.

In general, Identity management requires you to create a cohesive, jelled team that feels like a family, so that people have a sense of loyalty and commitment to their coworkers.

The second part, though, is to give people the information they need to steer the organization in the right direction.

Earlier today, Brett came into my office to discuss ship dates for FogBugz 6.0. He was sort of leaning toward April 2007; I was sort of leaning toward December 2006. Of course, if we shipped in April, we would have time to do a lot more polishing and improve many areas of the product; if we shipped in December, we'd probably have to cut a bunch of nice new features.

What I explained to Brett, though, is that we want to hire six new people in the spring, and the chances that we'll be able to afford them without FogBugz 6.0 are much smaller. So the way I concluded the meeting with Brett was to make him understand the exact financial motivations I have for shipping earlier, and now that he knows that, I'm confident he'll make the right decision . . . not necessarily *my* decision. Maybe we'll have a big upswing in sales without FogBugz 6.0, and now that Brett understands the basic financial parameters, he'll realize that maybe that means we can hold 6.0 for a few more features. The point being that by sharing information, I can get Brett to do the right thing for Fog Creek even if circumstances change. If I tried to push him around by offering him a cash reward for every day before April that he ships, his incentive would be to dump the existing buggy development build on the public *tonight*. If I tried to push him around using Command and Control management by ordering him to ship bug-free code on time, *dammit*, he might do it, but he'd hate his job and leave.

~

Conclusion

There are as many different styles of management as there are managers. I've identified three major styles: two easy, dysfunctional styles and one hard, functional style, but the truth is that many development shops manage in more of an ad hoc "whatever works" way that may change from day to day or person to person.

part two

Advice to Potential Programmers

eight

THE PERILS OF JAVASCHOOLS

Thursday, December 29, 2005

Lazy kids.

Whatever happened to hard work?

A sure sign of my descent into senility is bitchin' and moanin' about "kids these days," and how they won't or can't do anything hard any more.

When *I* was a kid, I learned to program on punched cards. If you made a mistake, you didn't have any of these modern features like a Backspace key to correct it. You threw away the card and started over.

When I started interviewing programmers in 1991, I would generally let them use any language they wanted to solve the coding problems I gave them. 99% of the time, they chose C.

Nowadays, they tend to choose Java.

Now, don't get me wrong: there's nothing wrong with Java as an implementation language.

Wait a minute, I want to modify that statement. I'm not claiming, *in this particular discussion*, that there's anything wrong with Java as an implementation language. There are lots of things wrong with it, but those will have to wait for another time.

Instead, what I'd like to claim is that Java is not, generally, a hard enough programming language that it can be used to discriminate between great programmers and mediocre programmers. It may be a fine language to work in, but that's not today's topic. I would even go so far as to say that the fact that Java is not hard enough is a feature, not a bug, but it does have this one problem.

If I may be so brash, it has been my humble experience that there are two things traditionally taught in universities as a part of a computer science curriculum that many people just never really fully comprehend: pointers and recursion.

You used to start out in college with a course in data structures, with linked lists and hash tables and whatnot, with extensive use of pointers. Those courses were often used as weed-out courses: they were so hard that anyone who couldn't handle the mental challenge of a CS degree would give up, which was a good thing, because if you thought pointers were hard, wait until you try to prove things about fixed point theory.

All the kids who did great in high school writing pong games in BASIC for their Apple II would get to college, take CompSci 101, a data structures course, and when they hit the pointers business, their brains would just totally explode, and the next thing you knew, they were majoring in political science because law school seemed like a better idea. I've seen all kinds of figures for dropout rates in CS, and they're usually between 40% and 70%. The universities tend to see this as a waste; I think it's just a necessary culling of the people who aren't going to be happy or successful in programming careers.

The other hard course for many young CS students was the course where you learned functional programming, including recursive programming. MIT set the bar very high for these courses, creating a required course (6.001) and a textbook (Abelson and Sussman's *Structure and Interpretation of Computer Programs* [The MIT Press, 1996]), which were used at dozens or even hundreds of top CS schools as the de facto introduction to computer science. (You can, and should, watch an older version of the lectures online.)

The difficulty of these courses is astonishing. In the first lecture, you've learned pretty much all of Scheme, and you're already being introduced to a fixed-point function that takes another function as its input. When I struggled through such a course, CSE 121 at Penn, I watched as many, if not most, of the students just didn't make it. The material was too hard. I wrote a long sob e-mail to the professor saying It Just Wasn't Fair. Somebody at Penn must have listened to me (or one of the other complainers), because that course is now taught in Java.

I wish they hadn't listened.

Therein lies the debate. Years of whinging by lazy CS undergrads like me, combined with complaints from industry about how few CS majors are graduating from American universities, have taken a toll, and in the last decade a large number of otherwise perfectly good schools have gone 100% Java. It's hip, the recruiters who use "grep" to evaluate resumes seem to like it, and, best of all, there's nothing hard enough about Java to really weed out the programmers without the part of the brain that does pointers or recursion, so the dropout rates are lower, and the computer science departments have more students and bigger budgets, and all is well.

The lucky kids of JavaSchools are never going to get weird segfaults trying to implement pointer-based hash tables. They're never going to go stark, raving mad trying to pack things into bits. They'll never have to get their head around how, in a purely functional program, the value of a variable never changes, and yet, it changes all the time! A paradox!

They don't need that part of the brain to get a 4.0 in their major.

Am I just one of those old-fashioned curmudgeons, like the Four Yorkshiremen, bragging about how tough I was to survive all that hard stuff?

Heck, in 1900, Latin and Greek were required subjects in college, not because they served any purpose, but because they were sort of considered an obvious requirement for educated people. In some sense, my argument is no different from the argument made by the pro-Latin people (all four of them). "[Latin] trains your mind. Trains your memory. Unraveling a Latin sentence is an excellent exercise in thought, a real intellectual puzzle, and a good introduction to logical thinking," writes Scott Barker (www.promotelatin.org/whylatin.htm). But I can't find a single university that requires Latin any more. Are pointers and recursion the Latin and Greek of computer science?

Now, I freely admit that programming with pointers is not needed in 90% of the code written today, and in fact, it's downright dangerous in production code. OK. That's fine. And functional programming is just not used much in practice. Agreed.

But it's still important for some of the most exciting programming jobs. Without pointers, for example, you'd never be able to work on the Linux kernel. You can't understand a line of code in Linux, or, indeed, any operating system, without really understanding pointers.

Without understanding functional programming, you can't invent MapReduce, the algorithm that makes Google so massively scalable. The terms "Map" and "Reduce" come from Lisp and functional programming. MapReduce is, in retrospect, obvious to anyone who remembers from their 6.001-equivalent programming class that purely functional programs have no side effects and are thus trivially paralleliz-able. The very fact that Google invented MapReduce, and Microsoft didn't, says something about why Microsoft is still playing catch-up try-ing to get basic search features to work, while Google has moved on to the next problem: building Skynet^H^H^H^H^H^H, the world's largest massively parallel supercomputer. I don't think Microsoft com-pletely understands just how far behind they are on that wave.

But beyond the prima facie importance of pointers and recursion, their real value is that building big systems requires the kind of mental flexibility you get from learning about them and the mental aptitude you need to avoid being weeded out of the courses in which they are taught. Pointers and recursion require a certain ability to reason, to think in abstractions, and, most importantly, to view a problem at several levels of abstraction simultaneously. And thus, the ability to understand point-ers and recursion is directly correlated with the ability to be a great programmer.

Nothing about an all-Java CS degree really weeds out the students who lack the mental agility to deal with these concepts. As an employer, I've seen that the 100% JavaSchools have started churning out quite a few CS graduates who are simply not smart enough to work as pro-grammers on anything more sophisticated than Yet Another Java Accounting Application, although they did manage to squeak through the newly dumbed-down coursework. These students would never sur-vive 6.001 at MIT or CS 323 at Yale, and frankly, that is one reason why, as an employer, a CS degree from MIT or Yale carries more weight than a CS degree from Duke, which recently went All Java, or Penn, which replaced Scheme and ML with Java in trying to teach the class that nearly killed me and my friends, CSE 121. Not that I don't want to hire smart kids from Duke and Penn—I do—it's just a lot harder for me to figure out who they are. I used to be able to tell the smart kids because they could rip through a recursive algorithm in seconds, or implement linked-list manipulation functions using pointers as fast as they could write on the whiteboard. But with a JavaSchool grad, I can't tell whether they're struggling with these problems because they are undereducated or because they don't actually have that special part of the brain that they're going to need to do great programming work. Paul Graham calls them "Blub programmers" (www.paulgraham.com/avg.html).

It's bad enough that JavaSchools fail to weed out the kids who are never going to be great programmers, which the schools could justifiably say is not their problem. Industry or, at least, the recruiters-who-use-grep are surely clamoring for Java to be taught.

But JavaSchools also fail to train the brains of kids to be adept, agile, and flexible enough to do good software design (and I don't mean object-oriented "design," where you spend countless hours rewriting your code to rejiggle your object hierarchy, or you fret about faux "problems" like "has-a" vs. "is-a"). You need training to think of things at multiple levels of abstraction simultaneously, and that kind of thinking is exactly what you need to design great software architecture.

You may be wondering if teaching object-oriented programming (OOP) is a good weed-out substitute for pointers and recursion. The quick answer: no. Without debating OOP on the merits, it is just not hard enough to weed out mediocre programmers. OOP in school consists mostly of memorizing a bunch of vocabulary terms like "encapsulation" and "inheritance" and taking multiple-choice quizzicles on the difference between polymorphism and overloading. Not much harder than memorizing famous dates and names in a history class, OOP poses inadequate mental challenges to scare away first-year students. When you struggle with an OOP problem, *your program still works*, it's just sort of hard to maintain. Allegedly. But when you struggle with pointers, your program produces the line Segmentation Fault, and you have no idea what's going on, until you stop and take a deep breath and really try to force your mind to work at two different levels of abstraction simultaneously.

The recruiters-who-use-grep, by the way, are ridiculed here, and for good reason. I have never met anyone who can do Scheme, Haskell, and C pointers who can't pick up Java in two days and create better Java code than people with five years of experience in Java, but try explaining that to the average HR drone.

But what about the CS mission of CS departments? They're not vocational schools! It shouldn't be their job to train people to work in industry. That's for community colleges and government retraining programs for displaced workers, they will tell you. They're supposed to be giving students the fundamental tools to live their lives, not preparing them for their first weeks on the job. Right?

Still. CS is proofs (recursion), algorithms (recursion), languages (lambda calculus), operating systems (pointers), compilers (lambda calculus)—and so the bottom line is that a JavaSchool that won't teach C and won't teach Scheme is not really teaching computer science either. As useless as the concept of function currying may be to the real world, it's obviously a prereq for CS grad school. I can't understand why the professors on the curriculum committees at CS schools have allowed their programs to be dumbed down to the point where not only can't they produce *working programmers*, they can't even produce CS grad students who might get PhDs and compete for their jobs. Oh wait. Never mind. Maybe I do understand.

Actually, if you go back and research the discussion that took place in academia during the Great Java Shift, you'll notice that the biggest concern was whether Java was *simple* enough to use as a teaching language.

My God, I thought, *they're trying to dumb down the curriculum even further!* Why not spoonfeed everything to the students? Let's have the TAs take their tests for them, too, and then nobody will switch to American studies. How is anyone supposed to learn anything if the curriculum has been carefully designed to make everything easier than it already is? There seems to be a task force underway to figure out a simple subset of Java that can be taught to students, producing simplified documentation that carefully hides all that EJB/J2EE crap from their tender minds, so they don't have to worry their little heads with any classes where they don't need to do the ever-easier CS problem sets.

The most sympathetic interpretation of why CS departments are so enthusiastic to dumb down their classes is that it leaves them more time to teach actual CS concepts, if they don't need to spend two whole lectures unconfusing students about the difference between, say, a Java int and an Integer. Well, if that's the case, 6.001 has the perfect answer for you: Scheme, a teaching language so simple that the entire language can be taught to bright students in about ten minutes; then you can spend the rest of the semester on fixed points.

Feh.

I'm going back to ones and zeros.

(You had ones? Lucky bastard! All we got were zeros.)

nine

TALK AT YALE

Monday, December 3, 2007

This is part one of the text of a talk delivered to the Yale Computer Science department on November 28, 2007.

I graduated with a BS in computer science in 1991. Sixteen years ago. What I'm going to try to do today is relate my undergraduate years in the CS department to my career, which consists of developing software, writing about software, and starting a software company. And, of course, that's a little bit absurd; there's a famous part at the beginning of MIT's Introduction to Computer Science where Hal Abelson gets up and explains that computer science isn't about computers and it isn't a science, so it's a little bit presumptuous of me to imply that CS is supposed to be training for a career in software development, any more than, say, media studies or cultural anthropology would be.

I'll press ahead anyway. One of the most useful classes I took was a course that I dropped after the first lecture. Another one was a class given by Roger Schank that was so disdained by the CS faculty that it was not allowed to count toward a degree in computer science. But I'll get to that in a minute.

The third was this little gut called CS 322, which you know of as CS 323. Back in my day, CS 322 took so much work that it was a 1 1/2 credit class. And Yale's rule is that extra half credit could only be combined with other half credits from the same department. Apparently, there were two other 1 1/2 credit courses, but they could only be taken together. So through that clever trickery, the half credit was therefore completely useless, but it did justify those weekly problem sets that took forty hours to complete. After years of students' complaining, the course was adjusted to be a 1 credit class, it was renumbered CS 323, and still had weekly forty-hour problem sets. Other than that, it's pretty much the same thing. I loved it, because I love programming. The best thing about CS 323 is it teaches a lot of people that they just ain't never gonna be programmers. This is a good thing. People who don't have the benefit of Stan Eisenstat teaching them that they can't be programmers have miserable careers cutting and pasting a lot of Java. By the way, if you took CS 323 and got an A, we have great summer internships at Fog Creek. See me afterward.

As far as I can tell, the core curriculum hasn't changed at all. 201, 223, 240, 323, 365, 421, 422, 424, 429 appear to be almost the same courses we took sixteen years ago. The number of CS majors is actually up since I went to Yale, although a temporary peak during the dot-com days makes it look like it's down. And there are a lot more interesting electives now than there were in my time. So: progress.

For a moment there, I actually thought I'd get a PhD. Both my parents are professors. So many of their friends were academics that I grew up assuming that all adults eventually got PhDs. In any case, I was thinking pretty seriously of going on to graduate school in computer science. Until I tried to take a class in dynamic logic right here in this very department. It was taught by Lenore Zuck, who is now at UIC.

I didn't last very long, nor did I understand much of anything that was going on. From what I gather, dynamic logic is just like formal logic: Socrates is a man, all men are mortal, therefore Socrates is mortal. The difference is that in dynamic logic, truth values can change over time. Socrates was a man, now he's a cat, etc. In theory, this should be an interesting way to prove things about computer programs, in which state, i.e., truth values, change over time.

In the first lecture, Dr. Zuck presented a few axioms and some transformation rules and set about trying to prove a very simple thing. She had a computer program, $f := not\ f$, where f is a Boolean that simply flipped a bit; the goal was to prove that if you ran this program an even number of times, f would finish with the same value as it started out with.

The proof went on and on. It was in this very room, if I remember correctly, it looks like the carpet hasn't been changed since then, and all of these blackboards were completely covered in the steps of the proof. Dr. Zuck used proof by induction, proof by reductio ad absurdum, proof by exhaustion—the class was late in the day and we were already running forty minutes over—and, in desperation, proof by graduate student, whereby, she says, "I can't really remember how to prove this step," and a graduate student in the front row says, "Yes, yes, professor, that's right."

And when all was said and done, she got to the end of the proof and somehow was getting exactly the opposite result of the one that made sense, until that same graduate student pointed out where, 63 steps earlier, some bit had been accidentally flipped due to a little bit of dirt on the board, and all was well.

For our homework, she told us to prove the converse: that if you run the program f := not f n times, and the bit is in the same state as it started, that n must be even.

I worked on that problem for hours and hours. I had her original proof in front of me, going in one direction, which, upon closer examination, turned out to have all kinds of missing steps that were "trivial," but not to me. I read every word about dynamic logic that I could find in Becton Center, and I struggled with the problem late into the night. I was getting absolutely nowhere and increasingly despairing of theoretical computer science. It occurred to me that when you have a proof that goes on for pages and pages, it's far more likely to contain errors than your own intuition about the trivial statements that it's trying to prove; and I decided that this dynamic logic stuff was really not a fruitful way of proving things about actual, interesting computer programs, because you're more likely to make a mistake in the proof than you are to make a mistake in your own intuition about what the program f := not f is going to do. So I dropped the course, thank God for shopping period, but not only that, I decided on the spot that graduate school in computer science was just not for me, which made this the single most useful course I ever took.

Now this brings me to one of the important themes that I've learned in my career. Time and time again, you'll see programmers redefining problems so that they can be solved algorithmically. By redefining the problem, it often happens that they're left with something that can be solved, but which is actually a trivial problem. They don't solve the real problem, because that's intractable. I'll give you an example.

You will frequently hear the claim that software engineering is facing a quality crisis of some sort. I don't happen to agree with that claim—

the computer software most people use most of the time is of ridiculously high quality compared to everything else in their lives—but that's beside the point. This claim about the "quality crisis" leads to a lot of proposals and research about making higher quality software. And at this point, the world divides into the geeks and the suits.

The geeks want to solve the problem automatically, using software. They propose things like unit tests, test-driven development, automated testing, dynamic logic, and other ways to "prove" that a program is bug free.

The suits aren't really aware of the problem. They couldn't care less if the software is buggy, as long as people are buying it.

Currently, in the battle between the geeks and the suits, the suits are winning, because they control the budget, and honestly, I don't know if that's such a bad thing. The suits recognize that there are diminishing returns to fixing bugs. Once the software hits a certain level of quality that allows it to solve someone's problem, that person will pay for it and derive benefit out of it.

The suits also have a broader definition of "quality." Their definition is about as mercenary as you can imagine: the quality of software is defined by how much it increases their bonus this year. Accidentally, this definition of quality incorporates a lot more than just making the software bug free. For example, it places a lot of value on adding more features to solve more problems for more people, which the geeks tend to deride by calling it "bloatware." It places value on aesthetics: a cool-looking program sells more copies than an ugly program. It places value on how happy a program makes its users feel. Fundamentally, it lets the users define their own concept of quality and decide on their own if a given program meets their needs.

Now, the geeks are interested in the narrowly technical aspects of quality. They focus on things they can see in the code, rather than waiting for the users to judge. They're programmers, so they try to automate everything in their life, and of course they try to automate the QA process. This is how you get unit testing, which is not a bad thing, don't get me wrong, and it's how you get all these attempts to mechanically "prove" that a program is "correct." The trouble is that anything that can't be automated has to be thrown out of the definition of quality. Even though we know that users prefer software that looks cooler, there's no automated way to measure how cool looking a program is, so that gets left out of the automated QA process.

In fact, what you'll see is that the hard-core geeks tend to give up on all kinds of useful measures of quality, and basically they get left with the only one they can prove mechanically, which is, does the program behave according to specification. And so we get a very narrow, geeky definition of quality: how closely the program corresponds to the spec. Does it produce the defined outputs given the defined inputs?

The problem here is very fundamental. In order to mechanically prove that a program corresponds to some spec, the spec itself needs to be extremely detailed. In fact, the spec has to define everything about the program; otherwise, nothing can be proven automatically and mechanically. Now, if the spec does define everything about how the program is going to behave, then, lo and behold, it contains all the information necessary to generate the program! And now certain geeks go off to a very dark place where they start thinking about automatically compiling specs into programs, and they start to think that they've just invented a way to program computers without programming.

Now, this is the software engineering equivalent of a perpetual motion machine. It's one of those things that crackpots keep trying to do, no matter how much you tell them it could never work. If the spec defines precisely what a program will do, with enough detail that it can be used to generate the program itself, this just begs the question: how do you write the spec? Such a complete spec is just as hard to write as the underlying computer program, because just as many details have to be answered by the spec writer as the programmer. To use terminology from information theory: the spec needs just as many bits of Shannon entropy as the computer program itself would have. Each bit of entropy is a decision taken by the spec writer or the programmer.

So, the bottom line is that if there really were a mechanical way to prove things about the correctness of a program, all you'd be able to prove is whether that program is identical to some other program that must contain the same amount of entropy as the first program; otherwise, some of the behaviors are going to be undefined, and thus unproven. So now the spec writing is just as hard as writing a program, and all you've done is moved one problem from over here to over there, and accomplished nothing whatsoever.

This seems like a kind of brutal example, but nonetheless, this search for the holy grail of program quality is leading a lot of people to a lot of dead ends. The Windows Vista team at Microsoft is a case in point. Apparently—and this is all based on blog rumors and innuendo—Microsoft has had a long-term policy of eliminating all software testers who don't know how to write code, replacing them with what they call SDETs, Software Development Engineers in Test, programmers who write automated testing scripts.

The old testers at Microsoft checked lots of things: they checked whether fonts were consistent and legible, they checked that the location of controls on dialog boxes was reasonable and neatly aligned, they checked whether the screen flickered when you did things, they looked at how the UI flowed, they considered how easy the software was to use and how consistent the wording was, they worried about performance, they checked the spelling and grammar of all the error messages, and they spent a lot of time making sure that the user interface was consistent from one part of the product to another, because a consistent user interface is easier to use than an inconsistent one.

None of those things could be checked by automated scripts. And so one result of the new emphasis on automated testing was that the Vista release of Windows was extremely inconsistent and unpolished. Lots of obvious problems got through in the final product . . . none of which was a "bug" by the definition of the automated scripts, but every one of which contributed to the general feeling that Vista was a downgrade from XP. The geeky definition of quality won out over the suit's definition; I'm sure the automated scripts for Windows Vista are running at 100% success right now at Microsoft, but it doesn't help when just about every tech reviewer is advising people to stick with XP for as long as humanly possible. It turns out that nobody wrote the automated test to check whether Vista provided users with a compelling reason to upgrade from XP.

I don't hate Microsoft, really I don't. In fact, my first job out of school was actually at Microsoft. In those days, it was not really a respectable place to work. Sort of like taking a job in the circus. People looked at you funny. Really? Microsoft? On campus, in particular, it was perceived as corporate, boring, buttoned-down, making inferior software so that accountants can do, oh I don't know, spreadsheets or whatever it is that accountants do. Perfectly miserable. And it all ran on a pathetic single-tasking operating system, called MS-DOS, full of arbitrary stupid limitations like 8-character file names and no e-mail and no telnet and no Usenet. Well, MS-DOS is long gone, but the cultural gap between the Unixheads and the Windows users has never been wider. This is a culture war. The disagreements are very byzantine but very fundamental. To Yale, Microsoft was this place that made toy business operating systems using three-decades-old computer science. To Microsoft, "computer sciency" was a bad term used to make fun of new hires with their bizarre hypotheses about how Haskell is the next major programming language.

Just to give you one tiny example of the Unix-Windows cultural war. Unix has this cultural value of separating user interface from functionality. A righteous Unix program starts out with a command-line interface, and if you're lucky, someone else will come along and write a pretty front end for it, with shading and transparency and 3D effects, and this pretty front end just launches the command-line interface in the background, which then fails in mysterious ways, which are then not reflected properly in the pretty front end, which is now hung waiting for some input that it's never going to get.

But the good news is that you can use the command-line interface from a script.

Whereas the Windows culture would be to write a GUI app in the first place, and all the core functionality would be tangled up hopelessly with the user interface code, so you could have this gigantic application like Photoshop that's absolutely brilliant for editing photos, but if you're a programmer, and you want to use Photoshop to resize a folder of 1,000 pictures so that each one fits in a 200-pixel box, you just can't write that code, because it's all very tightly bound to a particular user interface.

Anyway, the two cultures roughly correspond to highbrow vs. lowbrow, and in fact, it's reflected accurately in the curriculum of computer science departments throughout the country. At Ivy League institutions, everything is Unix, functional programming, and theoretical stuff about state machines. As you move down the chain to less and less selective schools, Java starts to appear. Move even lower, and you literally start to see classes in topics like Microsoft Visual Studio 2005 101, three credits. By the time you get to the two-year institutions, you see the same kind of SQL-Server-in-21-days "certification" courses you see advertised on the weekends on cable TV. Isn't it time to start your career in (different voice) Java Enterprise Beans!

TUESDAY, DECEMBER 4, 2007

This is part two of the text of a talk delivered to the Yale Computer Science department on November 28, 2007.

After a few years in Redmond, Washington, during which I completely failed to adapt to my environment, I beat a hasty retreat to New York City. I stayed on with Microsoft in New York for a few months, where I was a complete and utter failure as a consultant at Microsoft Consulting, and then I spent a few years in the mid-90s, when the Internet was first starting to happen, at Viacom. That's this big corporate conglomerate which owned MTV, VH1, Nickelodeon, Blockbuster, Paramount Studios, Comedy Central, CBS, and a bunch of other entertainment companies. New York was the first place I got to see what most computer programmers do for a living. It's this scary thing called "in-house software." It's terrifying. You never want to do in-house software. You're a programmer for a big corporation that makes, oh, I don't know, aluminum cans, and there's nothing quite available off the shelf that does the exact kind of aluminum can processing that they need, so they have these in-house programmers, or they hire companies like Accenture and IBM to send them overpriced programmers, to write this software. And there are two reasons this is so frightening: one, because it's not a very fulfilling career if you're a programmer, for a list of reasons that I'll enumerate in a moment, and two, it's frightening because this is what probably 80% of programming jobs are like, and if you're not very, very careful when you graduate, you might find yourself working on in-house software, by accident, and let me tell you, it can drain the life out of you.

OK, so, why does it suck to be an in-house programmer?

Number one: you never get to do things the right way. You always have to do things the expedient way. It costs so much money to hire these programmers—typically a company like Accenture or IBM would charge $300 an hour for the services of some recent Yale political science grad who took a six-week course in .NET programming, and who is earning $47,000 a year and hoping that it'll provide enough experience to get into business school—anyway, it costs so much to hire these programmers who are not going to be allowed to build things with Ruby on Rails no matter how cool Ruby is and no matter how spiffy the Ajax is going to be. You're going into Visual Studio, you're going to click the wizard, you're going to drag the little Grid control onto the page, you're going to hook it up to the database, and presto, you're done. It's good enough. Get out of there and onto the next thing. That's the second reason these jobs suck: as soon as your program gets good enough, you have to stop working on it. Once the core functionality is there, the main problem is solved, there is absolutely no return on investment, no business reason to make the software any better. So all of these in-house programs look like a dog's breakfast: because it's just not worth a penny to make them look nice. Forget any pride in workmanship or craftsmanship you learned in CS 323. You're going to churn out embarrassing junk, and then, you're going to rush off to patch up last year's embarrassing junk, which is starting to break down because it wasn't done right in the first place, twenty-seven years of that and you get a gold watch. Oh, and they don't give gold watches any more. Twenty-seven years and you get carpal tunnel syndrome. Now, at a product company, for example, if you're a software developer working on a software product or even an online product like Google or Facebook, the better you make the product, the better it sells. The key point about in-house development is that once it's "good enough," you stop. When you're working on products, you can keep refining and polishing and refactoring and improving, and if you work for Facebook, you can spend a whole month optimizing the Ajax name-choosing gizmo so that it's really fast and really cool, and all that effort is worthwhile because it makes your product better than the competition. So, the number two reason product work is better than in-house work is that you get to make beautiful things.

Number three: when you're a programmer at a software company, the work you're doing is directly related to the way the company makes money. That means, for one thing, that management cares about you. It means you get the best benefits and the nicest offices and the best chances for promotion. A programmer is never going to rise to become CEO of Viacom, but you might well rise to become CEO of a tech company.

Anyway. After Microsoft, I took a job at Viacom, because I wanted to learn something about the Internet, and Microsoft was willfully ignoring it in those days. But at Viacom, I was just an in-house programmer, several layers removed from anybody who did anything that made Viacom money in any way.

And I could tell that no matter how critical it was for Viacom to get this Internet thing right, when it came time to assign people to desks, the in-house programmers were stuck with three people per cubicle in a dark part of the office with no line of sight to a window, and the "producers," I don't know what they did exactly, but they were sort of the equivalent of Turtle on *Entourage*, the producers had their own big windowed offices overlooking the Hudson River. Once at a Viacom Christmas party, I was introduced to the executive in charge of interactive strategy or something. A very lofty position. He said something vague and inept about how interactivity was very important. It was the future. It convinced me that he had no flipping idea whatsoever what it was that was happening and what the Internet meant or what I did as a programmer, and he was a little bit scared of it all, but who cares, because he's making two million dollars a year and I'm just a typist or "HTML operator" or whatever it is that I did, how hard can it be, his teenage daughter can do that.

So I moved across the street to Juno Online Services. This was an early Internet provider that gave people free dial-up accounts that could only be used for e-mail. It wasn't like Hotmail or Gmail, which didn't exist yet, because you didn't need Internet access to begin with, so it was really free.

Juno was, allegedly, supported by advertising. It turned out that advertising to the kinds of people who won't pay $20 a month for AOL is not exactly the most lucrative business in the world, so in reality, Juno was supported by rich investors. But at least Juno was a product company where programmers were held in high regard, and I felt good about their mission to provide e-mail to everyone. And indeed, I worked there happily for about three years as a C++ programmer. Eventually, though, I started to discover that the management philosophy at Juno was old fashioned. The assumption there was that managers exist to tell people what to do. This is quite upside-down from the way management worked in typical West Coast high-tech companies. What I was used to from the West Coast was an attitude that management is just an annoying, mundane chore someone has to do so that the smart people can get their work done. Think of an academic department at a university, where being the chairperson of the department is actually something of a burden that nobody really wants to do; they'd much rather be doing research. That's the Silicon Valley style of management. Managers exist to get furniture out of the way so the real talent can do brilliant work.

Juno was founded by very young, very inexperienced people—the president of the company was 24 years old, and it was his first job, not just his first management job—and somewhere in a book or a movie or a TV show, he had gotten the idea that managers exist to DECIDE.

If there's one thing I know, it's that managers have the least information about every technical issue, and they are the last people who should be deciding anything. When I was at Microsoft, Mike Maples, the head of the applications division, used to have people come to him to resolve some technical debate they were having. And he would juggle some bowling pins, tell a joke, and tell them to get the hell out of his office and solve their own damned problems instead of coming to him, the least qualified person to make a technical decision on its merits. That was, I thought, the only way to manage smart, highly qualified people. But the Juno managers, like George Bush, were the deciders, and there were too many decisions to be made, so they practiced something I started calling hit-and-run micromanagement: they dive in from nowhere, micromanage some tiny little issue, like how dates should be entered in a dialog box, overriding the opinions of all the highly qualified technical people on the team who had been working on that problem for weeks, and then they disappear, so that's the hit-and-run part, because there's some other little brush fire elsewhere that needs micromanagement.

So, I quit, without a real plan.

WEDNESDAY, DECEMBER 5, 2007

This is part three of the text of a talk delivered to the Yale Computer Science department on November 28, 2007.

I despaired of finding a company to work for where programmers were treated like talent and not like typists, and decided I would have to start my own. In those days, I was seeing lots of really dumb people with really dumb business plans making Internet companies, and I thought, hey, if I can be, say, 10% less dumb than them, that should be easy, maybe I can make a company too, and in my company, we'd do things right for a change. We'd treat programmers with respect, we'd make high-quality products, we wouldn't take any shit from VCs or 24-year-olds playing president, we'd care about our customers and solve their problems when they called, instead of blaming everything on Microsoft, and we'd let our customers decide whether or not to pay us. At Fog Creek, we'll give anyone their money back with no questions asked under any circumstances whatsoever. Keeps us honest.

So, it was the summer of 2000, and I had taken some time off from work while I hatched the plans for Fog Creek Software and went to the beach a lot. During that period, I started writing up some of the things I had learned over the course of my career on a web site called *Joel on Software*. In those early days before blogs were invented, a programmer named Dave Winer had set up a system called EditThisPage.com where anyone could post things to the Web in a sort-of blog like format. *Joel on Software* grew quickly and gave me a pulpit where I could write about software development and actually get some people to pay attention to what I was saying. The site consists of fairly unoriginal thoughts combined with jokes. It was successful because I used a slightly larger font than the average web site, making it easy to read. It's always hard to figure out how many people read the site, especially when you don't bother counting them, but typical articles on that site get read by somewhere between 100,000 and a million people, depending on how popular the topic is.

What I do on *Joel on Software*—writing articles about somewhat technical topics—is something I learned here in the CS department, too. Here's the story behind that. In 1989, Yale was pretty good at AI, and one of the big name professors, Roger Schank, came and gave a little talk at Hillel about some of his AI theories about scripts and schemas and slots and all that kind of stuff. Now essentially, I suspect from reading his work that it was the same speech he'd been giving for twenty years, and he had spent twenty years of his career writing little programs using these theories, presumably to test them, and they didn't work, but somehow the theories never got discarded. He did seem like a brilliant man, and I wanted to take a course with him, but he was well known for hating undergraduates, so the only option was to take this course called Algorithmic Thinking—CS 115—basically, a watered-down gut group

IV class designed for poets. It was technically in the CS department, but the faculty was so completely unimpressed that you were not allowed to count it toward a CS major. Although it was the largest class by enrollment in the CS department, I cringed every time I heard my history-major friends referring to the class as "computer science." A typical assignment was to write an essay on whether machines can think or not. You can see why we weren't allowed to count it toward a CS degree. In fact, I would not be entirely surprised if you revoke my degree today, retroactively, upon learning that I took this class.

The best thing about the Algorithmic Thinking course was that you had to write a lot. There were thirteen papers—one every week. You didn't get grades. Well, you did. Well, OK, there's a story there. One of the reasons Schank hated undergrads so much was that they were obsessed with grades. He wanted to talk about whether computers could think, and all undergrads wanted to talk about was why their paper got a B instead of an A. At the beginning of the term, he made a big speech about how grades are evil and decided that the only grade you could get on a paper was a little check mark to signify that some grad student read it. Over time, he wanted to recognize the really good papers, so he added check-plus, and then there were some really lame papers, so he started giving out check-minuses, and I think I got a check-plus-plus once. But grades: never.

And despite the fact that CS 115 didn't count toward the major, all this experience writing about slightly technical topics turned out to be the most useful thing I got out of the CS department. Being able to write clearly on technical topics is the difference between being a grunt individual contributor programmer and being a leader. My first job at Microsoft was as a program manager on the Excel team, writing the technical specification for this huge programming system called Visual Basic for Applications. This document was something like 500 pages long, and every morning literally hundreds of people came into work and read my spec to figure out what to do next. That included programmers, testers, marketing people, documentation writers, and localizers around the world. I noticed that the really good program managers at Microsoft were the ones who could write really well. Microsoft flipped its corporate strategy 180 degrees based on a single compelling e-mail that Steve Sinofsky wrote called "Cornell is Wired" (www.cornell. edu/about/wired/). The people who get to decide the terms of the debate are the ones who can write. The C programming language took over because *The C Programming Language* by Brian Kernighan and Dennis Ritchie (Prentice Hall, 1988) was such a great book.

So anyway, those were the highlights of CS: CS 115, in which I learned to write, one lecture in dynamic logic, in which I learned not to go to graduate school, and CS 322, in which I learned the rites and rituals of the Unix church and had a good time writing a lot of code. The main thing you don't learn with a CS degree is how to develop software, although you will probably build up certain muscles in your brain that may help you later if you decide that developing software is what you want to do. The other thing you can do, if you want to learn how to develop software, is send your resume to jobs@fogcreek.com and apply for a summer internship, and we'll teach you a thing or two about the subject.

Thank you very much for your time.

ten

ADVICE FOR COMPUTER SCIENCE COLLEGE STUDENTS

SUNDAY, JANUARY 2, 2005

Despite the fact that it was only a year or two ago that I was blubbering about how rich Windows GUI clients were the wave of the future, college students nonetheless do occasionally e-mail me asking for career advice, and since it's recruiting season, I thought I'd write up my standard advice, which they can read, laugh at, and ignore.

Most college students, fortunately, are brash enough never to bother asking their elders for advice, which, in the field of computer science, is a good thing, because their elders are apt to say goofy, antediluvian things like "The demand for keypunch operators will exceed 100,000,000 by the year 2010," and "Lisp careers are really very hot right now."

I, too, have no idea what I'm talking about when I give advice to college students. I'm so hopelessly out of date that I can't really figure out AIM and still use (horrors!) this quaint old thing called e-mail, which was popular in the days when music came on flat round plates called CDs.

So you'd be better off ignoring what I'm saying here and instead building some kind of online software thing that lets other students find people to go out on dates with.

Nevertheless.

If you enjoy programming computers, count your blessings: you are in a very fortunate minority of people who can make a great living doing work they enjoy. Most people aren't so lucky. The very idea that you can "love your job" is a modern concept. Work is supposed to be something unpleasant you do to get money to do the things you actually like doing, when you're 65 and can finally retire, if you can afford it, and if you're not too old and infirm to do those things, and if those things don't require reliable knees, good eyes, and the ability to walk twenty feet without being out of breath, etc.

What was I talking about? Oh yeah. Advice.

Without further ado, then, here are Joel's Seven Pieces Of Free Advice For Computer Science College Students (worth what you paid for them):

1. Learn how to write before graduating.

2. Learn C before graduating.

3. Learn microeconomics before graduating.

4. Don't blow off non-CS classes just because they're boring.

5. Take programming-intensive courses.

6. Stop worrying about all the jobs going to India.

7. No matter what you do, get a good summer internship.

Now for the explanations, unless you're gullible enough to do all that stuff just because I tell you to, in which case add this: 8. Seek professional help for that self-esteem thing.

~

Learn how to write before graduating

Would Linux have succeeded if Linus Torvalds hadn't evangelized it? As brilliant a hacker as he is, it was Linus's ability to convey his ideas in written English via e-mail and mailing lists that made Linux attract a worldwide brigade of volunteers.

Have you heard of the latest fad, Extreme Programming? Well, without getting into what I think about XP, the reason you've heard of it is because it is being promoted by people who are very gifted writers and speakers.

Even on the small scale, when you look at any programming organization, the programmers with the most power and influence are the ones who can write and speak in English clearly, convincingly, and comfortably. Also, it helps to be tall, but you can't do anything about that.

The difference between a tolerable programmer and a great programmer is not how many programming languages they know, and it's not whether they prefer Python or Java. It's whether they can communicate their ideas. By persuading other people, they get leverage. By writing clear comments and technical specs, they let other programmers understand their code, which means other programmers can use and work with their code instead of rewriting it. Absent this, their code is worthless. By writing clear technical documentation for end users, they allow people to figure out what their code is supposed to do, which is the only way those users can see the value in their code. There's a lot of wonderful, useful code buried on SourceForge somewhere that nobody uses because it was created by programmers who don't write very well (or don't write at all), and so nobody knows what they've done, and their brilliant code languishes.

I won't hire a programmer unless they can write, and write well, in English. If you can write, wherever you get hired, you'll soon find that you're getting asked to write the specifications, and that means you're already leveraging your influence and getting noticed by management.

Most colleges designate certain classes as "writing intensive," meaning you have to write an awful lot to pass them. Look for those classes and take them! Seek out classes in any field that have weekly or daily written assignments.

Start a journal or weblog. The more you write, the easier it will be, and the easier it is to write, the more you'll write, in a virtuous circle.

~

Learn C before graduating

Part two: C. Notice I didn't say C++. Although C is becoming increasingly rare, it is still the lingua franca of working programmers. It is the language they use to communicate with one another, and, more importantly, it is much closer to the machine than "modern" languages that you'll be taught in college like ML, Java, Python, or whatever trendy junk they teach these days. You need to spend at least a semester getting close to the machine, or you'll never be able to create efficient code in higher level languages. You'll never be able to work on compilers and operating systems, which are some of the best programming jobs around. You'll never be trusted to create architectures for large-scale projects. I don't care how much you know about continuations and closures and exception handling: if you can't explain why while (*s++ = *t++); copies a string, or if that isn't the most natural thing in the world to you, well, you're programming based on superstition, as far as I'm concerned: a medical doctor who doesn't know basic anatomy, passing out prescriptions based on what the pharma sales babe said would work.

~

Learn microeconomics before graduating

Super-quick review if you haven't taken any economics courses: econ is one of those fields that starts off with a bang, with many useful theories and facts that make sense, can be proven in the field, etc., and then it's all downhill from there. The useful bang at the beginning is microeconomics, which is the foundation for literally every theory in business that matters. After that things start to deteriorate: you get into macroeconomics (feel free to skip this if you want) with its interesting theories about things like the relationship of interest rates to unemployment which, er, seem to be disproven more often than they are proven, and after that it just gets worse and worse, and a lot of econ majors switch out to physics, which gets them better Wall Street jobs, anyway. But make sure you study microeconomics, because you have to know about supply and demand, you have to know about competitive advantage, and you have to understand NPVs and discounting and marginal utility before you'll have any idea why business works the way it does.

Why should CS majors learn econ? Because a programmer who understands the fundamentals of business is going to be a more valuable programmer, to a business, than a programmer who doesn't. That's all there is to it. I can't tell you how many times I've been frustrated by programmers with crazy ideas that make sense in code but don't make sense in capitalism. If you understand this stuff, you're a more valuable programmer, and you'll get rewarded for it, for reasons that you'll also learn in microeconomics.

~

Don't blow off non-CS classes just because they're boring

B lowing off your non-CS courses is a great way to get a lower GPA. Never underestimate how big a deal your GPA is. Lots and lots of recruiters and hiring managers, myself included, go straight to the GPA when they scan a resume, and we're not going to apologize for it. Why? Because the GPA, more than any other one number, reflects the sum of what dozens of professors over a long period of time in many different situations think about your work. SAT scores? Ha! That's one test over a few hours. The GPA reflects hundreds of papers and midterms and classroom participations over four years. Yeah, it's got its problems. There has been grade inflation over the years. Nothing about your GPA says whether you got that GPA taking easy classes in home economics at Podunk Community College or studying graduate-level quantum mechanics at Caltech. Eventually, after I screen out all the 2.5 GPAs from Podunk Community, I'm going to ask for transcripts and recommendations. And then I'm going to look for *consistently* high grades, not just high grades in computer science.

Why should I, as an employer looking for software developers, care about what grade you got in European History? After all, history is *boring*. Oh, so, you're saying I should hire you because you don't work very hard when the work is boring? Well, there's boring stuff in programming, too. Every job has its boring moments. And I don't want to hire people who only want to do the fun stuff.

I took this course in college called Cultural Anthropology because I figured, what the heck, I need to learn *something* about anthropology, and this looked like an interesting survey course.

Interesting? Not even close! I had to read these incredibly monotonous books about Indians in the Brazilian rain forest and Trobriand Islanders, who, with all due respect, are not very interesting to me. At some point, the class was so incredibly wearisome that I longed for something more exciting, like *watching grass grow*. I had completely lost interest in the subject matter. Completely, and thoroughly. My *eyes teared*, I was so tired of the endless discussions of piling up yams. I don't know why the Trobriand Islanders spend so much time piling up yams, I can't remember any more, it's incredibly boring, but It Was Going To Be On The Midterm, so I plowed through it. I eventually decided that cultural anthropology was going to be my Boredom Gauntlet: my personal obstacle course of tedium. If I could get an A in a class where the tests required me to learn all about potlatch blankets, I could handle anything, no matter how boring. The next time I accidentally get stuck in Lincoln Center sitting through all eighteen hours of Wagner's "Ring Cycle," I could thank my studies of the Kwakiutl for making it seem pleasant by comparison.

I got an A. And if I could do it, you can do it.

~

Take programming-intensive courses

I remember the exact moment I vowed never to go to graduate school. It was in a course on dynamic logic, taught by the dynamic Lenore Zuck at Yale, one of the brightest of an array of very bright CS faculty.

Now, my murky recollections are not going to do proper credit to this field, but let me muddle through anyway. The idea of formal logic is that you prove things are true because other things are true. For example, thanks to formal logic, "Everyone who gets good grades will get hired" plus "Johnny got good grades" allows you to discover the new true fact "Johnny will get hired." It's all very quaint, and it only takes ten seconds for a deconstructionist to totally tear apart everything useful in formal logic so you're left with something fun, but useless.

Now, *dynamic* logic is the same thing, with the addition of time. For example, "*After* you turn the light on, you can see your shoes" plus "The light went on in the past" implies "You can see your shoes."

Dynamic logic is appealing to brilliant theoreticians like Professor Zuck because it holds up the hope that you might be able to *formally* prove things about computer programs, which could be very useful, if, for example, you could formally prove that the Mars Rover's flash card wouldn't overflow and cause itself to be rebooted again and again all day long when it's supposed to be driving around the red planet looking for Marvin the Martian.

So in the first day of that class, Dr. Zuck filled up two entire whiteboards and quite a lot of the wall *next to* the whiteboards proving that if you have a light switch, and the light was off, and you flip the switch, the light will then be on.

The proof was insanely complicated, and very error-prone. It was harder to prove that the *proof* was correct than to convince yourself of the fact that switching a light switch turns on the light. Indeed, the multiple whiteboards of proof included many skipped steps, skipped because they were too tedious to go into formally. Many steps were reached using the long-cherished method of proof by induction, others by proof by reductio ad absurdum, and still others using proof by graduate student.

For our homework, we had to prove the converse: *if* the light was off, *and* it's on now, prove that you flipped it.

I tried, I really did.

I spent hours in the library trying.

After a couple of hours, I found a mistake in Dr. Zuck's original proof, which I was trying to emulate. Probably I copied it down wrong, but it made me realize something: if it takes three hours of filling up blackboards to prove something trivial, allowing hundreds of opportunities for mistakes to slip in, this mechanism would never be able to prove things that are *interesting*.

Not that that matters to dynamic logicians: they're not in it for *useful*, they're in it for tenure.

I dropped the class and vowed never to go to graduate school in computer science.

The moral of the story is that computer science is not the same as software development. If you're really, really lucky, your school might have a decent software development curriculum, although they might not, because elite schools think that teaching practical skills is better left to the technical-vocational institutes and the prison rehabilitation programs. You can learn mere *programming* anywhere. We are Yale University, and we Mold Future World Leaders. You think your $160,000 tuition entitles you to learn about *while loops*? What do you think this is, some fly-by-night *Java seminar* at the Airport Marriott? Pshaw.

The trouble is, we don't really have professional schools in software development, so if you want to be a programmer, you probably majored in computer science. Which is a fine subject to major in, but it's a *different subject* from software development.

If you're lucky, though, you can find lots of programming-intensive courses in the CS department, just like you can find lots of courses in the History department where you'll write enough to learn how to write. And those are the best classes to take. If you love programming, don't feel bad if you don't understand the point of those courses in lambda calculus or linear algebra where you never touch a computer. Look for the 400-level courses with "Practicum" in the name. This is an attempt to hide a useful (*shudder*) course from the Liberal Artsy Fartsy Administration by dolling it up with a Latin name.

Stop worrying about all the jobs going to India

Well, OK, first of all, if you're already *in* India, you never really had to worry about this, so don't even *start* worrying about all the jobs going to India. They're wonderful jobs, enjoy them in good health.

But I keep hearing that enrollment in CS departments is dropping perilously, and one reason I hear for it is "Students are afraid to go into a field where all the jobs are going to India." That's so wrong for so many reasons. First, trying to choose a career based on a current business fad is foolish. Second, programming is incredibly good training for all kinds of fabulously interesting jobs, such as business process engineering, even if every single programming job does go to India and China. Third, and trust me on this, there's still an incredible shortage of the really good programmers, here *and* in India. Yes, there are a bunch of out-of-work IT people making a lot of noise about how long they've been out of work, but you know what? At the risk of pissing them off, really good programmers *do* have jobs. Fourth, you got any better ideas? What are you going to do, major in history? Then you'll have no choice but to go to law school. And there's one thing I do know: 99% of working lawyers *hate* their jobs, hate every waking minute of it, and they're working ninety-hour weeks, too. Like I said: if you love to program computers, count your blessings: you are in a very fortunate minority of people who can make a great living doing work they love.

Anyway, I don't think students really think about this. The drop in CS enrollment is merely a resumption of historically normal levels after a big bubble in enrollment caused by dot-com mania. That bubble consisted of people who didn't really like programming but thought the sexy high-paid jobs and the chances to IPO at age 24 were to be found in the CS department. Those people, thankfully, are long gone.

~

No matter what you do, get a good summer internship

Smart recruiters know that the people who love programming wrote a database for their dentist in eighth grade, and taught at computer camp for three summers before college, and built the content management system for the campus newspaper, and had summer internships at software companies. That's what they're looking for on your resume.

If you enjoy programming, the biggest mistake you can make is to take any kind of job—summer, part time, or otherwise—that is not a programming job. I know, every other 19-year-old wants to work in the mall folding shirts, but you have a skill that is incredibly valuable even when you're 19, and it's foolish to waste it folding shirts. By the time you graduate, you really should have a resume that lists a whole bunch of programming jobs. The A&F graduates are going to be working at Enterprise Rent-a-Car "helping people with their rental needs." (Except for Tom Welling. He plays Superman on TV.)

To make your life really easy, and to underscore just how completely self-serving this whole essay is, my company, Fog Creek Software, has summer internships in software development that look *great* on resumes. "You will most likely learn more about software coding, development, and business with Fog Creek Software than any other internship out there," says Ben, one of the interns from last summer, and not entirely because I sent a goon out to his dorm room to get him to say that. The application deadline is February 1. Get on it.

If you follow my advice, you, too, may end up selling stock in Microsoft way too soon, turning down jobs at Google because you want your own office with a door, and other stupid life decisions, but they won't be my fault. I told you not to listen to me.

part three

The Impact of Design

eleven

FONT SMOOTHING, ANTI-ALIASING, AND SUBPIXEL RENDERING

Tuesday, June 12, 2007

Apple and Microsoft have always disagreed in how to display fonts on computer displays. Today, both companies are using subpixel rendering to coax sharper-looking fonts out of typical low-resolution screens. Where they differ is in philosophy.

- Apple generally believes that the goal of the algorithm should be to preserve the design of the typeface as much as possible, even at the cost of a little bit of blurriness.

- Microsoft generally believes that the shape of each letter should be hammered into pixel boundaries to prevent blur and improve readability, even at the cost of not being true to the typeface.

Now that Safari for Windows is available, which goes to great trouble to use Apple's rendering algorithms, you can actually compare the philosophies side by side on the very same monitor and see what I mean, as in the following illustration. I think you'll notice the difference. Apple's fonts are indeed fuzzy, with blurry edges; but at small font sizes, there seems to be much more variation between different font families, because their rendering is truer to what the font would look like if it were printed at high resolution. (For the on screen view, visit `http://www.joelonsoftware.com/items/2007/06/12.html`.)

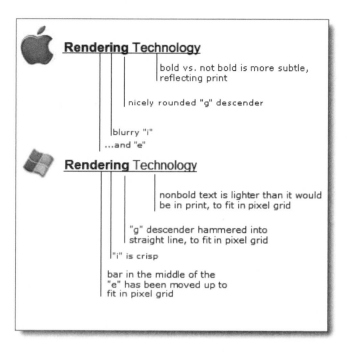

The difference originates from Apple's legacy in desktop publishing and graphic design. The nice thing about the Apple algorithm is that you can lay out a page of text for print, and onscreen, you get a nice approximation of the finished product. This is especially significant when you consider how dark a block of text looks. Microsoft's mechanism of hammering fonts into pixels means that they don't really mind using thinner lines to eliminate blurry edges, even though this makes the entire paragraph lighter than it would be in print.

The advantage of Microsoft's method is that it works better for onscreen reading. Microsoft pragmatically decided that the design of the typeface is not so holy, and that sharp onscreen text that's comfortable to read is more important than the typeface designer's idea of how light or dark an entire block of text should feel. Indeed, Microsoft actually designed font faces for onscreen reading, like Georgia and Verdana, around the pixel boundaries; these are beautiful onscreen but don't have much character in print.

Typically, Apple chose the stylish route, putting art above practicality, because Steve Jobs has taste, while Microsoft chose the comfortable route, the measurably pragmatic way of doing things that completely lacks in panache. To put it another way, if Apple were Target, Microsoft would be Wal-Mart.

Now, on to the question of what people prefer. Jeff Atwood's post (www.codinghorror.com/blog/archives/000884.html) comparing the two font technologies side by side generated rather predictable heat: Apple users liked Apple's system, while Windows users liked Microsoft's system. This is not just standard fanboyism; it reflects the fact that when you ask people to choose a style or design that they prefer, unless they are trained, they will generally choose the one that looks most familiar. In most matters of taste, when you do preference surveys, you'll find that most people don't really know what to choose and will opt for the one that seems most familiar. This goes for anything from silverware (people pick out the patterns that match the silverware they had growing up) to typefaces to graphic design: unless people are trained to know what to look for, they're going to pick the one that is most familiar.

Which is why Apple engineers probably feel like they're doing a huge service to the Windows community, bringing their "superior" font rendering technology to the heathens, and it explains why Windows users are generally going to think that Safari's font rendering is blurry and strange, and they don't know why, they just don't like it. Actually, they're thinking, "Whoa! That's different. I don't like different. Why don't I like these fonts? Oh, when I look closer, they look blurry. *That must be why.*"

twelve

A GAME OF INCHES

THURSDAY, JUNE 7, 2007

"Did someone leave the radio on in the bathroom?" I asked Jared. There was a faint sound of classical music.

"No. It's coming from outside. It started while you were away and happens every night."

We live in an apartment building in New York. There are neighbors on all sides. We're used to hearing TV shows from below, and the little kid in the apartment directly above us has a favorite game: throwing a bunch of marbles on the floor and then throwing *himself* around the room violently. I'm not sure how you keep score. As I write this, he's running rapidly from room to room crashing into things. I can't wait until he's old enough for paintball.

Anyway. This classical-music-late-at-night thing had never happened before.

Worse, it was some kind of Sturm-und-Drang romantic crap that was making me angry right when I wanted to fall asleep.

Eventually, the music stopped, and I was able to drift off to sleep. But the next night, when the music resumed at midnight, I was really worn out, and it was *more* self-important Wagner rubbish, with pompous crescendos that consistently woke me up every time I finally drifted off to sleep, and I had no choice but to go sit in the living room and look at pictures of lolcats until it stopped, which it finally did, around 1 a.m.

The next night I had had enough. When the music started at about midnight, I got dressed and started exploring the apartment building. I crept around the halls, listening at every door, trying to figure out where the music was coming from. I poked my head out windows and found an unlocked door leading to an airshaft where the music was amazingly loud. I climbed up and down the stairs, and listened closely from the window on each and every landing, until I was pretty convinced that the problem was from dear old Mrs. C's apartment, #2B, directly below us.

I didn't think Mrs. C, who is probably in her 60s, was even awake that late, let alone listening to music loudly, but I briefly entertained the possibility that the local classical music station was doing the "Ring Cycle" or something, and she was staying up late to hear it.

Not bloody likely.

One thing I had noticed was that the music seemed to go on at midnight every night and off at 1:00 a.m. Somehow, that made me think it was a clock radio, which probably had the alarm factory set to 12:00.

I couldn't bring myself to wake up an old lady downstairs on the mere *suspicion* that music was coming from her apartment. Frustrated, I went back to my apartment and caught up on *xkcd*. I was depressed and angry, because I hadn't solved the problem. I festered and scowled all the next day.

The next evening, I knocked on Mrs. C's door. The super had told me she was going away for the entire summer the next day, so if the problem was coming from her apartment, I better find out pronto.

"Sorry to bother you," I said. "I've noticed that every night around midnight there's loud classical music coming from the airshaft behind our apartments, and it's keeping me awake."

"Oh no, it's not me!" she insisted, as I suspected she would. Of course not: she probably goes to sleep at a completely normal hour and certainly never plays loud music that bothers the neighbors!

I thought she was a little hard of hearing and probably never noticed the thing blaring away from her spare room in the middle of the night. Or maybe she was a good sleeper.

It took a few minutes, but I finally convinced her to check if there was any kind of clock radio in the room below my window.

Turns out there was. Right in an open window beneath my own bedroom window. When I saw that it was tuned to 96.3, WQXR, I knew I had found the culprit.

"Oh, that thing? I have no idea how to use that thing. I never use it," she said. "I'll disconnect it completely."

"Not necessary," I said, and turned off the alarm, set the volume to zero, and, in my late-onset OCD, set the clock to the exact time.

Mrs. C was terribly apologetic, but it really wasn't her fault. It took me—me!—quite a while to figure out how to operate the damn clock radio, and let me tell you, sonny boy, I know a thing or two about *clock radios*. The UI was terrible. Your average little old lady didn't stand a chance.

Is it the clock radio's fault? Sort of. It was too hard to use. It had an alarm that continued to go off daily even if nobody touched it the day before, which is not the greatest idea. And there's no reason to reset the alarm time to *midnight* after a power outage. 7:00 a.m. would be a completely civilized default.

Somehow, over the last few weeks, I've become hypercritical. I'm always looking for flaws in things, and when I find them, I become single-minded about fixing them. It's a particular frame of mind, actually, that software developers get into when they're in the final debugging phase of a new product.

Over the last few weeks, I've been writing all the documentation for the next big version of FogBugz. As I write things, I try them out, either to make sure they work the way I think they should or to get screenshots. And every hour or so, bells go off. "Wait a minute! What just happened? That's not supposed to work like that!"

And since it's software, I can always fix it. HA HA! Just kidding! I can't make head or tail out of the code any more. I enter a bug, and someone with a clue fixes it.

Dave Winer says, "To create a usable piece of software, you have to fight for every fix, every feature, every little accommodation that will get one more person up the curve. There are no shortcuts. Luck is involved, but you don't win by being lucky, it happens because you fought for every inch" (www.scripting.com/2002/01/12.html).

Commercial software—the kind you sell to other people—is a game of inches.

Every day you make a tiny bit of progress. You make one thing just a smidgen better. You make the alarm clock default to 7:00 a.m. instead of 12:00 midnight. A tiny improvement that will barely benefit anyone. One inch.

There are thousands and tens of thousands of these tiny things.

It takes a mindset of constant criticism to find them. You have to reshape your mind until you're finding fault with *everything*. Your significant others go nuts. Your family wants to kill you. When you're walking to work and you see a driver do something stupid, it takes all your willpower to resist going up to the driver and explaining to him why he nearly killed that poor child in the wheelchair.

And as you fix more and more of these little details, as you polish and shape and shine and *craft* the little corners of your product, something magical happens. The inches add up to feet, the feet add up to yards, and the yards add up to miles. And you ship a truly great product. The kind of product that feels great, that works intuitively, that blows people away. The kind of product where that one-in-a-million user doing that one-in-a-million unusual thing finds that not only does it work, but it's beautiful: even the janitor's closets of your software have marble floors and solid-core oak doors and polished mahogany wainscoting.

And that's when you know it's great software.

Congratulations to the FogBugz 6.0 team, outlandishly good players of the game of inches, who shipped their first beta today, on track for final release at the end of the summer. This is the best product they've ever produced. It will blow you away.

thirteen

THE BIG PICTURE

SUNDAY, JANUARY 21, 2007

A review of Dreaming in Code, *by Scott Rosenberg (Three Rivers Press, 2007)*

Eyes work using a page-fault mechanism. They're so good at it that you don't even notice.

You can only see at a high resolution in a fairly small area, and even that has a big fat blind spot right exactly in the middle, but you still walk around *thinking* you have an ultra-high-resolution panoramic view of everything. Why? Because your eyes move *really* fast, and, under ordinary circumstances, they are happy to jump instantly to wherever you need them to jump to. And your mind supplies this really complete abstraction, providing you with the illusion of complete vision when all you *really* have is a very small area of high-res vision, a large area of extremely low-res vision, and the ability to page-fault-in anything you want to see—so quickly that you walk around all day thinking you have the whole picture projected internally in a little theater in your brain.

This is really, really useful, and lots of other things work this way, too. Your ears are good at tuning in important parts of conversations. Your fingers reach around and touch anything they need to, whether it's a fine merino wool sweater or the inside of your nose, giving you a full picture of what everything feels like. When you dream, your mind asks all kinds of questions that it's used to asking the senses (What's that? Look over there!), but your senses are temporarily turned off (you are, after all, *asleep*), so they get back sort of random answers, which you combine into a funny story in your brain called a dream. And then when you try to recount the dream to your boyfriend in the morning, even though it *seemed* totally, completely realistic, you suddenly realize that you *don't know what happened, actually*, so you have to make shit up. If you had stayed asleep for another minute or two, your brain would have asked your senses what *kind* of mammal was swimming with you in the rose bush, and gotten back some retarded, random answer (a *platypus!*), but you woke up, so until you tried to tell the story, you didn't even realize that you needed to know what was in the rose bushes with you to make the story coherent to your partner. Which it never is. So please don't tell me about your dreams.

One of the unfortunate side effects is that your mind gets into a bad habit of overestimating how clearly it understands things. It *always* thinks it has The Big Picture even when it doesn't.

This is a particularly dangerous trap when it comes to software development. You get some big picture idea in your head for what you want to do, and it all seems so *crystal clear* that it doesn't even seem like you need to *design* anything. You can just dive in and start implementing your vision.

Say, for example, that your vision is to rebuild an old DOS personal information manager, which was *really really great* but *totally unappreciated*. It seems easy. Everything about how the whole thing works seems so obvious, you don't even try to design the thing . . . you just hire a bunch of programmers and start banging out code.

Now you've made two mistakes.

Number one, you fell for that old overconfidence trick of your mind. "Oh, yeah, we totally know how to do this! It's all totally clear to us. No need to spec it out. Just write the code."

Number two, you hired programmers before you designed the thing. Because the only thing harder than trying to design software is trying to design software *as a team*.

I can't tell you how many times I've been in a meeting with even one or two other programmers, trying to figure out how something should work, and we're just not getting anywhere. So I go off in my office and take out a piece of paper and figure it out. The very act of interacting with a second person was keeping me from concentrating enough to design the dang feature.

What kills me is the teams who get into the bad habit of holding *meetings* every time they need to figure out how something is going to work. Did you ever try to write poetry in a committee meeting? It's like a bunch of fat construction guys trying to write an opera while sitting on the couch watching *Baywatch*. The more fat construction guys you add to the couch, the less likely you are to get opera out of it.

At least turn off the TV!

Now, it would be shockingly presumptuous of me to try to guess what happened on the Chandler team, and why it's taken them millions of dollars and several years to get to where they are now, which is, they have a pretty buggy and incomplete calendar application that's not very impressive compared to the fifty-eight me-too Web 2.0 calendars that came out last year, each of which was developed by two college kids in their spare time, one of whom really mostly just drew mascots.

Chandler doesn't even have a mascot!

Like I say, I can't presume to know what went wrong. Maybe nothing. Maybe they feel like they're right on track. Scott Rosenberg's excellent new book, which was supposed to be a *Soul of a New Machine* for the hottest open source startup of the decade, ends up, in frustration, with Scott cutting the story short because Chandler 1.0 was just not going to happen any time soon (and presumably Rosenberg couldn't run the risk that we wouldn't be using books at all by the time it shipped, opting instead to absorb knowledge by taking a pill).

Still, it's a great look at one particular type of software project: the kind that ends up spinning and spinning its wheels without really going anywhere because the vision was too grand and the details were a little short. Near as I can tell, Chandler's original vision was pretty much just to be "revolutionary." Well, I don't know about you, but I can't code "revolutionary." I need more details to write code. Whenever the spec describes the product in terms of adjectives ("It will be extremely cool") rather than specifics ("It will have brushed-aluminum title bars and all the icons will be reflected a little bit, as if placed on a grand piano"), you know you're in trouble.

The only concrete design ideas, as far as I could tell from Rosenberg's book, were "peer-to-peer," "no silos," and "natural language date interpretation." This may be a limitation of the book, but the initial design sure seemed to be extremely vague.

"Peer-to-peer" was the raison d'être of Chandler . . . why should you have to buy Microsoft Exchange Server to coordinate schedules? It turned out that peer-to-peer synchronization was too hard, or something, and this feature was cut. Now there's a server called Cosmo.

"No silos" was supposed to mean that instead of having your e-mail in one silo, and your calendar in another silo, and your reminder notes in a third, there would just be a single unified silo holding everything.

As soon as you start asking questions about "no silos," you realize it's not going to work. Do you put your e-mail on the calendar? Where? On the day when it arrived? So now I have 200 Viagra ads on Friday obscuring the one really important shareholder meeting?

Eventually, "no silos" got designed into this idea of *stamps*, so, for example, you could "stamp" any document or note or calendar item with an e-mail stamp, and suddenly that item could be mailed to anyone. Guess what? That feature has been in Microsoft Office for the last decade or so. They finally took it *out* in Office 2007 because nobody cared. There are too many easy ways to e-mail people things.

Indeed, I think the idea of "no silos" is most appealing to architecture astronauts, the people who look at subclasses and see abstract base classes, and who love to move functionality from the subclass into the base class for no good reason other than architectural aesthetics. This is usually a terrible user interface design technique. The way you make users understand your program model is with metaphors. When you make things look, feel, and, most importantly, behave like things in the real world, users are more likely to figure out how to use the program, and the app will be easier to use. When you try to combine two very dramatically different real-world items (e-mail and appointments) into the same kind of thing in the user interface, usability suffers because there's no longer a real-world metaphor that applies.

The other cool thing that Mitchell Kapor kept telling everyone who would listen is that Agenda would let you type things like "Next Tuesday," and magically you'd get an appointment for next Tuesday. This is slicker than heck, but every half-decent calendar program for the last decade has done this. Not revolutionary.

The Chandler team also overestimated how much help they would get from volunteers. Open source doesn't quite work like that. It's really good at implementing copycat features, because there's a spec to work from: the implementation you're copying. It's really good at Itch Scratching features. I need a command-line argument for EBCDIC, so I'll add it and send in the code. But when you have an app that doesn't do anything yet, nobody finds it itchy. *They're not using it.* So you don't get volunteers. Almost everyone on the Chandler dev team got paid.

Again, I must forcefully apologize to the Chandler team if Rosenberg missed the point somehow, or if he gave a completely incorrect impression of what was really holding up progress, and my bias—to blame these kinds of debacles on a failure to design—is showing.

All that said, one good thing did come out of the project: a fascinating book in the style of *Soul of a New Machine* and *Showstopper* about a software development project that failed to converge. Highly recommended.

fourteen

CHOICES = HEADACHES

Tuesday, November 21, 2006

I'm sure there's a whole *team* of UI designers, programmers, and testers who worked very hard on the Off button in Windows Vista, but seriously, is this the best you could come up with?

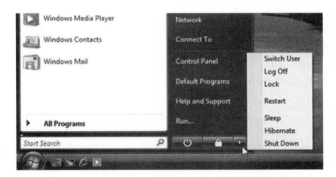

Every time you want to leave your computer, you have to choose between nine, count them, nine options: two icons and seven menu items. The two icons, I think, are shortcuts to menu items. I'm guessing the lock icon does the same thing as the Lock menu item, but I'm not sure which menu item the on/off icon corresponds to.

On many laptops, there are also four FN+key combinations to power off, hibernate, sleep, etc. That brings us up to thirteen choices, and, oh, yeah, there's an on/off button, fourteen, and you can close the lid, fifteen. A total of fifteen different ways to shut down a laptop that you're expected to choose from.

The more choices you give people, the harder it is for them to choose, and the unhappier they'll feel. See, for example, Barry Schwartz's book,

The Paradox of Choice: Why More Is Less (Harper Perennial, 2005). Let me quote from the *Publishers Weekly* review: "Schwartz, drawing extensively on his own work in the social sciences, shows that a bewildering array of choices floods our exhausted brains, ultimately restricting instead of freeing us. We normally assume in America that more options ('easy fit' or 'relaxed fit'?) will make us happier, but Schwartz shows the opposite is true, arguing that having all these choices actually goes so far as to erode our psychological well-being."

The fact that you have to choose between nine different ways of turning off your computer every time *just on the Start menu*, not to mention the choice of hitting the physical on/off button or closing the laptop lid, produces just a little bit of unhappiness every time.

Can anything be done? It must be possible. iPods don't even *have* an on/off switch. Here are some ideas.

If you've spoken to a nongeek recently, you may have noticed that they have no idea what the difference is between Sleep and Hibernate. They could be trivially merged. One option down.

Switch User and Lock can be combined by letting a second user log on when the system is locked. That would probably save a lot of forced logouts anyway. Another option down.

Once you've merged Switch User and Lock, do you really need Log Off? The only thing Log Off gets you is that it exits all running programs. But so does powering off, so if you're really concerned about exiting all running programs, just power off and on again. One more option gone.

Restart can be eliminated. 95% of the time you need this because of an installation that prompted you to restart anyway. For the other cases, you can just turn the power off and then turn it on again. Another option goes away. Less choice, less pain.

Of course, you should eliminate the distinction between the icons and the menu. That eliminates two more choices. We are down to

Sleep/Hibernate

Switch User/Lock

Shut Down

What if we combined Sleep, Hibernate, Switch User, and Lock modes? When you go into this mode, the computer flips to the Switch

User screen. If nobody logs on for about 30 seconds, it sleeps. A few minutes later, it hibernates. In all cases, it's locked. So now we've got two options left:

1. I am going away from my computer now.

2. I am going away from my computer now, but I'd like the power to be really off.

Why do you want the power off? If you're concerned about power usage, let the power management software worry about that. It's smarter than you are. If you're going to open the box and don't want to get shocked, well, just powering off the system doesn't really completely make it safe to open the box; you have to unplug it anyway. So, if Windows used RAM that was effectively nonvolatile, by swapping memory out to flash drives during idle time, effectively you would be able to remove power whenever you're in "away" mode without losing anything. Those new hybrid hard drives can make this super fast.

So now we've got exactly one log off button left. Call it "b'bye". When you click b'bye, the screen is locked, and any RAM that hasn't already been copied out to flash is written. You can log back on, or anyone else can log on and get their own session, or you can unplug the whole computer.

Inevitably, you are going to think of a long list of intelligent, defensible reasons why each of these options is absolutely, positively essential. Don't bother. I know. Each additional choice makes complete sense until you find yourself explaining to your uncle that he has to choose between fifteen different ways to turn off a laptop.

This highlights a style of software design shared by Microsoft and the open source movement, in both cases driven by a desire for consensus and for Making Everybody Happy, but it's based on the misconceived notion that lots of choices make people happy, which we really need to rethink.

fifteen

IT'S NOT JUST USABILITY

For years and years, self-fashioned pundits, like, uh, me, have been nattering endlessly about usability and how important it is to make software usable. Jakob Nielsen has a *mathematical formula* he'll reveal to you in exchange for $122 that you can use to calculate the value of usability. (If the expected value of usability is greater than $122, I guess you make a profit.)

I have a book you can buy for a lot less—*User Interface Design for Programmers* (Apress, 2001)—that tells you some of the principles of designing usable software, but there's no math involved, and you'll be out the price of the book.

In that book, on page 31, I showed an example from what was, at the time, the most popular software application on earth, Napster. The main Napster window used buttons to flip between the five screens. Due to a principle in usability called *affordance*, instead of buttons, it really should have had tabs, which was the point I was trying to make.

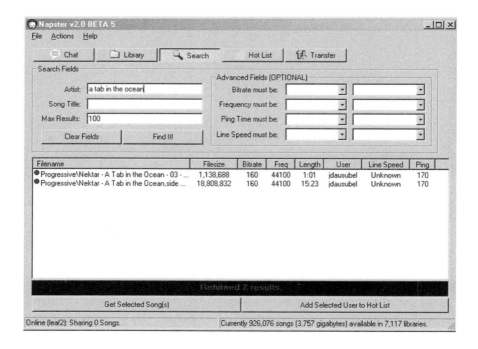

And yet, Napster was the most popular software application on earth.

In an early version of the manuscript, I actually wrote something like "This just goes to show you that usability ain't all that important," which was an odd thing to be writing in a book about usability. I was sort of relieved when the typesetter announced that I had to shorten that paragraph. So I deleted the sentence.

But there's a scary element of truth to it—scary to UI professionals, at least: an application that does something really great that people really want to do can be pathetically unusable, and it will still be a hit. And an application can be the easiest thing in the world to use, but if it doesn't do anything anybody wants, it will flop. UI consultants are constantly on the defensive, working up improbable ROI formulas about the return on investment clients will get from their $75,000 usability project, precisely because usability is perceived as "optional," and the scary thing is, in a lot of cases, *it is*. In a lot of cases. The CNN web site has nothing to be gained from a usability consultant. I'll go out on a limb and say that there is not a single content-based web site online that would gain even one dollar in revenue by improving usability, because content-based web sites (by which I mean web sites that are not also applications) are already so damn usable.

Anyway.

My goal today is not to whine about how usability is not important . . . usability *is* important at the margins, and there are lots of examples where bad usability kills people in small planes, creates famine and pestilence, etc.

My goal today is to talk about the *next* level of software design issues, after you've got the UI right: designing the *social interface*.

I need to explain that, I guess.

Software in the 1980s, when usability was "invented," was all about computer-human interaction. A lot of software still is. But the Internet brings us a new kind of software: software that's about human-human interaction.

Discussion groups. Social networking. Online classifieds. Oh, and, uh, e-mail. It's all software that mediates between *people*, not between the human and the computer.

When you're writing software that mediates between people, after you get the usability right, you have to get the social interface right. And the social interface is *more important*. The best UI in the world won't save software with an awkward social interface.

The best way to illustrate social interfaces is with a few examples of failures and successes.

~

Some examples

First, a failing social interface. Every week I get an e-mail from somebody I've never heard of asking me to become a part of their social network. I usually don't know the person, so I feel a little bit miffed and delete the message. Someone told me why this happens: one of those social networking software companies has a tool that goes through your e-mail address book and sends e-mail to everyone asking them to join in. Now, combine this with the feature that some e-mail software saves the sender's address of every incoming message and the feature that when you go to sign up for the *Joel on Software* e-mail bulletin you get a confirmation message asking if you really want to join, and voilà: all kinds of people whom I don't know are running software that is inadvertently asking me to confirm that I'm their friend. Thank you for subscribing to my newsletter, but no, I'm not going to introduce you to Bill Gates. I currently have a policy of not joining any of these social networks, because they strike me as going strongly against the grain of how human networks really work.

Now, let's look at a successful social interface. Many humans are less inhibited when they're typing than when they are speaking face to face. Teenagers are less shy. With cellphone text messages, they're more likely to ask each other out on dates. That genre of software was so successful socially that it's radically improving millions of people's love lives (or at least their social calendars). Even though text messaging has a ghastly user interface, it became extremely popular with the kids. The joke of it is that there's a much better user interface *built into every cellphone* for human-to-human communication: this clever thing called phone calls. You dial a number, after which everything you say can be heard by the other person and vice versa. It's that simple. But it's not as popular in some circles as this awkward system where you break your thumbs typing huge strings of numbers just to say "Damn you're hot," because that string of numbers gets you a date, and you would never have the guts to say "Damn you're hot" using your larynx.

Another social software success is eBay. When I first heard about eBay, I said, "Nonsense! That will never work. Nobody's going to send money to some random person they encountered on the Internet in hopes that person will, out of the goodness of their hearts, actually ship them some merchandise." A lot of people thought this. We were all wrong. Wrong, wrong, wrong. eBay made a big bet on the cultural anthropology of human beings and *won*. The great thing about eBay is that it was a huge success *precisely because* it seemed like a terrible idea at the time, and so nobody else tried it, until eBay locked in the network effects and first-mover advantage.

In addition to absolute success and failures in social software, there are also social software side effects. The way social software behaves determines a huge amount about the type of community that develops. Usenet clients have this big-R command, which is used to reply to a message *while quoting the original message* with those elegant >'s in the left column. And the early newsreaders were not threaded, so if you wanted to respond to someone's point coherently, you *had* to quote them using the big-R feature. This led to a particularly Usenet style of responding to an argument: the line-by-line nitpick. It's fun for the nitpicker but never worth reading. (By the way, the political bloggers, newcomers to the Internet, have reinvented this technique, thinking they were discovering something fun and new, and called it *fisking*, for reasons I won't go into. Don't worry, it's not dirty.) Even though human beings had been debating for centuries, a tiny feature of a software product produced a whole new style of debating.

Small changes in software can make big differences in the way that software supports, or fails to support, its social goals. Danah Boyd has a great critique of social software networks, "Autistic Social Software" (www.danah.org/papers/Supernova2004.html), blasting the current generation of this software for forcing people to behave autistically:

> *Consider, for a moment, the recent surge of interest in articulated social networks such as Friendster, Tribe, LinkedIn, Orkut, and the like. These technologies attempt to formalize how people should construct and manage their relationships. They assume that you can rate your friends. In some cases, they procedurally direct how people can engage with new people by giving you an absolute process through which you can contact others.*

> *While this approach certainly has its merits because it is computationally possible, I'm terrified when people think that this models social life. It's so simplistic that people are forced to engage as though they have autism, as though they must interact procedurally. This approach certainly aids people who need that kind of systematization, but it is not a model that universally makes sense. Furthermore, what are the implications of having technology prescribe mechanistic engagement? Do we really want a social life that encourages autistic interactions?*

When software implements social interfaces while disregarding cultural anthropology, it's creepy and awkward and doesn't really work.

~

Designing social software

Let me give you an example of social interface design.
Suppose your user does something they shouldn't have done.

Good usability design says that you should tell them what they did wrong and tell them how to correct it. Usability consultants are marketing this under the brand name "Defensive Design."

When you're working on social software, this is too naive.

Maybe the thing that they did wrong was to post an advertisement for Viagra on a discussion group.

Now you tell them, "Sorry, Viagra is not a suitable topic. Your post has been rejected."

Guess what they'll do? They'll post an advertisement for Viagra (either that, or they'll launch into a long boring rant about censorship and the First Amendment).

With social interface engineering, you have to look at sociology and anthropology. In societies, there are freeloaders, scammers, and other miscreants. In social software, there will be people who try to abuse the software for their own profit at the expense of the rest of the society. Unchecked, this leads to something economists call *the tragedy of the commons*.

Whereas the goal of user interface design is to help the user succeed, the goal of social interface design is to help the society succeed, even if it means one user has to fail.

So a good social interface designer might say, "Let's not display an error message. Let's just pretend that the post about Viagra was accepted. Show it to the original poster, so he feels smug and moves on to the next inappropriate discussion group. But don't show it to anyone else."

Indeed, one of the best ways to deflect attacks is to make it look like they're succeeding. It's the software equivalent of playing dead.

No, it doesn't work 100% of the time. It works 95% of the time, and it reduces the problems you'll have twentyfold. Like everything else in sociology, it's a fuzzy heuristic. It kind of works a lot of the time, so it's worth doing, even if it's not foolproof. The Russian mafia with their phishing schemes will eventually work around it. The idiot Floridians in trailer parks trying to get rich quick will move on. 90% of the spam I get today is still so hopelessly naive about spam filters that it would even get caught by the pathetic junk filter built into Microsoft Outlook, and you've got to have really lame spam to get caught by *that* scrawny smattering of simplistic search phrases.

~

Marketing social interfaces

A few months ago, I realized that a common theme in the software we've built at Fog Creek is an almost obsessive attention to getting the social interfaces right. For example, FogBugz has lots of features, and even more **non**features, designed to make bug tracking *actually happen*. Time and time again, customers tell me that their old bug tracking software was never getting used because it did not align with the way people wanted to work together, but when they rolled out FogBugz, people actually starting using it, and became addicted to it, and it changed the way they worked together. I know that FogBugz works because we have a very high upgrade rate when there's a new version, which tells me FogBugz is not just shelfware, and because even customers who buy huge blocks of licenses keep coming back for more user licenses as the product spreads around their organization and really gets used. This is something I'm really proud of. Software used in teams usually fails to take hold, because it requires everyone on the team to change the way they work simultaneously, something which anthropologists will tell you is vanishingly unlikely. For that reason, FogBugz has lots of design decisions that make it useful even for a *single person* on a team and lots of design features that encourage it to spread to other members of the team gradually until everyone is using it.

The discussion group software used on my site, which will soon be for sale as a feature of FogBugz, is even more obsessed with getting the social interface aspects exactly right. There are dozens of features and nonfeatures and design decisions that collectively lead to a very high level of interesting conversation with the best signal-to-noise ratio of any discussion group I've ever participated in. I write a lot about this in the next chapter.

Since then, I've become even more devoted to the idea of the value of good social interface design: we bring in experts like Clay Shirky (a pioneer in the field), we do bold experiments on the poor citizens of the *Joel on Software* discussion group (many of which are so subtle as to be virtually unnoticeable, for example, the fact that we don't show you the post you're replying to while you type your reply in hopes of cutting down quoting, which makes it easier to read a thread), and we're investing heavily in advanced algorithms to reduce discussion group spam.

∼

A new field

Social interface design is still a field in its infancy. I'm not aware of *any* books on the subject; there are only a few people working in the research side of the field, and there's no organized science of social interface design. In the early days of usability design, software companies recruited ergonomics experts and human factors experts to help design usable products. Ergonomics experts knew a lot about the right height for a desk, but they didn't know how to design GUIs for file systems, so a new field arose. Eventually, the new discipline of user interface design came into its own and figured out concepts like consistency, affordability, feedback, etc., which became the cornerstone of the science of UI design.

Over the next decade, I expect that software companies will hire people trained as anthropologists and ethnographers to work on social interface design. Instead of building usability labs, they'll go out into the field and write ethnographies. And hopefully, we'll figure out the new principles of social interface design. It's going to be fascinating . . . as fun as user interface design was in the 1980s . . . so stay tuned.

sixteen

BUILDING COMMUNITIES WITH SOFTWARE

In his book, *The Great Good Place* (Da Capo Press, 1999), social scientist Ray Oldenburg talks about how humans need a third place, besides work and home, to meet with friends, have a beer, discuss the events of the day, and enjoy some human interaction. Coffee shops, bars, hair salons, beer gardens, pool halls, clubs, and other hangouts are as vital as factories, schools, and apartments. But capitalist society has been eroding those third places, and society is left impoverished. In *Bowling Alone* (Simon & Schuster, 2001), Robert Putnam brings forth, in riveting and well-documented detail, reams of evidence that American society has all but lost its third places. Over the last 25 years, Americans "belong to fewer organizations that meet, know our neighbors less, meet with friends less frequently, and even socialize with our families less often." For too many people, life consists of going to work, and then going home and watching TV. Work-TV-Sleep-Work-TV-Sleep. It seems to me that the phenomenon is far more acute among software developers, especially in places like Silicon Valley and the suburbs of Seattle. People graduate from college, move across country to a new place where they don't know anyone, and end up working twelve-hour days basically out of loneliness.

So it's no surprise that so many programmers, desperate for a little human contact, flock to online communities—chat rooms, discussion forums, open source projects, and Ultima Online. In creating community software, we are, to some extent, trying to create a third place. And like any other architecture project, the design decisions we make are crucial. Make a bar too loud, and people won't be able to have conversations.

That makes for a very different kind of place from a coffee shop. Make a coffee shop without very many chairs, as Starbucks does, and people will carry their coffee back to their lonely rooms, instead of staying around and socializing like they do in the fantasy TV coffeehouse of *Friends*, a program we watch because an ersatz third place is less painful than none at all.

In software, as in architecture, design decisions are just as important to the type of community that develops or fails to develop. When you make something easy, people do it more often. When you make something hard, people do it less often. In this way, you can gently encourage people to behave in certain ways that determine the character and quality of the community. Will it feel friendly? Is there thick conversation, a European salon full of intellectuals with interesting ideas? Or is the place deserted, with a few dirty advertising leaflets lying around on the floor that nobody has bothered to pick up?

Look at a few online communities, and you'll instantly notice the different social atmosphere. Look more closely, and you'll see this variation is most often a byproduct of software design decisions.

On Usenet, threads last for months and months and go off onto so many tangents that you never know where they've been. Whenever a newbie stumbles by and asks a germane question, the old timers shout him down and tell him to read the FAQ. Quoting, with the > symbol, is a disease that makes it impossible to read any single thread without boring yourself to death by rereading the whole history of a chain of argument that you just read in the original, seconds ago, again and again and again. Shlemiel the Painter reading.

On IRC, you can't own your nickname, and you can't own a channel—once the last person leaves a room, anyone can take it over. That's the way the software works. The social result was that it was often impossible to find your friends when you came back the next day, because someone else might have locked you out of your chatroom, and your friends might have been forced to choose different nicknames. The only way to prevent gay bashers in Perth, Australia, from taking over gay chat channels when the boys went to sleep was to create a software robot to hang around 24 hours a day and guard the channel. Many IRC participants put more effort into complicated bot wars, attempts to take over channels, and general tomfoolery than actually having a conversation, often ruining things for the rest of us.

On most investment discussion boards, it's practically impossible to follow a thread from beginning to end, because every post is its own page, which makes for a lot of banner ad inventory, but the latency in reading a conversation will eventually drive you nuts. The huge amount of flashing commercial crap on all four sides of the conversation makes you feel like you were trying to make friends in Times Square, but the neon lights keep demanding all the attention.

On Slashdot, every thread has hundreds of replies, many of which are identical, so the conversation there feels insipid and stupid. In a moment, I'll reveal why Slashdot has so many identical replies, and the *Joel on Software* forum doesn't.

And on FuckedCompany.com, the discussion board is completely, utterly worthless; the vast majority of posts consist of irrelevant profanity and general abusiveness, and it feels like a fraternity rudeness contest, without any fraternity.

So, we have discovered the primary axiom of online communities:

Small software implementation details result in big differences in the way the community develops, behaves, and feels.

IRC users organize themselves around bot warfare because the software doesn't let you reserve a channel. Usenet threads are massively redundant because the original Usenet reader, "rn," designed for 300-baud modems, never shows you old posts, only new ones, so if you want to nitpick about something someone said, you had to quote them or your nitpick wouldn't make sense.

With that in mind, I'd like to answer the most common questions about the *Joel on Software* forum, why it was designed the way it was designed, how that makes it work, and how it could be improved.

Q. Why is the software so dang simplistic?

A. In the early days of the *Joel on Software* forum, achieving a critical mass to get the conversation off the ground was important to prevent the empty restaurant phenomenon (nobody goes into an empty restaurant, they'll always go into the full one next door even if it's totally rubbish.) Thus a design goal was to eliminate impediments to posting. That's why there's no registration and there are literally no features, so there's nothing to learn.

The business goal of the software that runs the forum was to provide tech support for Fog Creek's products. That's what paid for
the development. To achieve that goal, nothing was more important
than making the software super simple so that anyone could be
comfortable using it. Everything about how the forum works is
incredibly obvious. I don't know of anyone who hasn't been able
to figure out how to use it immediately.

Q. Could you make a feature where I check a box that says "E-mail
me if somebody replies to my post?"

A. This one feature, so easy to implement and thus so tempting to
programmers, is the best way to kill dead any young forum.
Implement this feature, and you may never get to critical mass.
Philip Greenspun's LUSENET has this feature, and you can watch
it sapping the life out of young discussion groups.

Why?

What happens is that people go to the group to ask a question. If
you offer the "Notify me" check box, these people will post their
question, check the box, and never come back. They'll just read the
replies in their mailbox. The end.

If you eliminate the check box, people are left with no choice but to
check back every once in a while. And while they're checking back,
they might read another post that looks interesting. And they might
have something to contribute to that post. And in the critical early
days when you're trying to get the discussion group to take off,
you've increased the "stickiness" and you've got more people
hanging around, which helps achieve critical mass a lot quicker.

Q. OK, but can't you at least have branching? If someone gets off
on a tangent, that should be its own branch, which you can follow
or go back to the main branch.

A. Branching is very logical to a programmer's mind, but it doesn't
correspond to the way conversations take place in the real world.
Branched discussions are disjointed to follow and distracting. You
know what I find distracting? When I'm trying to do something on
my bank's web site, and the site is so slow I can't remember what
I'm doing from one click to the next. That reminds me of a joke.
Three old ladies talking. Lady 1: "I'm so forgetful, the other day I
was on the steps to my apartment with a bag, and I couldn't

remember if I was taking out the trash or going upstairs with the groceries." Lady 2: "I'm so forgetful, I was in my car in the driveway, and I couldn't remember if I was coming home or going to shul." Lady 3: "Thank God, I still have my memory, clear as a bell, knock on wood (knock, knock, knock). Come in, door's open!" Branching makes discussions get off track, and reading a thread that is branched is discombobulating and unnatural. Better to force people to start a new topic if they want to get off topic. Which reminds me . . .

Q. Your list of topics is sorted wrong. It should put the topic with the most recent reply first, rather than listing them based on the time of the original post.

A. It could do that; that's what many web-based forums do. But when you do that, certain topics tend to float near the top forever, because people will be willing to argue about H1B visas, or what's wrong with computer science in college, until the end of the universe. Every day, a hundred new people arrive in the forum for the first time, and they start at the top of the list, and they dive into that topic with gusto.

The way I do it has two advantages. One, topics rapidly go away, so conversation remains relatively interesting. Eventually, people have to just stop arguing about a given point.

Two, the order of topics on the home page is stable, so it's easier to find a topic again that you were interested in because it stays in the same place relative to its neighbors.

Q. Why don't you have some kind of system so I can see what posts I've already read?

A. We have the best system that can be implemented in a distributed, scalable fashion: we let everyone's browser keep track of it. Web browsers will change the color of the links you've already visited from blue to purple. So all we have to do is subtly change the URL for each topic to include the number of replies available; that way when there are additional replies, the post will appear in the "unread" color again.

Anything more elaborate than this would be harder to build and would needlessly complicate the UI.

Q. The damn "Reply" link is all the way at the bottom. This is a usability annoyance because you have to scroll all the way to the bottom.

A. This is intentional. I would prefer that you read all the posts before you reply; otherwise, you may post something that is repetitive or that sounds disjointed coming after the previous last post. Of course, I can't physically grab your eyeballs and move them from left to right, forcing you to read the entire thread before letting you post, but if I put a "Reply" link anywhere but the bottom of the page, that would positively encourage people to spew their little gems before they've read what's already there. This is why Slashdot topics have 500 replies but only 17 interesting replies, and it's why nobody likes to read Slashdot discussions: they sound like a classroom full of children all shouting out the same answer at the same time. ("Ha ha . . . Bill Gates! That's an oxymoron!")

Q. The damn "Start a New Topic" link is all the way at the bottom . . .

A. Uh huh, same thing.

Q. Why don't you show people their posts to confirm them before you post them? Then people wouldn't make mistakes and typos.

A. Empirically, that is not true. Not only is it not true, it's the opposite of true.

Part one: when you have a confirmation step, most people just click past it. Very few people reread their post carefully. If they wanted to reread their post carefully, they could have done it while they were editing it, but they are bored by their post already, it's yesterday's newspaper, they are ready to move on.

Part two: the lack of the confirmation step actually makes people more cautious. It's like those studies they did that showed that it's safer, on twisty mountain roads, to remove the crash barrier, because it makes people scared and so they drive more carefully, and any way, that little flimsy aluminum crash barrier ain't gonna stop a two-ton SUV moving at 50 mph from flying off the cliff. You're better off, statistically, just scaring the bejesus out of drivers so they creep along at 2 miles per hour around the hairpins.

Q. Why don't you show me the post I'm replying to, while I compose my reply?

A. Because that will tempt you to quote a part of it in your own reply. Anything I can do to reduce the amount of quoting will increase the fluidity of the conversation, making topics interesting to read. Whenever someone quotes something from above, the person who reads the topic has to read the same thing twice in a row, which is pointless and automatically guaranteed to be boring.

Sometimes people still try to quote things, usually because they are replying to something from three posts ago, or because they're mindlessly nitpicking and they need to rebut twelve separate points. These are not bad people, they're just programmers, and programming requires you to dot every i and cross every t, so you get into a frame of mind where you can't leave any argument unanswered any more than you would ignore an error from your compiler. But I'll be damned if I make it EASY on you. I'm almost tempted to try to find a way to show posts as images so you can't cut and paste them. If you really need to reply to something from three posts ago, kindly take a moment to compose a decent English sentence ("When Fred said blah, he must not have considered . . . "); don't litter the place with your <<<>>>s.

Q. Why do posts disappear sometimes?

A. The forum is moderated. That means that a few people have the magick powah to delete a post. If the post they delete is the first one in a thread, the thread itself appears deleted because there's no way to get to it.

Q. But that's censorship!

A. No, it's picking up the garbage in the park. If we didn't do it, the signal-to-noise ratio would change dramatically for the worse. People post spam and get-rich schemes, people post antisemitic comments about me, people post nonsense that doesn't make any sense. Some idealistic youngsters may imagine a totally uncensored world as one in which the free exchange of intelligent ideas raises everyone's IQ, an idealized Oxford Debate Society or Speakers' Corner. I am pragmatic and understand that a totally uncensored world just looks like your inbox: 80% spam, advertising, and fraud, rapidly driving away the few interesting people.

If you are looking for a place to express yourself in which there will be no moderation, my advice to you would be to (a) create a new forum and (b) make it popular. (Apologies to Larry Wall.)

Q. How do you decide what to delete?

A. First of all, I remove radically off-topic posts or posts that, in my opinion, are only of interest to a very small number of people. If something is not about the same general topics as *Joel on Software* is about, it may be interesting as all heck to certain people, but it's not likely to interest the majority of people who came to my site to hear about software development.

My policy in the past has been that "off topic" includes any discussion of the forum itself, its design or usability. There's a slightly different reason for this, almost another axiom. Every forum, mailing list, discussion group, and BBS will, all else being equal, lapse into conversations about the forum itself every week or two. Literally once a week, somebody strolls in and announces his list of improvements to the forum software, which he demands be made right away. And then somebody says, "Look buddy, you're not paying for it, Joel's doing us a favor, get lost." And somebody else says "Joel's not doing this out of the goodness of his heart, it's marketing for Fog Creek." And it's just SOOOO BORING because it happens EVERY WEEK. It's like talking about the weather when you have nothing else to talk about. It may be exciting to the new person who just appeared on the board, but it is only barely about software development, so, as Strong Bad says, "DELETED." Unfortunately, what I have learned is that trying to get people to stop talking about the forum is like trying to stop a river. But please, if you're reading this article and you want to discuss it on the forum, please, please, do me a *huge* favor, and resist the urge.

We will delete posts that are personal, ad hominem attacks on non-public personalities. I better define that. Ad hominem means it is an attack on the individual, rather than on his ideas. If you say, "That is a stupid idea because . . . " it's OK. If you say, "You are stupid," then it's an ad hominem attack. If it's vicious or uncivil or libelous, I delete it. There's one exception: because the *Joel on Software* forum is the best place to criticize Joel, vicious or uncivil posts about Joel are allowed to stand, but only if they contain some tiny sliver of a useful argument or idea.

I automatically delete posts that comment on the spelling or grammar of a previous poster. We'll be talking about interviews and someone will say, "It's a wonder you can get a job with spelling like that." It's just super boring to talk about other people's spelling. SUPER, SUPER boring.

Q. Why don't you just post the rules instead of leaving it as a mystery?

A. The other day I was taking the train from Newark International Airport back to Manhattan. Besides being in general disrepair, the only thing to read was a large sign that explained very sternly and in great detail that if you misbehaved, you would be put off the train at the next stop, and the police would be summoned. And I thought, 99.99999% of the people who read that sign ain't gonna be misbehavin', and the misbehavers couldn't care less what the sign says. So the net result of the sign is to make honest citizens feel like they're being accused of something, and it doesn't deter the sociopaths at all, and it just reminds the good citizens of New Jersey endlessly that they're in Newark, Crime Capital, where sociopaths get on the train and do Unpleasant Things and Make A Scene and Have To Be Put Off and the Police Summoned.

Almost everyone on the *Joel on Software* forum, somehow, was born with the part of the brain that tells them that it's not civilized to post vicious personal attacks, or to post questions about learning French on a software forum, or to conduct an argument by criticizing someone's spelling. And the other .01% don't care about the rules. So posting rules is just a way to insult the majority of the law-abiding citizens, and it doesn't deter the morons who think their own poo smells delicious and nothing they post could possibly be against the rules.

When you address troublemakers in public, everyone else thinks you're paranoid or feels angry at being scolded when they did nothing wrong. It's like being in grade school again, and one idiot-child has broken a window, and now everyone has to sit there listening to the teacher giving the whole class a stern lecture on why you mustn't break windows. So any public discussion of why a particular post got deleted, for example, is taboo.

Q. Instead of deleting posts, why don't you have a moderation scheme, where people vote on how much they like a post, and people can choose how high the vote has to be before they read it?

A. This is, of course, how Slashdot works, and I'll bet you 50% of the people who read Slashdot regularly have never figured it out.

There are three things I don't like about this. One: it's more UI complication, a feature that people need to learn how to use. Two: it creates such complicated politics that it make the Byzantine Empire look like third-grade school government. And three: when you read Slashdot with the filters turned up high enough that you see only the interesting posts, the narrative is completely lost. You just get a bunch of random disjointed statements with no context.

Q. Why don't you have a registration scheme to eliminate rude posters?

A. As I explained earlier, the goal of the forum is to make it easy to post. (Remember, the software was written for tech support.) Registration schemes eliminate at least 90% of the people who might have posted, and in a tech support scenario, those 90% are going to call my toll-free number.

Besides, I don't think registration would help. If somebody is being abusive, it doesn't help to ban them, they can trivially reregister. The idea of improving the community by requiring registration is an old one, and it's appropriate, I think, for the Echo/Well type of conferences where you're creating a network of people as much as you're discussing a topic, and you charge people cash money to belong.

But requiring registration does NOT improve the quality of the conversation or the average quality of the participants. If you look closely at the signal-to-noise ratio on the *Joel on Software* forum, you might start to notice that the noisiest people (i.e., the people who post the most words while contributing the fewest ideas) are often the long-time, hardcore members who visit the forum every ten minutes. These are the people who feel the need to chime in with an "I agree with that" and replies to Every Single Topic even when they haven't got an original thought to contribute. And they would certainly register.

Q. Any plans for the future?

A. Working on the software for the discussion forum is not a priority for me or my company: it's good enough, it works, it has created an interesting place to talk about hard computer management problems and get ideas from some of the smartest people in the world. And I've got too many better things to work on. Somebody else can create the next big leap in usability for discussion forums.

I just created a New York City forum, to see if geographically based forums encourage people to get to know each other in person as well as online. In my experience, regionally based communities cause the community to take a giant leap from a simple web site to a real society, a true third place.

Creating community, in any case, is a noble goal, because it's sorely missing for so many of us. Let's keep plugging away at it.

part four

MANAGING LARGE PROJECTS

seventeen

MARTIAN HEADSETS

MONDAY, MARCH 17, 2008

You're about to see the mother of all flame wars on Internet groups where web developers hang out. It'll make the Battle of Stalingrad look like that time your sister-in-law stormed out of afternoon tea at your grand-mother's and wrapped the Mustang around a tree.

This upcoming battle will be presided over by Dean Hachamovitch, the Microsoft veteran currently running the team that's going to bring you the next version of Internet Explorer, 8.0. The IE 8 team is in the process of making a decision that lies perfectly, exactly, precisely on the fault line smack in the middle of two different ways of looking at the world. It's the difference between conservatives and liberals, it's the difference between "idealists" and "realists," it's a huge global jihad dividing members of the same family, engineers against computer scientists, and Lexuses vs. olive trees.

And there's no solution. But it will be really, really entertaining to watch, because 99% of the participants in the flame wars are not going to understand what they're talking about. It's not just entertainment: it's required reading for every developer who needs to design interoperable systems.

The flame war will revolve around the issue of something called web standards. I'll let Dean introduce the problem (blogs.msdn.com/ie/ archive/2008/03/03/microsoft-s-interoperability-principles-and-ie8.aspx):

*All browsers have a "Standards" mode, call it "Standards mode,"
and use it to offer a browser's best implementation of web standards. Each version of each browser has its own Standards mode,
because each version of each browser improves on its web standards support. There's Safari 3's Standards mode, Firefox 2's
Standards mode, IE 6's Standards mode, and IE 7's Standards
mode, and they're all different. We want to make IE 8's Standards
mode much, much better than IE 7's Standards mode.*

And the whole problem hinges on the little tiny decision of what IE 8
should do when it encounters a page that claims to support "standards,"
but has probably only been tested against IE 7.

What the hell *is* a standard?

Don't they have standards in all kinds of engineering endeavors?
(Yes.)

Don't they usually work? (Mmmm . . .)

Why are "web standards" so frigging messed up? (It's not *just*
Microsoft's fault. It's your fault too. And Jon Postel's [1943–1998]. I'll
explain that later.)

There is no solution. Each solution is terribly wrong. Eric Bangeman
at *Ars Technica* writes, "The IE team has to walk a fine line between
tight support for W3C standards and making sure sites coded for earlier
versions of IE still display correctly" (arstechnica.com/news.ars/
post/20071219-ie8-goes-on-an-acid2-trip-beta-due-in-first-half-
of-2008.html). This is incorrect. It's not a fine line. It's a line of negative
width. There is no place to walk. They are damned if they do and
damned if they don't.

That's why I can't take sides on this issue, and I'm not going to. But
every working software developer should understand, at least, how standards work, how standards should work, how we got into this mess, so
I want to try to explain a little bit about the problem here, and you'll see
that it's the same reason Microsoft Vista is selling so poorly, and it's the
same issue I wrote about when I referred to the Raymond Chen camp
(pragmatists) at Microsoft vs. the MSDN camp (idealists), the MSDN
camp having won, and now nobody can figure out where their favorite
menu commands went in Microsoft Office 2007, and nobody wants
Vista, and it's all the same debate: whether you are an idealist ("red") or
a pragmatist ("blue").

Let me start at the beginning. Let's start by thinking about *how to get things to work together*.

What kinds of things? Anything, really. A pencil and a pencil sharpener. A telephone and a telephone system. An HTML page and a web browser. A Windows GUI application and the Windows operating system. Facebook and a Facebook application. Stereo headphones and stereos.

At the point of contact between those two items, there are all kinds of things that have to be agreed on, or they won't work together.

I'll work through a simple example.

Imagine that you went to Mars, where you discovered that the beings who live there don't have portable music players. They're still using boom boxes.

You realize this is a huge business opportunity and start selling portable MP3 players (except on Mars they're called Qxyzrhjjjjukltks) and compatible headphones. To connect the MP3 player to the headphones, you invent a neat kind of metal jack that looks like this:

Because you control the player and the headphone, you can ensure that your player works with your headphones. This is a ONE-TO-ONE market. One player, one headphone.

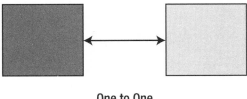

One to One

Maybe you write up a spec, hoping that third parties will make different color headphones, since Marslings are very particular about the color of things that they stick in their earlings.

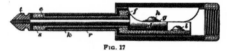

may not touch the connecting block *f*, an insulating washer *g*, is placed under the screw and washer *h*. The insulating washer is made large enough so that there will be no stray strands to short-circuit the plug. The sleeve *s* is made from brass tubing and passes through the insulating tube *k* to its

FIG. 17

connecting block *f*, within which it is screwed; the connection is made to the sleeve under the screw and washer *l*. The sleeve connection is made by bending back one of the conductors, when the cord is screwed into the shank of the plug. The strand is thus pinched tightly against the threads,

And you forgot, when you wrote the spec, to document that the voltage should be around 1.4 volts. You just forgot. So the first aspiring manufacturer of 100% compatible headphones comes along, his speaker is only expecting 0.014 volts, and when he tests his prototype, it either blows out the headphones or the eardrums of the listener, whichever comes first. And he makes some adjustments and eventually gets a headphone that works fine and is just a couple of angstroms more fierce than your headphones.

More and more manufacturers show up with compatible headphones, and soon we're in a ONE-TO-MANY market.

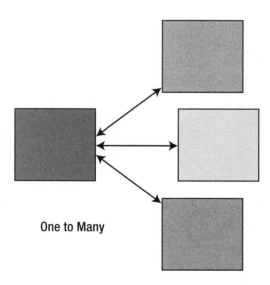

One to Many

So far, all is well. We have a de facto standard for headphone jacks here. The written spec is not complete and not adequate, but anybody who wants to make a compatible headphone just has to plug it into your personal stereo device and test it, and if it works, all is well, they can sell it, and it will work.

Until you decide to make a new version, the Qxyzrhjjjjukltk 2.0.

The Qxyzrhjjjjukltk 2.0 is going to include a *telephone* (turns out Marslings didn't figure out cellphones on their own, either), and the headphone is going to have to have a built-in microphone, which requires one more conductor, so you rework the connector into something totally incompatible and kind of ugly, with all kinds of room for expansion:

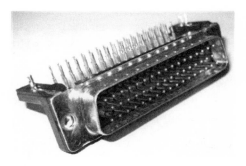

And the Qxyzrhjjjjukltk 2.0 is a complete and utter failure in the market. Yes, it has a nice telephone thing, but nobody cared about that. They cared about their large collections of headphones. It turns out that when I said Marslings are very particular about the color of things that they stick in their ears, I meant it. Most trendy Marslings at this point have a whole *closet* full of nice headphones. They all look the same to you (red), but Marslings are very, very finicky about shades of red in a way that you never imagined. The newest high-end apartments on Mars are being marketed with a headphone closet. I kid you not.

So the new jack is not such a success, and you quickly figure out a new scheme:

New!

Notice that you've now split the main shaft to provide another conductor for the microphone signal, but the trouble is, your Qxyzrhjjjjukltk 2.1 doesn't really know whether the headset that's plugged in has a mic or not, and it needs to know this so it can decide whether to enable phone calls. And so you invent a little protocol . . . the new device puts a signal on the mic pin and looks for it on the ground, and if it's there, it must be a three-conductor plug, and therefore they don't have a mic, so you'll go into backward-compatibility mode where you only play music. It's simple, but it's a protocol negotiation.

It's not a ONE-TO-MANY market any more. All the stereo devices are made by the same firm, one after the other, so I'm going to call this a SEQUENCE-TO-MANY market:

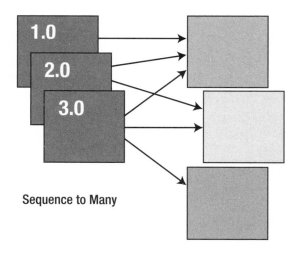

Sequence to Many

Here are some SEQUENCE-TO-MANY markets you already know about:

1. Facebook: about 20,000 Facebook apps

2. Windows: about 1,000,000 Windows apps

3. Microsoft Word: about 1,000,000,000 Word documents

There are hundreds of other examples. The key thing to remember is that when a new version of the left-hand device comes out, it has to maintain auto-backward-compatibility with all the old right-hand accessories meant to work with the old device, because those old accessories could not possibly have been designed with the new product in mind. The Martian headphones are already made. You can't go back and change them all. It's much easier and more sensible to change the newly invented device so that it *acts like* an old device when confronted with an old headphone.

And because you want to make progress, adding new features and functionality, you also need a new protocol for new devices to use, and the sensible thing to do is to have both devices negotiate a little bit at the beginning to decide whether they both understand the latest protocol.

SEQUENCE-TO-MANY is the world Microsoft grew up in.

But there's one more twist, the MANY-TO-MANY market.

A few years pass; you're still selling Qxyzrhjjjjukltks like crazy; but now there are lots of Qxyzrhjjjjukltk clones on the market, like the open source FireQx, and lots of headphones, and you all keep inventing new features that require changes to the headphone jack, and it's driving the headphone makers *crazy* because they have to test their new designs out against *every Qxyzrhjjjjukltk clone*, which is costly and time consuming, and frankly most of them don't have time and just get it to work on the most popular version of Qxyzrhjjjjukltk, 5.0, and if that works, they're happy; but of course when you plug the headphones into FireQx 3.0, lo and behold, they explode in your hands because of a slight misunderstanding about some obscure thing in the spec that nobody really understands called *hasLayout*, and everybody understands that when it's *raining* the *hasLayout* property is *true* and the voltage is supposed to increase to support the windshield-wiper feature, but there seems to be some debate over whether hail and snow are *rain* for the purpose of *hasLayout*, because the spec just doesn't say. FireQx 3.0 treats snow as rain, because you need windshield wipers in the snow, Qxyzrhjjjjukltk 5.0 does not, because the programmer who worked on that feature lives in a warm part of Mars without snow and doesn't have a driver's license anyway. Yes, they have driver's licenses on Mars.

And eventually some tedious bore writes a lengthy article on her blog explaining a trick you can use to make Qxyzrhjjjjukltk 5.0 behave just like FireQx 3.0 through taking advantage of a bug in Qxyzrhjjjjukltk 5.0 in which you trick Qxyzrhjjjjukltk into deciding that it's raining when it's snowing by melting a little bit of the snow, and it's ridiculous, but everyone does it, because they have to solve the *hasLayout* incompatibility. Then the Qxyzrhjjjjukltk team fixes that bug in 6.0, and you're screwed again, and you have to go find some new bug to exploit to make your windshield-wiper-equipped headphone work with either device.

NOW. This is the MANY-TO-MANY market. Many players on the left-hand side who *don't* cooperate, and SCRILLIONS of players on the right-hand side. And they're *all making mistakes* because To Err Is Human.

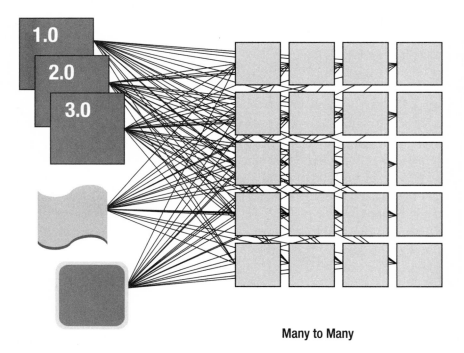

Many to Many

And of course, this is the situation we find ourselves in with HTML. Dozens of common browsers, literally *billions* of web pages.

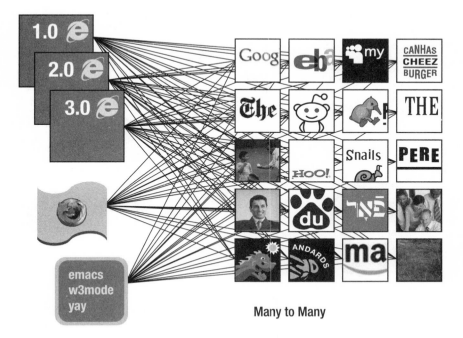

Many to Many

And over the years what happens in a MANY-TO-MANY market is that there is a hue and cry for "standards" so that "all the players" (meaning the small players) have an equal chance at being able to display all eight billion web pages correctly, and, even more importantly, so that the *designers* of those eight billion pages only have to test against one browser, and use "web standards," and then they will know that their page will also work in *other* browsers, without having to test every page against every browser.

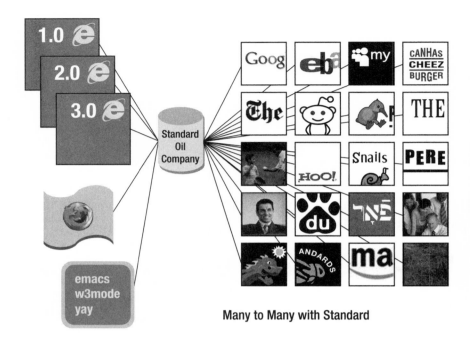

Many to Many with Standard

See, the idea is, instead of many-to-many testing, you have many-to-standard and standard-to-many testing, and you need radically fewer tests. Not to mention that your web pages don't need any browser-specific code to work around bugs in individual browsers, because in this platonic world there are no bugs.

That's the ideal.

In practice, with the Web, there's a bit of a problem: no way to test a web page against the standard, because there's no reference implementation that guarantees that if it works, all the browsers work. This just doesn't exist.

So you have to "test" in your own head, purely as a thought experiment, against a bunch of standards documents, which you probably never read and couldn't completely understand even if you did.

Those documents are *super* confusing. The specs are full of statements like "If a sibling block box (that does not float and is not absolutely positioned) follows the run-in box, the run-in box becomes the first inline box of the block box. A run-in cannot run in to a block that already starts with a run-in or that itself is a run-in." Whenever I read things like that, I wonder how *anyone* correctly conforms to the spec.

There is no practical way to check whether the web page you just coded conforms to the spec. There are validators, but they won't tell you what the page is supposed to look like, and having a "valid" page where all the text is overlapping, nothing lines up, and you can't see anything is not very useful. What people do is check their pages against one browser, maybe two, until it looks right. And if they've made a mistake that just happens to look OK in IE and Firefox, they're not even going to know about it.

And their pages may break when a future web browser comes out.

If you've ever visited the ultra-orthodox Jewish communities of Jerusalem, all of whom agree in complete and utter adherence to every iota of Jewish law, you will discover that despite general agreement on what constitutes kosher food, you will not find a rabbi from one ultra-orthodox community who is willing to eat at the home of a rabbi from a different ultra-orthodox community. And the web designers are discovering what the Jews of Mea Shearim have known for decades: just because you all agree to follow one book doesn't ensure compatibility, because the laws are so complex and complicated and convoluted that it's almost impossible to understand them all well enough to avoid traps and landmines, and you're safer just asking for the fruit plate.

Standards are a great goal, of course, but before you become a standards fanatic, you have to understand that due to the failings of human beings, standards are sometimes misinterpreted, sometimes confusing and even ambiguous.

The precise problem here is that you're pretending that there's one standard, but since nobody has a way to test against the standard, it's not a real standard: it's a platonic ideal and a set of misinterpretations, and therefore the standard is not serving the desired goal of reducing the test matrix in a MANY-TO-MANY market.

DOCTYPE is a myth.

A mortal web designer who attaches a DOCTYPE tag to their web page saying, "This is standard HTML," is committing an act of hubris. There is no way they know that. All they are really saying is that the page was *meant* to be standard HTML. All they *really* know is that they tested it with IE, Firefox, maybe Opera and Safari, and it seems to work. Or, they copied the DOCTYPE tag out of a book and don't know what it means.

In the real world, where people are imperfect, you can't have a standard with just a spec—you *must have* a super-strict reference implementation, and everybody has to test against the reference implementation. Otherwise, you get seventeen different "standards," and you might as well not have one at all.

And this is where Jon Postel caused a problem, back in 1981, when he coined the robustness principle: "Be conservative in what you do, be liberal in what you accept from others" (tools.ietf.org/html/rfc793). What he was trying to say was that the best way to make the protocols work robustly would be if everyone was very, very careful to conform to the specification, but they should be also be extremely forgiving when talking to partners that don't conform exactly to the specification, as long as you can kind of figure out what they meant.

So, technically, the way to make a paragraph with small text is <p><small>, but a lot of people wrote <small><p>, which is technically incorrect for reasons most web developers don't understand, and the web browsers forgave them and made the text small anyway, because that's obviously what they wanted to happen.

Now there are all these web pages out there with errors, because all the early web browser developers made super-liberal, friendly, accommodating browsers that loved you for *who you were* and didn't care if you made a mistake. And so there were lots of mistakes. And Postel's robustness principle didn't really work. The problem wasn't noticed for many years. In 2001, Marshall Rose finally wrote the following (tools.ietf.org/html/rfc3117):

Counter-intuitively, Postel's robustness principle ("be conservative in what you send, liberal in what you accept") often leads to deployment problems. Why? When a new implementation is initially fielded, it is likely that it will encounter only a subset of existing implementations. If those implementations follow the robustness principle, then errors in the new implementation will likely go undetected. The new implementation then sees some, but not widespread, deployment. This process repeats for several new implementations. Eventually, the not-quite-correct implementations run into other implementations that are less liberal than the initial set of implementations. The reader should be able to figure out what happens next.

Jon Postel should be honored for his enormous contributions to the invention of the Internet, and there is really no reason to fault him for the infamous robustness principle. 1981 is prehistoric. If you had told Postel that there would be 90 million untrained people, not engineers, creating web sites, and they would be doing all kinds of awful things, and some kind of misguided charity would have caused the early browser makers to accept these errors and display the page anyway, he would have understood that this is the wrong principle, and that, actually, the web standards idealists are right, and the way the web "should have" been built would be to have very, very strict standards, and every web browser should be positively *obnoxious* about pointing them *all out to you*, and web developers who couldn't figure out how to be "conservative in what they emit" should not be allowed to author pages that appear *anywhere* until they get their act together.

But, of course, if that had happened, maybe the web would never have taken off like it did, and maybe instead, we'd all be using a gigantic Lotus Notes network operated by AT&T. *Shudder.*

Shoulda woulda coulda. Who cares. We are where we are. We can't change the past, only the future. Heck, we can barely even change the future.

And if you're a pragmatist on the Internet Explorer 8.0 team, you might have these words from Raymond Chen seared into your cortex. He was writing about how Windows XP had to emulate buggy behavior from old versions of Windows (`blogs.msdn.com/oldnewthing/archive/2003/12/23/45481.aspx`):

> *Look at the scenario from the customer's standpoint. You bought programs X, Y, and Z. You then upgraded to Windows XP. Your computer now crashes randomly, and program Z doesn't work at all. You're going to tell your friends, "Don't upgrade to Windows XP. It crashes randomly, and it's not compatible with program Z." Are you going to debug your system to determine that program X is causing the crashes, and that program Z doesn't work because it is using undocumented window messages? Of course not. You're going to return the Windows XP box for a refund. (You bought programs X, Y, and Z some months ago. The 30-day return policy no longer applies to them. The only thing you can return is Windows XP.)*

And you're thinking, hmm, let's update this for today:

Look at the scenario from the customer's standpoint. You bought programs X, Y, and Z. You then upgraded to Windows ~~XP~~*Vista. Your computer now crashes randomly, and program Z doesn't work at all. You're going to tell your friends, "Don't upgrade to Windows* ~~XP~~*Vista. It crashes randomly, and it's not compatible with program Z." Are you going to debug your system to determine that program X is causing the crashes, and that program Z doesn't work because it is using* ~~undocumented~~*insecure window messages? Of course not. You're going to return the Windows* ~~XP~~*Vista box for a refund. (You bought programs X, Y, and Z some months ago. The 30-day return policy no longer applies to them. The only thing you can return is Windows* ~~XP~~*Vista.)*

The victory of the idealists over the pragmatists at Microsoft, which I reported in 2004, directly explains why Vista is getting terrible reviews and selling poorly.

And how does it apply to the IE team?

Look at the scenario from the customer's standpoint. You visit 100 web sites a day. You then upgraded to IE 8. On half of them, the page is messed up, and Google Maps doesn't work at all.

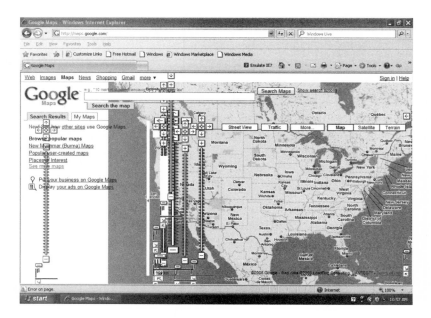

You're going to tell your friends, "Don't upgrade to IE 8. It messes up every page, and Google Maps doesn't work at all." Are you going to View Source to determine that web site X is using nonstandard HTML, and Google Maps doesn't work because it is using nonstandard JavaScript objects from old versions of IE that were never accepted by the standards committee? Of course not. You're going to uninstall IE 8. (Those web sites are out of your control. Some of them were developed by people who are now dead. The only thing you can do is go back to IE 7).

And so if you're a developer on the IE 8 team, your first inclination is going to be to do exactly what has always worked in these kinds of SEQUENCE-TO-MANY markets. You're going to do a little protocol negotiation and continue to emulate the old behavior for every site that doesn't *explicitly* tell you that they expect the new behavior, so that all existing web pages continue to work, and you're only going to have the nice new behavior for sites that put a little flag on the page saying, "Yo! I *grok* IE 8! Give me all the new IE 8 Goodness please!"

And indeed that was the first decision announced by the IE team on January 21. The web browser would accommodate existing pages silently so that nobody had to change their web site by acting like the old, buggy IE 7 that web developers hated.

A pragmatic engineer would have to come to the conclusion that the IE team's first decision was right. But the young idealist "standards" people went nuclear.

IE needed to provide a web standards experience *without* requiring a special "Yo! I'm tested with IE 8!" tag, they said. They were sick of special tags. Every frigging web page has to have thirty-seven ugly hacks in it to make it work with five or six popular browsers. Enough ugly hacks. Eight billion existing web pages be damned.

And the IE team flip-flopped. Their second decision, and I have to think it's not final, their second decision was to do the idealistic thing, and treat all sites that claim to be "standards compliant" as if they have been designed for and tested with IE 8.

Almost every web site I visited with IE 8 is broken in some way. Web sites that use a lot of JavaScript are generally completely dead. A lot of pages simply have visual problems: things in the wrong place, pop-up menus that pop under, mysterious scrollbars in the middle. Some sites have more subtle problems: they look OK, but as you go further, you find that critical form won't submit or leads to a blank page.

These are *not* web pages with errors. They are usually web sites that were carefully constructed to conform to web standards. But IE 6 and IE 7 didn't really conform to the specs, so these sites have little hacks in them that say, "On Internet Explorer . . . move this thing 17 pixels to the right to compensate for IE's bug."

And IE 8 *is* IE, but it no longer has the IE 7 bug where it moved that thing 17 pixels left of where it was supposed to be according to web standards. So now code that was written that was completely reasonable no longer works.

IE 8 can't display most web pages correctly until you give up and press the "ACT LIKE IE 7" button. The idealists don't care: they want those pages changed.

Some of those pages can't be changed. They might be burned onto CD-ROMs. Some of them were created by people who are now dead. Most of them were created by people who have no frigging idea what's going on and why their web page, which they paid a designer to create four years ago, is now not working properly.

The idealists rejoiced. Hundreds of them descended on the IE blog to actually say nice things about Microsoft for the first times in their lives.

I looked at my watch.

Tick, tick, tick.

Within a matter of seconds, you started to see people on the forums showing up like this one (forums.microsoft.com/MSDN/ShowPost. aspx?PostID=2972194&SiteID=1):

> *I have downloaded IE 8 and with it some bugs. Some of my web sites like "HP" are very difficult to read as the whole page is very very small . . . The speed of my Internet has also been reduced on some occasions. When I use Google Maps, there are overlays everywhere, enough so it makes it awkward to use!*

Mmhmm. All you smug idealists are laughing at this newbie/idjit. The consumer is not an idiot. She's your wife. So stop laughing. 98% of the world will install IE 8 and say, "It has bugs and I can't see my sites." They don't give a flicking flick about your stupid religious enthusiasm for making web browsers that conform to some mythical, platonic "standard" that is not actually implemented anywhere. They don't want to hear your stories about messy hacks. They want web browsers that work with actual web sites.

So you see, we have a terrific example here of a gigantic rift between two camps.

The web standards camp seems kind of Trotskyist. You'd think they're the left wing, but if you happened to make a web site that claims to conform to web standards but doesn't, the idealists turn into Joe Arpaio, America's Toughest Sheriff: "YOU MADE A MISTAKE AND YOUR WEB SITE SHOULD BREAK. I don't care if 80% of your web sites stop working. I'll put you all in jail, where you will wear pink pajamas and eat 15-cent sandwiches and work on a chain gang. And I don't care if the whole county is in jail. The law is the law."

On the other hand, we have the pragmatic, touchy feely, warm and fuzzy engineering types: "Can't we just default to IE 7 mode? One line of code . . . Zip! Solved!"

Secretly? Here's what I think is going to happen. The IE 8 team is going to tell everyone that IE 8 will use web standards by default, and run a nice long beta during which they beg people to test their pages with IE 8 and get them to work. And when they get closer to shipping, and only 32% of the web pages in the world render properly, they'll say, "Look guys, we're really sorry, we really wanted IE 8 standards mode to be the default, but we can't ship a browser that doesn't work," and they'll revert to the pragmatic decision. Or maybe they won't, because the pragmatists at Microsoft have been out of power for a long time. In which case, IE is going to lose a lot of market share, which would please the idealists to no end, and probably won't decrease Dean Hachamovitch's big year-end bonus by one cent.

You see? No right answer.

As usual, the idealists are 100% right in principle and, as usual, the pragmatists are right in practice. The flames will continue for years. This debate precisely splits the world in two. If you have a way to buy stock in Internet flame wars, now would be a good time to do that.

eighteen

WHY ARE THE MICROSOFT OFFICE FILE FORMATS SO COMPLICATED? (AND SOME WORKAROUNDS)

TUESDAY, FEBRUARY 19, 2008

Last week, Microsoft published the binary file formats for Office. These formats appear to be almost completely insane. The Excel 97-2003 file format is a 349-page PDF file. But wait, that's not all there is to it! This document includes the following interesting comment:

Each Excel workbook is stored in a compound file.

You see, Excel 97-2003 files are OLE compound documents, which are, essentially, file systems inside a single file. These are sufficiently complicated that you have to read another nine-page spec to figure that out. And these "specs" look more like C data structures than what we traditionally think of as a spec. It's a whole hierarchical file system.

If you started reading these documents with the hope of spending a weekend writing some spiffy code that imports Word documents into your blog system or creates Excel-formatted spreadsheets with your personal finance data, the complexity and length of the spec probably cured you of that desire pretty darn quickly. A normal programmer would conclude that Office's binary file formats

- Are deliberately obfuscated
- Are the product of a demented Borg mind

- Were created by insanely bad programmers
- And are impossible to read or create correctly

You'd be wrong on all four counts. With a little bit of digging, I'll show you how those file formats got so unbelievably complicated, why it doesn't reflect bad programming on Microsoft's part, and what you can do to work around it.

The first thing to understand is that the binary file formats were designed with very different design goals than, say, HTML.

They were designed to be fast on very old computers. For the early versions of Excel for Windows, 1MB of RAM was a reasonable amount of memory, and an 80386 at 20 MHz had to be able to run Excel comfortably. There are a lot of optimizations in the file formats that are intended to make opening and saving files much faster:

- These are binary formats, so loading a record is usually a matter of just copying (blitting) a range of bytes from disk to memory, where you end up with a C data structure you can use. There's no lexing or parsing involved in loading a file. Lexing and parsing are orders of magnitude slower than blitting.

- The file format is contorted, where necessary, to make common operations fast. For example, Excel 95 and 97 have something called Simple Save, which they use sometimes as a faster variation on the OLE compound document format, which just wasn't fast enough for mainstream use. Word had something called Fast Save. To save a long document quickly, fourteen out of fifteen times, only the changes are appended to the end of the file, instead of rewriting the whole document from scratch. On the hard drives of the day, this meant saving a long document took one second instead of thirty. (It also meant that deleted data in a document was still in the file. This turned out to be not what people wanted.)

They were designed to use libraries. If you wanted to write a from-scratch binary importer, you'd have to support things like the Windows Metafile Format (for drawing things) and OLE Compound Storage. If you're running on Windows, there's library support for these that makes it trivial . . . using these features was a shortcut for the Microsoft team.

But if you're writing everything on your own from scratch, you have to do all that work yourself.

Office has extensive support for compound documents; for example, you can embed a spreadsheet in a Word document. A perfect Word file format parser would also have to be able to do something intelligent with the embedded spreadsheet.

They were not designed with interoperability in mind. The assumption, and a fairly reasonable one at the time, was that the Word file format only had to be read and written by Word. That means that whenever a programmer on the Word team had to make a decision about how to change the file format, the only thing they cared about was (a) what was fast and (b) what took the fewest lines of code *in the Word code base*. The idea of things like SGML and HTML—interchangeable, standardized file formats—didn't really take hold until the Internet made it practical to interchange documents in the first place; this was a decade later than the Office binary formats were first invented. There was always an assumption that you could use importers and exporters to exchange documents. In fact, Word does have a format designed for easy interchange, called RTF, which has been there almost since the beginning. It's still 100% supported.

They have to reflect all the complexity of the applications. Every check box, every formatting option, and every feature in Microsoft Office has to be represented in file formats somewhere. That check box in Word's paragraph menu called "Keep With Next" that causes a paragraph to be moved to the next page if necessary so that it's on the same page as the paragraph after it? That has to be in the file format. And that means if you want to implement a perfect Word clone than can correctly read Word documents, you have to implement that feature. If you're creating a competitive word processor that has to load Word documents, it may only take you a minute to write the code to load that bit from the file format, but it might take you weeks to change your page layout algorithm to accommodate it. If you don't, customers will open their Word files in your clone, and all the pages will be messed up.

They have to reflect the history of the applications. A lot of the complexities in these file formats reflect features that are old, complicated, unloved, and rarely used. They're still in the file format for backward compatibility and because it doesn't cost anything for Microsoft to leave the code around. But if you really want to do a thorough and complete job of parsing and writing these file formats, you have to redo all that work that some intern did at Microsoft fifteen years ago. The bottom line is that there are **thousands of developer years** of work that went into the current versions of Word and Excel, and if you really want to clone those applications completely, you're going to have to do thousands of years of work. A file format is just a concise summary of all the features an application supports.

Just for kicks, let's look at one tiny example in depth. An Excel worksheet is a bunch of BIFF records of different types. I want to look at the very first BIFF record in the spec. It's a record called **1904**.

The Excel file format specification is remarkably obscure about this. It just says that the 1904 record indicates "if the 1904 date system is used." Ah. A classic piece of useless specification. If you were a developer working with the Excel file format, and you found this in the file format specification, you might be justified in concluding that Microsoft is hiding something. This piece of information does not give you enough information. You also need some outside knowledge, which I'll fill you in on now. There are two kinds of Excel worksheets: those where the epoch for dates is 1/1/1900 (with a leap-year bug deliberately created for Lotus 1-2-3 compatibility that is too boring to describe here), and those where the epoch for dates is 1/1/1904. Excel supports both because the first version of Excel, for the Mac, just used that operating system's epoch because that was easy, but Excel for Windows had to be able to import Lotus 1-2-3 files, which used 1/1/1900 for the epoch. It's enough to bring you to tears. At no point in history did a programmer ever not do the right thing, but there you have it.

Both 1900 and 1904 file types are commonly found in the wild, usually depending on whether the file originated on Windows or Mac. Converting from one to another silently can cause data integrity errors, so Excel won't change the file type for you. To parse Excel files, you have to handle both. That's not just a matter of loading this bit from the file. It means you have to rewrite all of your date display and parsing code to handle both epochs. That would take several days to implement, I think.

Indeed, as you work on your Excel clone, you'll discover all kinds of subtle details about date handling. When does Excel convert numbers to dates? How does the formatting work? Why is 1/31 interpreted as January 31 of this year, while 1/50 is interpreted as January 1, 1950? All of these subtle bits of behavior cannot be fully documented without writing a document that has the same amount of information as the Excel source code.

And this is only the first of hundreds of BIFF records you have to handle, and one of the simplest. Most of them are complicated enough to reduce a grown programmer to tears.

The only possible conclusion is this. It's very helpful of Microsoft to release the file formats for Microsoft and Office, but it's not really going to make it any easier to import or save to the Office file formats. These are insanely complex and rich applications, and you can't just implement the most popular 20% and expect 80% of the people to be happy. The binary file specification is, at most, going to save you a few minutes reverse engineering a remarkably complex system.

OK, I promised some workarounds. The good news is that for almost all common applications, trying to read or write the Office binary file formats is the wrong decision. There are two major alternatives you should seriously consider: letting Office do the work or using file formats that are easier to write.

Let Office do the heavy work for you. Word and Excel have extremely complete object models, available via COM Automation, which allow you to programmatically do *anything*. In many situations, you are better off reusing the code inside Office rather than trying to reimplement it. Here are a few examples:

1. You have a web-based application that needs to output existing Word files in PDF format. Here's how I would implement that: a few lines of Word VBA code loads a file and saves it as a PDF using the built-in PDF exporter in Word 2007. You can call this code directly, even from ASP or ASP.NET code running under IIS. It'll work. The first time you launch Word, it'll take a few seconds. The second time, Word will be kept in memory by the COM subsystem for a few minutes in case you need it again. It's fast enough for a reasonable web-based application.

2. Same as the preceding, but your web hosting environment is Linux. Buy one Windows 2003 server, install a fully licensed copy of Word on it, and build a little web service that does the work. Half a day of work with C# and ASP.NET.

3. Same as the preceding, but you need to scale. Throw a load balancer in front of any number of boxes that you built in step 2. No code required.

This kind of approach would work for all kinds of common Office types of applications you might perform on your server. For example:

- Opening an Excel workbook, storing some data in input cells, recalculating, and pulling some results out of output cells
- Using Excel to generate charts in GIF format
- Pulling just about any kind of information out of any kind of Excel worksheet without spending a minute thinking about file formats
- Converting Excel file formats to CSV tabular data (another approach is to use Excel ODBC drivers to suck data out using SQL queries)
- Editing Word documents
- Filling out Word forms
- Converting files between any of the many file formats supported by Office (there are importers for dozens of word processor and spreadsheet formats)

In all of these cases, there are ways to tell the Office objects that they're not running interactively, so they shouldn't bother updating the screen, and they shouldn't prompt for user input. By the way, if you go this route, there are a few gotchas, and it's not officially supported by Microsoft, so read their knowledge base article before you get started.

Use a simpler format for writing files. If you merely have to *produce* Office documents programmatically, there's almost always a better format than the Office binary formats that you can use which Word and Excel will open happily, without missing a beat.

- If you simply have to produce tabular data for use in Excel, consider CSV.
- If you really need worksheet calculation features that CSV doesn't support, the WK1 format (Lotus 1-2-3) is a heck of a lot simpler than Excel, and Excel will open it fine.

- If you really, really have to generate native Excel files, find an extremely old version of Excel (Excel 3.0 is a good choice) before all the compound document stuff, and save a minimum file containing only the exact features you want to use. Use this file to see the exact minimum BIFF records that you have to output and just focus on that part of the spec.

- For Word documents, consider writing HTML. Word will open those fine, too.

- If you really want to generate fancy formatted Word documents, your best bet is to create an RTF document. Everything that Word can do can be expressed in RTF, but it's a text format, not binary, so you can change things in the RTF document, and it'll still work. You can create a nicely formatted document with placeholders in Word, save as RTF, and then using simple text substitution, replace the placeholders on the fly. Now you have an RTF document that every version of Word will open happily.

Anyway, unless you're literally trying to create a competitor to Office that can read and write all Office files perfectly, in which case, you've got thousands of years of work cut out for you, chances are that reading or writing the Office binary formats is the most labor-intensive way to solve whatever problem it is that you're trying to solve.

nineteen

WHERE THERE'S MUCK, THERE'S BRASS

When I was a kid working in the bread factory, my nemesis was dough. It was sticky and hard to remove and got everywhere. I got home with specks of dough in my hair. Every shift included a couple of hours of scraping dough off of machinery. I carried dough-scrapers in my back pocket. Sometimes a huge lump of dough would go flying someplace where it shouldn't and gum up everything. I had dough nightmares.

I worked in the production side of the factory. The other side did packing and shipping. Their nemesis was crumbs. Crumbs got everywhere. The shipping crew went home with crumbs in their hair. Every shift included a couple of hours of brushing crumbs out of machinery. They carried little brushes in their back pockets. I'm sure they had crumb nightmares, too.

Pretty much any job that you can get paid for includes dealing with one gnarly problem. If you don't have dough or crumbs to deal with, maybe you work in a razor blade factory and go home with little cuts all over your fingers. Maybe you work for VMware and have nightmares about emulating bugs in sophisticated video cards that games rely on. Maybe you work on Windows, and your nightmare is that the simplest change can cause millions of old programs and hardware devices to stop working. That's the gnarly part of your job.

One of our gnarly problems is getting FogBugz to run on our customers' own servers. Jason Fried over at 37signals has a good summary of why this is no fun (www.37signals.com/svn/posts/724-ask-37signals-installable-software): ". . . You have to deal with endless operating environment variations that are out of your control. When something goes wrong, it's a lot harder to figure out why if you aren't in control of the OS or the third-party software or hardware that may be interfering with the install, upgrade, or general performance of your product. This is even more complicated with remote server installs when there may be different versions of Ruby, Rails, MYSQL, etc. at play." Jason concludes that if they had to sell installable software, they "definitely wouldn't be as happy." Yep. Work that makes you unhappy is what I mean by "a gnarly problem."

The trouble is, the market pays for solutions to gnarly problems, not solutions to easy problems. As the Yorkshire lads say, "Where there's muck, there's brass."

We offer both kinds of FogBugz—hosted and installable—and our customers opt 4 to 1 to install it at their own site. For us, the installable option gives us five times the sales. It costs us an extra salary or two (in tech support costs). It also means we have to use Wasabi, which has some serious disadvantages compared to off-the-shelf programming languages, but which we found to be the most cost-effective and efficient way, given our code base, to ship software that is installable on Windows, Linux, and Mac. Boy, I would love nothing more than to scrap installable FogBugz and run everything on our servers . . . we've got racks and racks of nice, well-managed Dell servers with plenty of capacity, and our tech support costs for the hosted version are zero. Life would be much easier. But we'd be making so much less money, we'd be out of business.

The one thing that so many of today's cute startups have in common is that all they have is a simple little Ruby-on-Rails Ajax site that has no barriers to entry and doesn't solve any gnarly problems. So many of these companies feel insubstantial and fluffy because, out of necessity (the whole company is three kids and an iguana), they haven't solved anything difficult yet. Until they do, they won't be solving problems for people. People pay for solutions to their problems.

Making an elegantly designed and easy-to-use application is just as gnarly, even though, like good ballet, it seems easy when done well. Jason and 37signals put effort into good design and get paid for that. Good design seems like the *easiest* thing to copy but, watching Microsoft trying to copy the iPod, turns out to be not so easy. Great design *is* a gnarly problem and can actually provide surprisingly sustainable competitive advantage.

Indeed, Jason probably made a good choice by picking the gnarly problem where he has a lot of talent (design) to solve, because it doesn't seem like a chore to him. I've been a Windows programmer for ages, so making a Windows Setup program for FogBugz, from scratch in C++, doing all kinds of gnarly COM stuff, doesn't seem like a chore to me.

The only way to keep growing—as a person and as a company—is to keep expanding the boundaries of what you're good at. At some point, the 37signals team might decide that hiring one person to write the Setup script and do installation support would pay for itself, and generate substantially more profit than it costs. So unless they deliberately want to keep the company small, which is a perfectly legitimate desire, they might eventually lose their reluctance to do things that seem gnarly.

Or maybe they won't. There's nothing wrong with choosing the fun part of your business to work on. I've certainly been guilty of that. And there's nothing wrong with deciding that you only want to solve a specific set of problems for a small, select group of people. Salesforce.com has managed to become big enough by sticking to hosted software. And there are plenty of smaller software shops providing a fantastic lifestyle for their crew with no desire to get any bigger.

But the great thing is that as you solve each additional gnarly problem, your business and market grow substantially. Good marketing, good design, good sales, good support, and solving lots of problems for customers all amplify each other. You start out with good design, then you add some good features and triple your customer base by solving lots of problems, and then you do some marketing and triple your customer base again because now lots of people learn about your solution to their pain, and then you hire salespeople and triple your customer base yet again because now the people who know about your solution are reminded to actually buy it, and then you add more features to solve more problems for even more people, and eventually you actually have a chance to reach enough people with your software to make the world a better place.

P.S. I'm not claiming here that 37signals would sell five times as many copies if they offered Installable Basecamp. First of all, one of the reasons we may sell so many more installable versions of FogBugz is that it appears, to some customers, to be cheaper. (It's not cheaper in the long run because you have to pay for the server and administer it yourself, but that's subjective.) Also, our support costs for the installable version are only as low as they are because 80% of our customers opt to run on Windows Server. Because Windows systems are so similar, it's much easier for us to support the lowest common denominator. The vast majority of our tech support costs are caused by the diversity in Unix platforms out there—I'd guess that the 20% of our Unix sales result in 80% of our support incidents. If an installable version of Basecamp required Unix, the support cost would be disproportionately expensive compared to a hypothetical installable Windows version. Finally, another reason our experience might not translate to 37signals is that we've been selling installable software for seven years now; the hosted version has only been out for about six months. So we have a big installed base used to running FogBugz on their own servers. If you only look at *new* FogBugz customers, the ratio of installable to hosted goes down to 3 to 1.

part five

Programming Advice

twenty

EVIDENCE-BASED SCHEDULING

Software developers don't really like to make schedules. Usually, they try to get away without one. "It'll be done when it's done!" they say, expecting that such a brave, funny zinger will reduce their boss to a fit of giggles, and in the ensuing joviality, the schedule will be forgotten.

Most of the schedules you do see are halfhearted attempts. They're stored on a file share somewhere and completely forgotten. When these teams ship, two years late, that weird guy with the file cabinet in his office brings the old printout to the post mortem, and everyone has a good laugh. "Hey look! We allowed two weeks for rewriting from scratch in Ruby!"

Hilarious! If you're still in business.

You want to be spending your time on things that get the most bang for the buck. And you can't figure out how much buck your bang is going to cost without knowing how long it's going to take. When you have to decide between the "animated paperclip" feature and the "more financial functions" feature, you really need to know how much time each will take.

Why won't developers make schedules? Two reasons. One: it's a pain in the butt. Two: nobody believes the schedule is realistic. Why go to all the trouble of working on a schedule if it's not going to be right?

Over the last year or so at Fog Creek, we've been developing a system that's so easy even our grouchiest developers are willing to go along with it. And as far as we can tell, it produces extremely reliable schedules. It's called Evidence-Based Scheduling, or EBS. You gather *evidence*, mostly from historical time sheet data, that you feed back into your schedules. What you get is not just one ship date: you get a confidence distribution curve, showing the probability that you will ship on any given date. It looks like this:

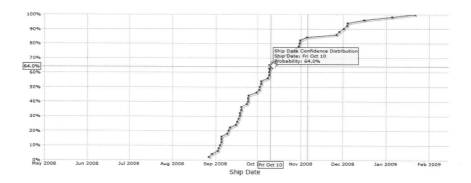

The steeper the curve, the more confident you are that the ship date is real.

Here's how you do it.

~

1. Break 'er down

When I see a schedule measured in days, or even weeks, I know it's not going to work. You have to break your schedule into very small tasks that can be measured in *hours*. Nothing longer than sixteen hours.

This forces you to actually figure out what you are going to do. Write subroutine foo. Create this dialog box. Parse the Fizzbott file. Individual development tasks are easy to estimate, because you've written subroutines, created dialog boxes, and parsed files before.

If you are sloppy and pick big three-week tasks (e.g., "Implement Ajax photo editor"), then you *haven't thought about what you are going to do*. In detail. Step by step. And when you haven't thought about what you're going to do, you can't know how long it will take.

Setting a sixteen-hour maximum forces you to *design* the damn feature. If you have a hand-wavy three-week feature called "Ajax photo editor" without a detailed design, I'm sorry to be the one to break it to you, but you are officially *doomed*. You never thought about the steps it's going to take, and you're sure to be forgetting a lot of them.

∿

2. Track elapsed time

It's hard to get individual estimates exactly right. How do you account for interruptions, unpredictable bugs, status meetings, and the semi-annual Windows Tithe Day when you have to reinstall everything from scratch on your main development box? Heck, even without all that stuff, how can you tell exactly how long it's going to take to implement a given subroutine?

You can't, really.

So, keep time sheets. Keep track of how long you spend working on each task. Then you can go back and see how long things took relative to the estimate. For each developer, you'll be collecting data like this:

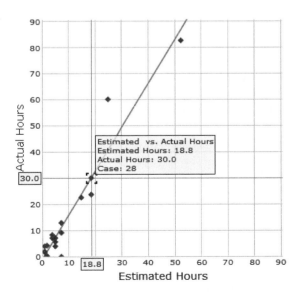

Each point on the chart is one completed task, with the estimated and actual times for that task. When you divide estimated by actual time, you get *velocity*: how fast the task was done relative to estimate. Over time, for each developer, you'll collect a history of velocities.

- The mythical *perfect estimator*, who exists only in your imagination, always gets every estimate exactly right. So their velocity history is {1, 1, 1, 1, 1, . . .}.

- A typical *bad estimator* has velocities all over the map, for example, {0.1, 0.5, 1.7, 0.2, 1.2, 0.9, 13.0}.

- Most estimators get the scale wrong but the relative estimates right. Everything takes longer than expected, because the estimate didn't account for bug fixing, committee meetings, coffee breaks, and that crazy boss who interrupts all the time. This *common estimator* has very consistent velocities, but they're below 1.0, for example, {0.6, 0.5, 0.6, 0.6, 0.5, 0.6, 0.7, 0.6}.

As estimators gain more experience, their estimating skills improve. So throw away any velocities older than, say, six months.

If you have a new estimator on your team who doesn't have a track record, assume the worst: give them a fake history with a wide range of velocities, until they've finished a half-dozen real tasks.

~

3. Simulate the future

Rather than just adding up estimates to get a single ship date, which sounds right but gives you a profoundly wrong result, you're going to use the Monte Carlo method to simulate many possible futures. In a Monte Carlo simulation, you can create 100 possible scenarios for the future. Each of these possible futures has 1% probability, so you can make a chart of the probability that you will ship by any given date.

While calculating each possible future for a given developer, you're going to divide each task's estimate by a *randomly-selected velocity* from that developer's historical velocities, which we've been gathering in step 2. Here's one sample future:

Estimate:	4	8	2	8	16	
Random Velocity:	0.6	0.5	0.6	0.6	0.5	**Total:**
E/V:	6.7	16	3.3	13.3	32	71.3

Do that 100 times; each total has 1% probability, and now you can figure out the probability that you will ship on any given date.

Now watch what happens:

- In the case of the mythical perfect estimator, all velocities are 1. Dividing by a velocity that is always 1 has no effect. Thus, all rounds of the simulation give the same ship date, and that ship date has 100% probability. Just like in the fairy tales!

- The bad estimator's velocities are all over the map. 0.1 and 13.0 are just as likely. Each round of the simulation is going to produce a very different result, because when you divide by random velocities, you get very different numbers each time. The probability distribution curve you get will be very shallow, showing an equal chance of shipping tomorrow or in the far future. That's still useful information to get, by the way: it tells you that you shouldn't have confidence in the predicted ship dates.

- The common estimator has a lot of velocities that are pretty close to each other, for example, {0.6, 0.5, 0.6, 0.6, 0.5, 0.6, 0.7, 0.6}. When you divide by these velocities, you increase the amount of time something takes, so in one iteration, an eight-hour task might take thirteen hours; in another it might take fifteen hours. That compensates for the estimator's perpetual optimism. And it compensates *precisely*, based *exactly* on this developer's *actual, proven, historical optimism*. And since all the historical velocities are pretty close, hovering around 0.6, when you run each round of the simulation, you'll get pretty similar numbers, so you'll wind up with a narrow range of possible ship dates.

In each round of the Monte Carlo simulation, of course, you have to convert the hourly data to calendar data, which means you have to take into account each developer's work schedule, vacations, holidays, etc. And then you have to see, for each round, which developer is finishing last, because that's when the whole team will be done. These calculations are painstaking, but luckily, painstaking is what computers are good at.

~

Obsessive-compulsive disorder not required

What do you do about the boss who interrupts you all the time with long-winded stories about his fishing trips? Or the sales meetings you're forced to go to even though you have no reason to be there? Coffee breaks? Spending half a day helping the new guy get his dev environment set up?

When Brett and I were developing this technique at Fog Creek, we worried a lot about things that take real time but can't be predicted in advance. Sometimes, this all adds up to more time than writing code. Should you have estimates for this stuff too, and track it on a time sheet?

Thursday 5/22/2008   ← ▦ →

Edit	Delete	Start	End	Case	Title
☑	☐	8:58 AM	9:14 AM	112	Reading Blogs
☑	☐	9:14 AM	11:53 AM	113	Company Mission Statement c'tee Meeting
☑	☐	12:51 PM	1:16 PM	114	Tracking Down Classpath Problems
☑	☐	1:16 PM	2:01 PM	110	Reinstalling Eclipse
☑	☐	2:01 PM	3:15 PM	109	Interviewing job candidates
☑	☐	3:15 PM	3:16 PM	115	HTML Work: Set page bg color to blue
☑	☐	3:16 PM	3:26 PM	111	Coffee Breaks
☑	☐	3:26 PM	4:15 PM	114	Tracking Down Classpath Problems

▯ **Add Interval**

Close

Well, yeah, you can, if you want. And Evidence-Based Scheduling will work.

But you don't have to.

It turns out that EBS works so well that all you have to do is *keep the clock running* on whatever task you were doing when the interruption occurred. As disconcerting as this may sound, EBS produces the best results when you do this.

Let me walk you through a quick example. To make this example as simple as possible, I'm going to imagine a very predictable programmer, John, whose whole job is writing those one-line getter and setter functions that inferior programming languages require. All day long this is all he does:

```
private int width;
public int getWidth () { return width; }
public void setWidth (int _width} { width = _width; }
```

I know, I know . . . it's a deliberately dumb example, but you *know* you've met someone like this.

Anyway. Each getter or setter takes him two hours. So his task estimates look like this:

{2, 2, 2, 2, 2, 2, 2, 2, 2, 2, 2, . . . }

Now, this poor guy has a boss who interrupts him every once in a while with a two-hour conversation about marlin fishing. Now, of course, John could have a task on his schedule called "Painful conversations about marlin" and put that on his time sheet, but this might not be politically prudent. Instead, John just keeps the clock running. So his actual times look like this:

{2, 2, 2, 2, 4, 2, 2, 2, 2, 4, 2, . . . }

And his velocities are

{1, 1, 1, 1, 0.5, 1, 1, 1, 1, 0.5, 1, . . . }

Now think about what happens. In the Monte Carlo simulation, the probability that each estimate will be divided by 0.5 *is exactly the same as the probability that John's boss would interrupt him during any given feature.* So EBS produces a correct schedule!

In fact, EBS is far more likely to have accurate evidence about these interruptions than even the most time sheet–obsessive developer. *Which is exactly why it works so well.* Here's how I explain this to people. When developers get interrupted, they can either

1. Make a big stink about putting the interruption on their time sheet and in their estimates, so management can see just how much time is being wasted on fishing conversation.

2. Make a big stink about refusing to put it on their time sheet, just letting the feature they were working on slip, because they refuse to pad *their* estimates, which were *perfectly correct*, with stupid conversation about fishing expeditions to which they *weren't even invited.*

and in either case, *EBS gives the same, exactly correct results*, no matter which type of passive-aggressive developer you have.

~

4. Manage your projects actively

Once you've got this set up, you can actively manage projects to ship on time. For example, if you sort features out into different priorities, it's easy to see how much it would help the schedule if you could cut the lower priority features.

Priority	50% Date
1 – Must Fix	5/30/2008
2 – Must Fix	6/30/2008
3 – Must Fix	10/2/2008
4 – Fix If Time	10/10/2008
5 – Fix If Time	10/19/2008
6 – Fix If Time	12/4/2008
7 – Don't Fix	3/1/2009

You can also look at the distribution of possible ship dates for *each developer*:

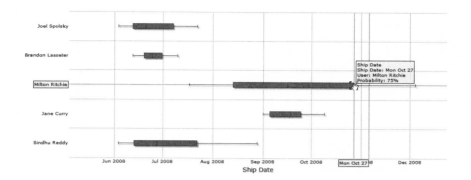

Some developers (like Milton in this picture) may be causing problems because their ship dates are so uncertain: they need to work on learning to estimate better. Other developers (like Jane) have very precise ship dates that are just too late: they need to have some of their work taken off their plate. Other developers (me! yay!) are not on the critical path at all, and can be left in peace.

~

Scope creep

A ssuming you had everything planned down to the last detail when you started work, EBS works great. To be honest, though, you may do some features that you hadn't planned. You get new ideas, your salespeople sell features you don't have, and somebody on the board of directors comes up with a cool new idea to make your golf cart GPS application monitor EKGs while golfers are buzzing around the golf course. All this leads to delays that could not have been predicted when you did the original schedule.

Ideally, you have a bunch of buffer for this. In fact, go ahead and build buffer into your original schedule for

1. New feature ideas

2. Responding to the competition

3. Integration (getting everyone's code to work together when it's merged)

4. Debugging time

5. Usability testing (and incorporating the results of those tests into the product)

6. Beta tests

So now, when new features come up, you can slice off a piece of the appropriate buffer and use it for the new feature.

What happens if you're still adding features and you've run out of buffer? Well, now the ship dates you get out of EBS start slipping. You should take a snapshot of the ship date confidence distribution every night, so that you can track this over time:

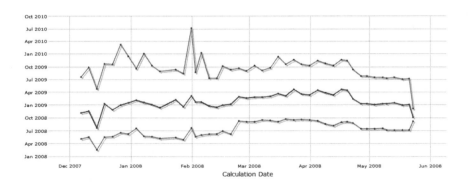

The x-axis is when the calculation was done; the y-axis is the ship date. There are three curves here: the top one is the 95% probability date, the middle is 50%, and the bottom is 5%. So, the closer the curves are to one another, the narrower the range of possible ship dates.

If you see the ship date getting later and later (rising curves), you're in trouble. If it's getting later by more than one day per day, you're adding work faster than you're completing work, and you'll never be done. You can also look and see whether the ship date confidence distribution is getting tighter (the curves are converging), which it should be if you're really converging on a date.

While we're at it

Here are a few more things I've learned over the years about schedules.

1. **Only the programmer doing the work can create the estimate.** Any system where management writes a schedule and hands it off to programmers is doomed to fail. Only the programmer who is going to implement a feature can figure out what steps they will need to take to implement that feature.

2. **Fix bugs as you find them, and charge the time back to the original task.** You can't schedule a single bug fix in advance, because you don't know what bugs you're going to have. When bugs are found in new code, charge the time to the original task that you implemented incorrectly. This will help EBS predict the time it takes to get *fully debugged* code, not just *working* code.

3. **Don't let managers badger developers into shorter estimates.** Many rookie software managers think that they can "motivate" their programmers to work faster by giving them nice, "tight" (unrealistically short) schedules. I think this kind of motivation is brain-dead. When I'm behind schedule, I feel doomed and depressed and unmotivated. When I'm working *ahead* of schedule, I'm cheerful and productive. The schedule is not the place to play psychological games.

   Why do managers try this?

When the project begins, the technical managers go off, meet with the business people, and come up with a list of features they *think* would take about three months, but which would really take twelve. When you think of writing code without thinking about all the steps you have to take, it always seems like it will take *n* time, when in reality it will probably take more like 4*n* time. When you do a real schedule, you add up all the tasks and realize that the project is going to take much longer than originally thought. The business people are unhappy.

Inept managers try to address this by figuring out how to get people to work faster. This is not very realistic. You might be able to hire more people, but they need to get up to speed and will probably be working at 50% efficiency for several months (and dragging down the efficiency of the people who have to mentor them).

You might be able to get 10% more raw code out of people *temporarily* at the cost of having them burn out 100% in a year. Not a big gain, and it's a bit like eating your seed corn. Of course, when you overwork people, debugging time *doubles* and a late project becomes later. Splendid karma.

But you can never get 4*n* from *n*, ever, and if you think you can, please e-mail me the stock symbol for your company so I can short it.

4. **A schedule is a box of wood blocks.** If you have a bunch of wood blocks, and you can't fit them into a box, you have two choices: get a bigger box or remove some blocks. If you wanted to ship in six months but you have twelve months on the schedule, you are going to have to either delay shipping or find some features to delete. You just can't shrink the blocks, and if you pretend you can, then you are merely depriving yourself of a useful opportunity to actually *see into the future* by lying to yourself about what you see there.

Now that I mention it, one of the great benefits of realistic schedules is that you *are* forced to delete features. Why is this good?

Suppose you have two features in mind. One is really useful and will make your product really great. The other is really easy and the programmers can't wait to code it up ("Look! <blink>!"), but it serves no useful purpose.

If you don't make a schedule, the programmers will do the easy/fun feature first. Then they'll run out of time, and you will have no choice but to slip the schedule to do the useful/important feature.

If you do make a schedule, even before you start working, you'll realize that you have to cut something, so you'll cut the easy/fun feature and just do the useful/important feature. By forcing yourself to choose some features to cut, you wind up making a more powerful, better product with a better mix of good features that ships sooner.

Way back when I was working on Excel 5, our initial feature list was huge and would have gone *way* over schedule. "Oh my!" we thought. "Those are *all* super important features! How can we live without a macro editing wizard?"

As it turns out, we had no choice, and we cut what we thought was "to the bone" to make the schedule. Everybody felt unhappy about the cuts. To make people feel better, we told ourselves that we weren't *cutting* the features, we were simply *deferring them* to Excel 6.

As Excel 5 was nearing completion, I started working on the Excel 6 spec with a colleague, Eric Michelman. We sat down to go through the list of Excel 6 features that had been punted from the Excel 5 schedule. Guess what? It was the shoddiest list of features you could imagine. Not *one* of those features was worth doing. I don't think a single one of them ever was. The process of culling features to fit a schedule was the best thing we could have done. If we hadn't done this, Excel 5 would have taken twice as long and included 50% useless crap features that would have had to be supported, for backward compatibility, until the end of time.

~

Summary

Using Evidence-Based Scheduling is pretty easy: it will take you a day or two at the beginning of every iteration to produce detailed estimates, and it'll take a few seconds every day to record when you start working on a new task on a time sheet. The benefits, though, are huge: realistic schedules.

Realistic schedules are the key to creating good software. It forces you to do the best features first and allows you to make the right decisions about what to build. Which makes your product better and your boss happier, delights your customers, and—best of all—lets you go home at 5 o'clock.

~

P.S.

Evidence-Based Scheduling is built into FogBugz 6.0.

twenty-one

STRATEGY LETTER VI

Tuesday, September 18, 2007

IBM just released an open source office suite called IBM Lotus Symphony. Sounds like Yet Another StarOffice distribution. But I suspect they're probably trying to wipe out the memory of the original Lotus Symphony, which had been hyped as the Second Coming and which fell totally flat. It was the software equivalent of *Gigli*.

In the late 1980s, Lotus was trying very hard to figure out what to do next with their flagship spreadsheet and graphics product, Lotus 1-2-3. There were two obvious ideas: first, they could add more features—word processing, say. This product was called Symphony. Another idea that seemed obvious was to make a 3-D spreadsheet. That became 1-2-3 version 3.0.

Both ideas ran head-first into a serious problem: the old DOS 640K memory limitation. IBM was starting to ship a few computers with 80286 chips, which could address more memory, but Lotus didn't think there was a big enough market for software that needed a $10,000 computer to run. So they squeezed and squeezed. They spent 18 months cramming 1-2-3 for DOS into 640K, and eventually, after a lot of wasted time, had to give up the 3D feature to get it to fit. In the case of Symphony, they just chopped features left and right.

Neither strategy was right. By the time 1-2-3 3.0 was shipping, everybody had 80386s with 2MB or 4MB of RAM. And Symphony had an inadequate spreadsheet, an inadequate word processor, and some other inadequate bits.

"That's nice, old man," you say. "Who gives a fart about some old character mode software?"

Humor me for a minute, because history is repeating itself, in three different ways, and the smart strategy is to bet on the same results.

~

Limited-memory, limited-CPU environments

From the beginning of time until about, say, 1989, programmers were extremely concerned with efficiency. There just wasn't that much memory and there just weren't that many CPU cycles.

In the late 1990s, a few companies, including Microsoft and Apple, noticed (just a little bit sooner than anyone else) that Moore's Law meant that they shouldn't think too hard about performance and memory usage . . . just build cool stuff, and wait for the hardware to catch up. Microsoft first shipped Excel for Windows when 80386s were too expensive to buy, but they were patient. Within a couple of years, the 80386SX came out, and anybody who could afford a $1,500 clone could run Excel.

As a programmer, thanks to plummeting memory prices and CPU speeds doubling every year, you had a choice. You could spend six months rewriting your inner loops in Assembler, or take six months off to play drums in a rock-and-roll band, and in either case, your program would run faster. Assembler programmers don't have groupies.

So, we don't care about performance or optimization much anymore.

Except in one place: JavaScript running on browsers in Ajax applications. And since that's the direction almost all software development is moving, that's a big deal.

A lot of today's Ajax applications have a meg or more of client-side code. This time, it's not the RAM or CPU cycles that are scarce: it's the download bandwidth and the compile time. Either way, you really have to squeeze to get complex Ajax apps to perform well.

History, though, is repeating itself. Bandwidth is getting cheaper. People are figuring out how to precompile JavaScript.

The developers who put a lot of effort into optimizing things and making them tight and fast will wake up to discover that effort was, more or less, wasted, or, at the very least, you could say that it "conferred no long-term competitive advantage," if you're the kind of person who talks like an economist.

The developers who ignored performance and blasted ahead adding cool features to their applications will, in the long run, have better applications.

~

A portable programming language

The C programming language was invented with the explicit goal of making it easy to port applications from one instruction set to another. And it did a fine job, but wasn't really 100% portable, so we got Java, which was even more portable than C. Mmmhmm.

Right now the big hole in the portability story is—tada!—client-side JavaScript, and especially the DOM in web browsers. Writing applications that work in all different browsers is a friggin' nightmare. There is simply no alternative but to test exhaustively on Firefox, IE 6, IE 7, Safari, and Opera, and guess what? I don't have time to test on Opera. Sucks to be Opera. Startup web browsers don't stand a chance.

What's going to happen? Well, you can try begging Microsoft and Firefox to be more compatible. Good luck with that. You can follow the p-code/Java model and build a little sandbox on top of the underlying system. But sandboxes are penalty boxes; they're slow and they suck, which is why Java applets are dead, dead, dead. To build a sandbox, you pretty much doom yourself to running at 1/10 the speed of the underlying platform, and you doom yourself to never supporting any of the cool features that show up on one of the platforms but not the others. (I'm still waiting for someone to show me a Java applet for phones that can access *any* of the phone's features, like the camera, the contacts list, the SMS messages, or the GPS receiver.)

Sandboxes didn't work then and they're not working now.

What's going to happen? The winners are going to do what worked at Bell Labs in 1978: build a programming language, like C, that's portable and efficient. It should compile down to "native" code (native code being JavaScript and DOMs) with different back ends for different target platforms, where the compiler writers obsess about performance so you don't have to. It'll have all the same performance as native JavaScript with full access to the DOM in a consistent fashion, and it'll compile down to IE native and Firefox native portably and automatically. And, yes, it'll go into your CSS and muck around with it in some frightening but provably correct way so you never have to think about CSS incompatibilities ever again. Ever. Oh joyous day that will be.

High interactivity and UI standards

The IBM 360 mainframe computer system used a user interface called CICS, which you can still see at the airport if you lean over the check-in counter. There's an 80-character by 24-character green screen, character mode only, of course. The mainframe sends down a form to the "client" (the client being a 3270 smart terminal). The terminal is smart; it knows how to present the form to you and let you input data into the form without talking to the mainframe at all. This was one reason mainframes were so much more powerful than Unix: the CPU didn't have to handle your line editing; it was offloaded to a smart terminal. (If you couldn't afford smart terminals for everyone, you bought a System/1 minicomputer to sit between the dumb terminals and the mainframe and handle the form editing for you.)

Anyhoo, after you filled out your form, you pressed SEND, and all your answers were sent back to the server to process. Then it sent you another form. And on and on.

Awful. How do you make a word processor in that kind of environment? (You really can't. There never was a decent word processor for mainframes.)

That was the first stage. It corresponds precisely to the HTML phase of the Internet. HTML is CICS with fonts.

In the second stage, everybody bought PCs for their desks, and suddenly, programmers could poke text anywhere on the screen willy-nilly, anywhere they wanted, any time they wanted, and you could actually read every keystroke from the users as they typed, so you could make a nice fast application that didn't have to wait for you to hit SEND before the CPU could get involved. So, for example, you could make a word processor that automatically wrapped, moving a word down to the next line when the current line filled up. Right away. Oh my god. You can do that?

The trouble with the second stage was that there were no clear UI standards . . . the programmers almost had too much flexibility, so everybody did things in different ways, which made it hard, if you knew how to use program X, to also use program Y. WordPerfect and Lotus 1-2-3 had completely different menu systems, keyboard interfaces, and command structures. And copying data between them was out of the question.

And that's exactly where we are with Ajax development today. Sure, yeah, the usability is much better than the first generation DOS apps, because we've learned some things since then. But Ajax apps can be inconsistent and have a lot of trouble working together—you can't really cut and paste objects from one Ajax app to another, for example, so I'm not sure how you get a picture from Gmail to Flickr. Come on guys, cut and paste was invented 25 years ago.

The third phase with PCs was Macintosh and Windows. A standard, consistent user interface with features like multiple windows and the Clipboard designed so that applications could work together. The increased usability and power we got out of the new GUIs made personal computing explode.

So if history repeats itself, we can expect some standardization of Ajax user interfaces to happen in the same way we got Microsoft Windows. Somebody is going to write a compelling SDK that you can use to make powerful Ajax applications with common user interface elements that work together. And whichever SDK wins the most developer mindshare will have the same kind of competitive stronghold as Microsoft had with their Windows API.

If you're a web app developer and you don't want to support the SDK everybody else is supporting, you'll increasingly find that people won't use your web app, because it doesn't, you know, support cut and paste and address book synchronization and whatever weird new interop features we'll want in 2010.

Imagine, for example, that you're Google with Gmail, and you're feeling rather smug. But then somebody you've never heard of, some bratty Y Combinator startup, maybe, is gaining ridiculous traction selling NewSDK, which combines a great portable programming language that compiles to JavaScript, and even better, a huge Ajaxy library that includes all kinds of clever interop features. Not just cut and paste: cool mashup features like synchronization and single-point identity management (so you don't have to tell Facebook and Twitter what you're doing, you can just enter it in one place). And you laugh at them, for their NewSDK is a honking 232 megabytes . . . 232 megabytes! . . . of JavaScript, and it takes 76 seconds to load a page. And your app, Gmail, doesn't lose any customers.

But then, while you're sitting on your googlechair in the googleplex sipping googleccinos and feeling smuggy smug smug smug, new versions of the browsers come out that support cached, compiled JavaScript. And suddenly NewSDK is really fast. And Paul Graham gives them another 6,000 boxes of instant noodles to eat, so they stay in business another three years perfecting things.

And your programmers are like, jeez Louise, Gmail is huge, we can't port Gmail to this stupid NewSDK. We'd have to change every line of code. Heck, it'd be a complete rewrite; the whole programming model is upside-down and recursive, and the portable programming language has more parentheses than even Google can buy. The last line of almost every function consists of a string of 3,296 right parentheses. You have to buy a special editor to count them.

And the NewSDK people ship a pretty decent word processor and a pretty decent e-mail app and a killer Facebook/Twitter event publisher that synchronizes with everything, so people start using it.

And while you're not paying attention, everybody starts writing NewSDK apps, and they're really good, and suddenly businesses ONLY want NewSDK apps, and all those old-school Plain Ajax apps look pathetic and won't cut and paste and mash and sync and play drums nicely with one another. And Gmail becomes a legacy, the WordPerfect of e-mail. And you'll tell your children how excited you were to get 2GB to store e-mail, and they'll laugh at you. Their *nail polish* has more than 2GB.

Crazy story? Substitute "Google Gmail" with "Lotus 1-2-3." The NewSDK will be the second coming of Microsoft Windows; this is exactly how Lotus lost control of the spreadsheet market. And it's going to happen again on the Web because all the same dynamics and forces are in place. The only thing we don't know yet are the particulars, but it'll happen.

twenty-two

CAN YOUR PROGRAMMING LANGUAGE DO THIS?

Tuesday, August 1, 2006

One day, you're browsing through your code, and you notice two big blocks that look almost exactly the same. In fact, they're exactly the same, except that one block refers to "Spaghetti" and one block refers to "Chocolate Mousse."

```
// A trivial example:

alert("I'd like some Spaghetti!");
alert("I'd like some Chocolate Mousse!");
```

These examples happen to be in JavaScript, but even if you don't know JavaScript, you should be able to follow along.

The repeated code looks wrong, of course, so you create a function:

```
function SwedishChef( food )
{
    alert("I'd like some " + food + "!");
}

SwedishChef("Spaghetti");
SwedishChef("Chocolate Mousse");
```

OK, it's a trivial example, but you can imagine a more substantial example. This is better code for many reasons, all of which you've heard a million times. Maintainability, Readability, Abstraction = Good!

Now you notice two other blocks of code that look almost the same, except that one of them keeps calling this function called BoomBoom and the other one keeps calling this function called PutInPot. Other than that, the code is pretty much the same.

```
alert("get the lobster");
PutInPot("lobster");
PutInPot("water");

alert("get the chicken");
BoomBoom("chicken");
BoomBoom("coconut");
```

Now you need a way to pass an argument to the function that itself is a function. This is an important capability, because it increases the chances that you'll be able to find common code that can be stashed away in a function.

```
function Cook( i1, i2, f )
{
    alert("get the " + i1);
    f(i1);
    f(i2);
}

Cook( "lobster", "water", PutInPot );
Cook( "chicken", "coconut", BoomBoom );
```

Look! We're passing in a function as an argument.

Can your language do this?

Wait . . . suppose you haven't already defined the functions PutInPot or BoomBoom. Wouldn't it be nice if you could just write them inline instead of declaring them elsewhere?

```
Cook( "lobster",
      "water",
      function(x) { alert("pot " + x); }  );
Cook( "chicken",
      "coconut",
      function(x) { alert("boom " + x); } );
```

Jeez, that is handy. Notice that I'm creating a function there on the fly, not even bothering to name it, just picking it up by its ears and tossing it into a function.

As soon as you start thinking in terms of anonymous functions as arguments, you might notice code all over the place that, say, does something to every element of an array.

```
var a = [1,2,3];

for (i=0; i<a.length; i++)
{
    a[i] = a[i] * 2;
}

for (i=0; i<a.length; i++)
{
    alert(a[i]);
}
```

Doing something to every element of an array is pretty common, and you can write a function that does it for you:

```
function map(fn, a)
{
    for (i = 0; i < a.length; i++)
    {
        a[i] = fn(a[i]);
    }
}
```

Now you can rewrite the preceding code as

```
map( function(x){return x*2;}, a );
map( alert, a );
```

Another common thing with arrays is to combine all the values of the array in some way.

```
function sum(a)
{
    var s = 0;
```

```
        for (i = 0; i < a.length; i++)
            s += a[i];
        return s;
}

function join(a)
{
    var s = "";
    for (i = 0; i < a.length; i++)
        s += a[i];
    return s;
}

alert(sum([1,2,3]));
alert(join(["a","b","c"]));
```

sum and join look so similar, you might want to abstract out their
essence into a generic function that combines elements of an array into
a single value:

```
function reduce(fn, a, init)
{
    var s = init;
    for (i = 0; i < a.length; i++)
        s = fn( s, a[i] );
    return s;
}

function sum(a)
{
    return reduce( function(a, b){ return a + b; },
                   a, 0 );
}

function join(a)
{
    return reduce( function(a, b){ return a + b; },
                   a, "" );
}
```

Many older languages simply had no way to do this kind of stuff. Other languages let you do it, but it's hard (for example, C has function pointers, but you have to declare and define the function somewhere else). Object-oriented programming languages aren't completely convinced that you should be allowed to do anything with functions.

Java required you to create a whole object with a single method called a functor if you wanted to treat a function like a first class object. Combine that with the fact that many OO languages want you to create a whole file for each class, and it gets really clunky fast. If your programming language requires you to use functors, you're not getting all the benefits of a modern programming environment. See if you can get some of your money back.

How much benefit do you really get out of writing itty-bitty functions that do nothing more than iterate through an array doing something to each element?

Well, let's go back to that map function. When you need to do something to every element in an array in turn, the truth is, it probably doesn't matter what order you do them in. You can run through the array forward or backward and get the same result, right? In fact, if you have two CPUs handy, maybe you could write some code to have each CPU do half of the elements, and suddenly map is twice as fast.

Or maybe, just hypothetically, you have hundreds of thousands of servers in several data centers around the world, and you have a really big array, containing, let's say, again, just hypothetically, the entire contents of the Internet. Now you can run map on thousands of computers, each of which will attack a tiny part of the problem.

So now, for example, writing some really fast code to search the entire contents of the Internet is as simple as calling the map function with a basic string searcher as an argument.

The really interesting thing I want you to notice here is that as soon as you think of map and reduce as functions that everybody can use, and they use them, you only have to get one supergenius to write the hard code to run map and reduce on a global massively parallel array of computers, and all the old code that used to work fine when you just ran a loop still works, only it's a zillion times faster, which means it can be used to tackle huge problems in an instant.

Lemme repeat that. By abstracting away the very concept of looping, you can implement looping any way you want, including implementing it in a way that scales nicely with extra hardware.

And now you understand something I wrote a while ago where I complained about CS students who are never taught anything but Java:

> *Without understanding functional programming, you can't invent MapReduce, the algorithm that makes Google so massively scalable. The terms "Map" and "Reduce" come from Lisp and functional programming. MapReduce is, in retrospect, obvious to anyone who remembers from their 6.001-equivalent programming class that purely functional programs have no side effects and are thus trivially parallelizable. The very fact that Google invented MapReduce, and Microsoft didn't, says something about why Microsoft is still playing catch-up trying to get basic search features to work, while Google has moved on to the next problem: building Skynet^H^H^H^H^H^H, the world's largest massively parallel supercomputer. I don't think Microsoft completely understands just how far behind they are on that wave.*

OK. I hope you're convinced, by now, that programming languages with first-class functions let you find more opportunities for abstraction, which means your code is smaller, tighter, more reusable, and more scalable. Lots of Google applications use MapReduce, and they all benefit whenever someone optimizes it or fixes bugs.

And now I'm going to get a little bit mushy, and argue that the most productive programming environments are the ones that let you work at *different levels of abstraction*. Crappy old FORTRAN really didn't even let you write functions. C had function pointers, but they were ugleeeeee and not anonymous and had to be implemented somewhere other than where you were using them. Java made you use functors, which is even uglier. As Steve Yegge points out, Java is the Kingdom of Nouns (steve-yegge.blogspot.com/2006/03/execution-in-kingdom-of-nouns.html).

Correction The last time I used FORTRAN was 27 years ago. Apparently, it's got functions. I must have been thinking about GW-BASIC.

---

twenty-three

MAKING WRONG CODE LOOK WRONG

Way back in September 1983, I started my first real job, working at Oranim, a big bread factory in Israel that made something like 100,000 loaves of bread every night in six giant ovens the size of aircraft carriers.

The first time I walked into the bakery I couldn't believe what a mess it was. The sides of the ovens were yellowing, machines were rusting, there was grease everywhere.

"Is it always this messy?" I asked.

"What? What are you talking about?" the manager said. "We just finished cleaning. This is the cleanest it's been in weeks."

Oh boy.

It took me a couple of months of cleaning the bakery every morning before I realized what they meant. In the bakery, clean meant no dough on the machines. Clean meant no fermenting dough in the trash. Clean meant no dough on the floors.

Clean did not mean the paint on the ovens was nice and white. Painting the ovens was something you did every decade, not every day. Clean did not mean no grease. In fact, there were a lot of machines that needed to be greased or oiled regularly, and a thin layer of clean oil was usually a sign of a machine that had just been cleaned.

The whole concept of clean in the bakery was something you had to learn. To an outsider, it was impossible to walk in and judge whether the place was clean or not. An outsider would never think of looking at the inside surfaces of the dough rounder (a machine that rolls square blocks of dough into balls) to see if they had been scraped clean. An outsider would obsess over the fact that the old oven had discolored panels, because those panels were *huge*. But a baker couldn't care less whether the paint on the outside of their oven was starting to turn a little yellow. The bread still tasted just as good.

After two months in the bakery, you learned how to "see" clean.

Code is the same way.

When you start out as a beginning programmer or you try to read code in a new language, it all looks equally inscrutable. Until you understand the programming language itself, you can't even see obvious syntactic errors.

During the first phase of learning, you start to recognize the things that we usually refer to as "coding style." So you start to notice code that doesn't conform to indentation standards and Oddly Capitalized variables.

It's at this point you typically say, "Blistering Barnacles, we've *got* to get some consistent coding conventions around here!" and you spend the next day writing up coding conventions for your team and the next six days arguing about the One True Brace Style and the next three weeks rewriting old code to conform to the One True Brace Style until a manager catches you and screams at you for wasting time on something that can never make money, and you decide that it's not really a bad thing to only reformat code when you revisit it, so you have about half of a True Brace Style, and pretty soon you forget all about that, and then you can start obsessing about something else irrelevant to making money like replacing one kind of string class with another kind of string class.

As you get more proficient at writing code in a particular environment, you start to learn to see other things. Things that may be perfectly legal and perfectly OK according to the coding convention, but which make you worry.

For example, in C

```
char* dest, src;
```

is legal code; it may conform to your coding convention, and it may even be what was intended, but when you've had enough experience writing C code, you'll notice that this declares dest as a char *pointer* while declaring src as merely a char, and even if this *might* be what you wanted, it probably isn't. That code smells a little bit dirty.

Even more subtle:

```
if (i != 0)
    foo(i);
```

In this case, the code is 100% correct; it conforms to most coding conventions, and there's nothing wrong with it, but the fact that the single-statement body of the `if` statement is not enclosed in braces may be bugging you, because you might be thinking in the back of your head, gosh, somebody might insert another line of code there:

```
if (i != 0)
    bar(i);
    foo(i);
```

and forget to add the braces, and thus accidentally make `foo(i)` unconditional! So when you see blocks of code that aren't in braces, you might sense just a tiny, wee, soupçon of uncleanliness, which makes you uneasy.

OK, so far I've mentioned three levels of achievement as a programmer:

1. You don't know clean from unclean.

2. You have a superficial idea of cleanliness, mostly at the level of conformance to coding conventions.

3. You start to smell subtle hints of uncleanliness beneath the surface, and they bug you enough to reach out and fix the code.

There's an even higher level, though, which is what I really want to talk about:

4. You deliberately architect your code in such a way that your nose for uncleanliness makes your code more likely to be correct.

This is the real art: making robust code by literally *inventing conventions* that make errors stand out on the screen.

So now I'll walk you through a little example, and then I'll show you a general rule you can use for inventing these code-robustness conventions, and in the end it will lead to a defense of a certain type of Hungarian notation, probably not the type that makes people carsick, though, and a criticism of exceptions in certain circumstances, though probably not the kind of circumstances you find yourself in most of the time.

But if you're so convinced that Hungarian notation is a Bad Thing and that exceptions are the best invention since the chocolate milkshake and you don't even want to hear any other opinions, well, head on over to Rory's and read the excellent comix instead (`www.neopoleon.com/home/blogs/neo/archive/2005/04/29/15699.aspx`); you probably won't be missing much here anyway. In fact, in a minute I'm going to have actual code samples that are likely to put you to sleep even before they get a chance to make you angry. Yep. I think the plan will be to lull you almost completely to sleep and then to sneak the Hungarian notation = good, Exceptions = bad thing on you when you're sleepy and not really putting up much of a fight.

$\sim$

An example

Right. On with the example. Let's pretend that you're building some kind of a web-based application, since those seem to be all the rage with the kids these days.

Now, there's a security vulnerability called the Cross-Site Scripting Vulnerability, a.k.a. XSS. I won't go into the details here: all you have to know is that when you build a web application, you have to be careful never to repeat back any strings that the user types into forms.

So, for example, if you have a web page that says, "What is your name?" with an edit box and then submitting that page takes you to another page that says, "Hello, Elmer!" (assuming the user's name is Elmer), well, that's a security vulnerability, because the user could type in all kinds of weird HTML and JavaScript instead of "Elmer," and their weird JavaScript could do narsty things, and now those narsty things appear to come from you, so, for example, they can read cookies that you put there and forward them on to Dr. Evil's evil site.

Let's put it in pseudo code. Imagine that

```
s = Request("name")
```

reads input (a POST argument) from the HTML form. If you ever write this code:

```
Write "Hello, " & Request("name")
```

your site is already vulnerable to XSS attacks. That's all it takes.

Instead, you have to encode it before you copy it back into the HTML. Encoding it means replacing " with ", replacing > with >, and so forth. So

```
Write "Hello, " & Encode(Request("name"))
```

is perfectly safe.

All strings that originate from the user are *unsafe*. Any unsafe string must not be output without encoding it.

Let's try to come up with a coding convention that will ensure that if you ever make this mistake, the code will just *look* wrong. If wrong code, at least, *looks* wrong, then it has a fighting chance of getting caught by someone working on that code or reviewing that code.

Possible solution #1

One solution is to encode all strings right away, the minute they come in from the user:

```
s = Encode(Request("name"))
```

So our convention says this: if you ever see Request that is not surrounded by Encode, the code must be wrong.

You start to train your eyes to look for naked Requests, because they violate the convention.

That works, in the sense that if you follow this convention you'll never have an XSS bug, but that's not necessarily the best architecture. For example, maybe you want to store these user strings in a database somewhere, and it doesn't make sense to have them stored HTML encoded in the database, because they might have to go somewhere that is not an HTML page, like to a credit card processing application that will get confused if they are HTML encoded. Most web applications are developed under the principle that all strings internally are *not* encoded until the *very last moment* before they are sent to an HTML page, and that's probably the right architecture.

We really need to be able to keep things around in unsafe format for a while.

OK. I'll try again.

Possible solution #2

What if we made a coding convention that said that when you *write out* any string you have to encode it?

```
s = Request("name")

// much later:
Write Encode(s)
```

Now whenever you see a naked `Write` without the `Encode`, you know something is amiss.

Well, that doesn't quite work . . . sometimes you have little bits of HTML around in your code and you *can't* encode them:

```
If mode = "linebreak" Then prefix = "<br>"
// much later:
Write prefix
```

This looks wrong according to our convention, which requires us to encode strings on the way out:

```
Write Encode(prefix)
```

But now the "`<br>`", which is supposed to start a new line, gets encoded to <br> and appears to the user as a literal < b r >. That's not right either.

So, sometimes you can't encode a string when you read it in, and sometimes you can't encode it when you write it out, so neither of these proposals works. And without a convention, we're still running the risk that you do this:

```
s = Request("name")
...pages later...
name = s
...pages later...
```

```
recordset("name") = name // store name in db in a column
"name"
...days later...
theName = recordset("name")
...pages or even months later...
Write theName
```

Did we remember to encode the string? There's no single place where you can look to see the bug. There's no place to sniff. If you have a lot of code like this, it takes a ton of detective work to trace the origin of every string that is ever written out to make sure it has been encoded.

The real solution

So let me suggest a coding convention that works. We'll have just one rule:

All strings that come from the user must be stored in variables (or database columns) with a name starting with the prefix "us" (for Unsafe String). All strings that have been HTML encoded or that came from a known-safe location must be stored in variables with a name starting with the prefix "s" (for Safe string).

Let me rewrite that same code, changing nothing but the variable names to match our new convention.

```
us = Request("name")
...pages later...
usName = us
...pages later...
recordset("usName") = usName
...days later...
sName = Encode(recordset("usName"))
...pages or even months later...
Write sName
```

The thing I want you to notice about the new convention is that now, if you make a mistake with an unsafe string, *you can always see it on some single line of code*, as long as the coding convention is adhered to:

```
s = Request("name")
```

is a priori wrong, because you see the result of Request being assigned to a variable whose name begins with s, which is against the rules. The result of Request is always unsafe, so it must always be assigned to a variable whose name begins with "us".

```
us = Request("name")
```

is always OK.

```
usName = us
```

is always OK.

```
sName = us
```

is certainly wrong.

```
sName = Encode(us)
```

is certainly correct.

```
Write usName
```

is certainly wrong.

```
Write sName
```

is OK, as is

```
Write Encode(usName)
```

Every line of code can be inspected *by itself*, and if every line of code is correct, the entire body of code is correct.

Eventually, with this coding convention, your eyes learn to see the Write usXXX and know that it's wrong, and you instantly know how to fix it, too. I know, it's a little bit hard to see the wrong code at first, but do this for three weeks, and your eyes will adapt, just like the bakery workers who learned to look at a giant bread factory and instantly say, "Jay-zuss, nobody cleaned insahd rounduh fo-ah! What the hayl kine a opparashun y'awls runnin' heey-uh?"

In fact, we can extend the rule a bit, and rename (or wrap) the Request and Encode functions to be UsRequest and SEncode . . . in other

words, functions that return an unsafe string or a safe string will start
with Us and S, just like variables. Now look at the code:

```
us = UsRequest("name")
usName = us
recordset("usName") = usName
sName = SEncode(recordset("usName"))
Write sName
```

See what I did? Now you can look to see that both sides of the equal
sign start with the same prefix to see mistakes.

```
us = UsRequest("name") // OK, both sides start with US
s = UsRequest("name")  // bug
usName = us            // OK
sName = us             // certainly wrong.
sName = SEncode(us)    // certainly correct.
```

Heck, I can take it one step further, by naming Write to WriteS and
renaming SEncode to SFromUs:

```
us = UsRequest("name")
usName = us
recordset("usName") = usName
sName = SFromUs(recordset("usName"))
WriteS sName
```

This makes mistakes even *more* visible. Your eyes will learn to "see"
smelly code, and this will help you find obscure security bugs just
through the normal process of writing code and reading code.

Making wrong code look wrong is nice, but it's not necessarily the
best possible solution to every security problem. It doesn't catch every
possible bug or mistake, because you might not look at every line of
code. But it's sure a heck of a lot better than nothing, and I'd much
rather have a coding convention where wrong code at least looked
wrong. You instantly gain the incremental benefit that every time a programmer's eyes pass over a line of code, that particular bug is checked
for and prevented.

~

A general rule

This business of making wrong code look wrong depends on getting the right things close together in one place on the screen. When I'm looking at a string, in order to get the code right, I need to know, everywhere I see that string, whether it's safe or unsafe. I don't want that information to be in another file or on another page that I would have to scroll to. I have to be able to see it *right there*, and that means a variable naming convention.

There are a lot of other examples where you can improve code by moving things next to each other. Most coding conventions include rules like

- Keep functions short.
- Declare your variables as close as possible to the place where you will use them.
- Don't use macros to create your own personal programming language.
- Don't use goto.
- Don't put closing braces more than one screen away from the matching opening brace.

What all these rules have in common is that they are trying to get the relevant information about what a line of code really does physically as close together as possible. This improves the chances that your eyeballs will be able to figure out everything that's going on.

In general, I have to admit that I'm a little bit scared of language features that hide things. When you see the code

```
i = j * 5;
```

in C, you know at least that j is being multiplied by five and the results stored in i.

But if you see that same snippet of code in C++, you don't know anything. Nothing. The only way to know what's really happening in C++

is to find out what types i and j are, something that might be declared somewhere altogether else. That's because j might be of a type that has operator* overloaded, and it does something terribly witty when you try to multiply it. And i might be of a type that has operator= overloaded, and the types might not be compatible, so an automatic type coercion function might end up being called. And the only way to find out is not only to check the type of the variables, but also to find the code that implements that type, and God help you if there's inheritance somewhere, because now you have to traipse all the way up the class hierarchy all by yourself trying to find where that code really *is*, and if there's polymorphism somewhere, you're *really* in trouble because it's not enough to know what type i and j are *declared*, you have to know what type they are *right now*, which might involve inspecting an arbitrary amount of code, and you can never really be sure if you've looked everywhere thanks to the halting problem (phew!).

When you see i=j*5 in C++, you are really on your own, bubby, and that, in my mind, reduces the ability to detect possible problems just by looking at code.

None of this was supposed to matter, of course. When you do clever-schoolboy things like override operator*, this is meant to help you provide a nice waterproof abstraction. Golly, j is a Unicode string type, and multiplying a Unicode string by an integer is *obviously* a good abstraction for converting Traditional Chinese to Standard Chinese, right?

The trouble is, of course, that waterproof abstractions aren't. I've already talked about this extensively in "The Law of Leaky Abstractions" in *Joel on Software* (Apress, 2004), so I won't repeat myself here.

Scott Meyers has made a whole career out of showing you all the ways they fail and bite you, in C++ at least. (By the way, the third edition of Scott's book *Effective C++* [Addison-Wesley Professional, 2005] just came out; it's completely rewritten, so get your copy today!)

OK.

I'm losing track. I better summarize The Story Until Now:

Look for coding conventions that make wrong code look wrong. Getting the right information collocated all together in the same place on screen in your code lets you see certain types of problems and fix them right away.

I'm Hungary

So now we get back to the infamous Hungarian notation.
Hungarian notation was invented by Microsoft programmer Charles
Simonyi. One of the major projects Simonyi worked on at Microsoft
was Word; in fact, he led the project to create the world's first WYSI-
WYG word processor, something called Bravo at Xerox PARC.

In WYSIWYG word processing, you have scrollable windows, so
every coordinate has to be interpreted as either relative to the window or
relative to the page, and that makes a big difference, and keeping them
straight is pretty important.

Which, I surmise, is one of the many good reasons Simonyi started
using something that came to be called Hungarian notation. It looked
like Hungarian, and Simonyi was from Hungary, thus the name. In
Simonyi's version of Hungarian notation, every variable was prefixed
with a lowercase tag that indicated the kind of thing that the variable
contained.

I'm using the word "kind" on purpose, there, because Simonyi
mistakenly used the word "type" in his paper, and generations of programmers misunderstood what he meant.

If you read Simonyi's paper closely, what he was getting at was the
same kind of naming convention as I used in my earlier example where
we decided that us meant "unsafe string" and s meant "safe string."
They're both of type string. The compiler won't help you if you assign
one to the other, and IntelliSense won't tell you bupkis. But they are
semantically different; they need to be interpreted differently and treated
differently, and some kind of conversion function will need to be called
if you assign one to the other, or you will have a *runtime* bug. *If* you're
lucky.

Simonyi's original concept for Hungarian notation was called, inside
Microsoft, Apps Hungarian, because it was used in the Applications
Division, to wit, Word and Excel. In Excel's source code, you see a lot of
rw and col, and when you see those, you know that they refer to rows
and columns. Yep, they're both integers, but it never makes sense to
assign between them. In Word, I'm told, you see a lot of xl and xw,
where xl means "horizontal coordinates relative to the layout" and xw

means "horizontal coordinates relative to the window." Both ints. Not interchangeable. In both apps, you see a lot of cb meaning "count of bytes." Yep, it's an int again, but you know so much more about it just by looking at the variable name. It's a count of bytes: a buffer size. And if you see xl = cb, well, blow the Bad Code Whistle, that is obviously wrong code, because even though xl and cb are both integers, it's completely crazy to set a horizontal offset in pixels to a count of bytes.

In Apps Hungarian, prefixes are used for functions, as well as variables. So, to tell you the truth, I've never seen the Word source code, but I'll bet you dollars to donuts there's a function called YlFromYw that converts from vertical window coordinates to vertical layout coordinates. Apps Hungarian requires the notation TypeFromType instead of the more traditional TypeToType so that every function name could begin with the type of thing that it was returning, just like I did earlier in the example when I renamed Encode SFromUs. In fact, in proper Apps Hungarian, the Encode function would *have* to be named SFromUs. Apps Hungarian wouldn't really give you a choice in how to name this function. That's a good thing, because it's one less thing you need to remember, and you don't have to wonder what kind of encoding is being referred to by the word Encode: you have something much more precise.

Apps Hungarian was extremely valuable, especially in the days of C programming where the compiler didn't provide a very useful type system.

But then something kind of wrong happened.

The dark side took over Hungarian notation.

Nobody seems to know why or how, but it appears that the documentation writers on the Windows team inadvertently invented what came to be known as Systems Hungarian.

Somebody, somewhere, read Simonyi's paper, where he used the word "type," and thought he meant type, like class, like in a type system, like the type checking that the compiler does. He did not. He explained very carefully exactly what he meant by the word "type," but it didn't help. The damage was done.

Apps Hungarian had very useful, meaningful prefixes like "ix" to mean an index into an array, "c" to mean a count, "d" to mean the difference between two numbers (for example "dx" meant "width"), and so forth.

Systems Hungarian had far less useful prefixes like "l" for long and "ul" for "unsigned long" and "dw" for double word, which is, actually, uh, an unsigned long. In Systems Hungarian, the only thing that the prefix told you was the actual data type of the variable.

This was a subtle but complete misunderstanding of Simonyi's intention and practice, and it just goes to show you that if you write convoluted, dense academic prose, nobody will understand it, and your ideas will be misinterpreted, and then the misinterpreted ideas will be ridiculed even when they weren't your ideas. So in Systems Hungarian, you got a lot of dwFoo meaning "double word foo," and doggone it, the fact that a variable is a double word tells you darn near nothing useful at all. So it's no wonder people rebelled against Systems Hungarian.

Systems Hungarian was promulgated far and wide; it is the standard throughout the Windows programming documentation; it was spread extensively by books like Charles Petzold's *Programming Windows* (Microsoft Press, 1998), the bible for learning Windows programming, and it rapidly became the dominant form of Hungarian, even inside Microsoft, where very few programmers outside the Word and Excel teams understood just what a mistake they had made.

And then came The Great Rebellion. Eventually, programmers who never understood Hungarian in the first place noticed that the misunderstood subset they were using was Pretty Dang Annoying and Well-Nigh Useless, and they revolted against it. Now, there are still some nice qualities in Systems Hungarian that help you see bugs. At the very least, if you use Systems Hungarian, you'll know the type of a variable at the spot where you're using it. But it's not nearly as valuable as Apps Hungarian.

The Great Rebellion hit its peak with the first release of .NET. Microsoft finally started telling people, "Hungarian Notation Is Not Recommended." There was much rejoicing. I don't even think they bothered saying why. They just went through the naming guidelines section of the document and wrote, "Do Not Use Hungarian Notation" in every entry. Hungarian notation was so doggone unpopular by this point that nobody really complained, and everybody in the world outside of Excel and Word were relieved at no longer having to use an awkward naming convention that, they thought, was unnecessary in the days of strong type checking and IntelliSense.

But there's still a tremendous amount of value to Apps Hungarian in that it increases collocation in code, which makes the code easier to read, write, debug, and maintain, and, most importantly, it makes wrong code look wrong.

Before we go, there's one more thing I promised to do, which is to bash exceptions one more time. The last time I did that, I got in a lot of trouble. In an off-the-cuff remark on the *Joel on Software* homepage, I wrote that I don't like exceptions because they are, effectively, an invisible goto, which, I reasoned, is even worse than a goto you can see. Of course, millions of people jumped down my throat. The only person in the world who leapt to my defense was, of course, Raymond Chen, who is, by the way, the best programmer in the world, so that has to say something, right?

Here's the thing with exceptions, in the context of this article. Your eyes learn to see wrong things, as long as there is something to see, and this prevents bugs. In order to make code really, really robust, when you code-review it, you need to have coding conventions that allow collocation. In other words, the more information about what code is doing is located right in front of your eyes, the better a job you'll do at finding the mistakes. When you have code that says

```
dosomething();
cleanup();
```

your eyes tell you, what's wrong with that? We always clean up! But the possibility that dosomething might throw an exception means that cleanup might not get called. And that's easily fixable, using finally or whatnot, but that's not my point: my point is that the only way to know that cleanup is definitely called is to investigate the entire call tree of dosomething to see whether there's anything in there, anywhere, that can throw an exception, and that's OK, and there are things like checked exceptions to make it less painful, but the real point is that exceptions eliminate collocation. You have to look *somewhere else* to answer a question of whether code is doing the right thing, so you're not able to take advantage of your eye's built-in ability to learn to see wrong code, because there's nothing to see.

Now, when I'm writing a dinky script to gather up a bunch of data and print it once a day, heck yeah, exceptions are great. I like nothing more than to ignore all possible wrong things that can happen and just wrap up the whole damn program in a big ol' try/catch that e-mails me if anything ever goes wrong. Exceptions are fine for quick-and-dirty code, for scripts, and for code that is neither mission critical nor life sustaining. But if you're writing software for an operating system, or a nuclear power plant, or the software to control a high-speed circular saw used in open heart surgery, exceptions are extremely dangerous.

I know people will assume that I'm a lame programmer for failing to understand exceptions properly and failing to understand all the ways they can improve my life if only I was willing to let exceptions into my heart, but, too bad. The way to write really reliable code is to try to use simple tools that take into account typical human frailty, not complex tools with hidden side effects and leaky abstractions that assume an infallible programmer.

~

More reading

If you're still all gung-ho about exceptions, read Raymond Chen's essay "Cleaner, More Elegant, and Harder to Recognize" (blogs. msdn.com/oldnewthing/archive/2005/01/14/352949.aspx): "It is extraordinarily difficult to see the difference between bad exception-based code and not-bad exception-based code . . . exceptions are too hard and I'm not smart enough to handle them."

Raymond's rant about Death by Macros, "A Rant Against Flow Control Macros" (blogs.msdn.com/oldnewthing/archive/2005/01/ 06/347666.aspx), is about another case where failing to get information all in the same place makes code unmaintainable. "When you see code that uses [macros], you have to go dig through header files to figure out what they do."

For background on the history of Hungarian notation, start with Simonyi's original paper, "Hungarian Notation" (msdn.microsoft.com/ en-us/library/aa260976(VS.60).aspx). Doug Klunder introduced this to the Excel team in a somewhat clearer paper, "Hungarian Naming Conventions" (www.byteshift.de/msg/hungarian-notation-doug-klunder). For more stories about Hungarian and how it got ruined by

documentation writers, read Larry Osterman's post (blogs.msdn.com/
larryosterman/archive/2004/06/22/162629.aspxf), especially Scott
Ludwig's comment (blogs.msdn.com/larryosterman/archive/2004/
06/22/162629.aspx#163721), or Rick Schaut's post (blogs.msdn.com/
rick_schaut/archive/2004/02/14/73108.aspx).

part six

Starting a Software Business

twenty-four

FOREWORD TO *ERIC SINK ON THE BUSINESS OF SOFTWARE*

FRIDAY, APRIL 7, 2006

Eric Sink has been hanging around Joel on Software *since the early days. He was one of the creators of the Spyglass web browser, he created the AbiWord open source word processor, and now he's a developer at SourceGear, which produces source code control software.*

But most of us around here know him from his contributions as host of The Business of Software, a discussion group that has become the hub for the software startup crowd. He coined the term "micro-ISV," he's been writing about the business of software on his blog for several years, and he wrote an influential series of articles for MSDN. He just published a full-fledged, dead-trees paper book called Eric Sink on the Business of Software *(Apress, 2006), and he asked me to write the foreword, which appears here.*

Did I ever tell you the story of my first business?

Let me see if I can remember the whole thing. I was fourteen, I think. They were running some kind of a TESOL summer institute at the University of New Mexico, and I was hired to sit behind a desk and make copies of articles from journals if anybody wanted them.

There was a big urn full of coffee next to the desk, and if you wanted coffee, you helped yourself and left a quarter in a little cup. I didn't drink coffee, myself, but I *did* like donuts and thought some nice donuts would go well with the coffee.

There were no donut stores within walking distance of my little world, so, being too young to drive, I was pretty much cut off from donuts in Albuquerque. Somehow, I persuaded a graduate student to buy a couple of dozen every day and bring them in. I put up a handwritten sign that said "Donuts: 25¢ (Cheap!)" and watched the money flow in.

Every day, people walked by, saw the little sign, dropped some money in the cup, and took a donut. We started to get regulars. The daily donut consumption was going up and up. People who didn't even need to be in the institute lounge veered off of their daily routes to get one of our donuts.

I was, of course, entitled to free samples, but that barely made a dent in the profits. Donuts cost, maybe, a dollar a dozen. Some people would even pay a dollar for a donut just because they couldn't be bothered to fish around in the money cup for change. I couldn't believe it!

By the end of the summer, I was selling two big trays a day . . . maybe a hundred donuts. Quite a lot of money had piled up . . . I don't remember the exact amount, but it was hundreds of dollars. This is 1979, you know. In those days, that was enough money to buy, like, *every donut in the world*, although by then I was sick of donuts and starting to prefer really, really spicy cheese enchiladas.

So, what did I do with the money? Nothing. The chairman of the Linguistics department took it all. He decided that the money should be used to hold a really big party for all the institute staff. I wasn't allowed to come to the party because I was too young.

The moral of the story?

Um, there is no moral.

But there is something incredibly exciting about watching a new business grow. It's the joy of watching the organic growth that every healthy business goes through. By "organic," I mean, literally, "of or designating carbon compounds." No, wait, that's not what I mean. I mean plant-like, gradual growth. Last week you made $24. This week you made $26. By this time next year, you might be making $100.

People love growing businesses for the same reason they love gardening. It's really fun to plant a little seed in the ground, water it every day, remove the weeds, and watch a tiny sprout grow into a big bushy plant full of gorgeous hardy mums (if you're lucky) or stinging nettles (if you got confused about what was a weed, but don't lose hope, you can make tea out of the nettles, just be careful not to touch 'em).

As you look at the revenues from your business, you'll say, "Gosh, it's only 3:00, and we've already had nine customers! This is going to be the best day ever!" And the next year nine customers will seem like a joke, and a couple of years later, you'll realize that that intranet report listing all the sales from the last week is unmanageably large.

One day, you'll turn off the feature that e-mails you every time someone buys your software. That's a huge milestone.

Eventually, you'll notice that one of the summer interns you hired is bringing in donuts on Friday morning and selling them for a buck. And I can only hope that you won't take his profits and use it for a party he's not invited to.

twenty-five

FOREWORD TO *MICRO-ISV: FROM VISION TO REALITY*

WEDNESDAY, JANUARY 11, 2006

This is my foreword to Bob Walsh's new book, Micro-ISV: From Vision to Reality *(Apress, 2006).*

How the heck did *I* become the poster child for the micro-ISV movement?

Of all people. Sheesh.

When I started Fog Creek Software, there was gonna be nothing "micro" about it. The plan was to build a big, multinational software company with offices in 120 countries and a skyscraper headquarters in

Manhattan, complete with a heliport on the roof for quick access to the Hamptons. It might take a few decades—after all, we were going to be bootstrapped and we always planned to grow slowly and carefully—but our ambitions were anything but small.

Heck, I don't even *like* the term micro-ISV. The "ISV" part stands for independent software vendor. It's a made-up word, made up by Microsoft, to mean "software company that is not Microsoft," or, more specifically, "software company that for some reason we have not yet bought or eliminated, probably because they are in some charming, twee line of business, like wedding table arrangements, the quaintness of which we are just *way* too cool to stoop down to, but you little people feel free to enjoy yourselves. Just remember to use .NET!"

It's like that other term, *legacy*, that Microsoft uses to refer to all non-Microsoft software. So when they refer to Google, say, as a "legacy search engine," they are trying to imply that Google is merely "an old, crappy search engine that you're still using by historical accident, until you bow to the inevitable and switch to MSN." What*ever*.

I prefer "software company," and there's nothing wrong with being a startup. *Startup software company*, that's how we describe ourselves, and we don't see any need to define ourselves in relation to Microsoft.

I suppose you're reading this book because you want to start a small software company, and it's a good book to read for that purpose, so let me use my pulpit here to provide you with my personal checklist of three things you should have before you start your micro . . . *ahem*, startup software company. There are some other things you should do; Bob covers them pretty well in the rest of the book, but before you get started, here's my contribution.

Number One. Don't start a business if you can't explain what pain it solves, for whom, and why your product will eliminate this pain, and how the customer will pay to solve this pain. The other day I went to a presentation of six high-tech startups, and not *one* of them had a clear idea for what pain they were proposing to solve. I saw a startup that was building a way to set a time to meet your friends for coffee, a startup that wanted you to install a plug-in in your browser to track your every movement online in exchange for being able to delete things from that history, and a startup that wanted you to be able to leave text messages for your friend that were tied to a particular location (so if they ever walked past the same bar, they could get a message you had left for them there). What they all had in common was that none of them solved a problem, and all of them were as doomed as a long-tailed cat in a room full of rocking chairs.

Number Two. Don't start a business by yourself. I know, there are lots of successful one-person startups, but there are even more failed one-person startups. If you can't even convince *one friend* that your idea has merit, um, maybe it doesn't? Besides, it's lonely and depressing, and you won't have anyone to bounce ideas off of. And when the going gets tough, which it will, as a one-person operation, you'll just fold up shop. With two people, you'll feel an obligation to your partner to push on through. P.S. Cats do not count.

Number Three. Don't expect much at first. People never know how much money they're going to make in the first month when their product goes on sale. I remember five years ago, when we started selling FogBugz, we had no idea if the first month of sales would be $0 or $50,000. Both figures seemed just as likely to me. I have talked to enough entrepreneurs and have enough data now to give you a definitive answer for *your* startup.

That's right, I have a crystal ball, and I can now tell you the one fact that you need to know more than anything else: exactly how much money you're going to make during the first month after your product goes live.

Ready?

OK.

In the first month, you are going to make,

about,

$364, *if you do everything right.* If you charge too little, you're going to make $40. If you charge too much, you're going to make $0. If you expect to make any more than that, you're going to be really disappointed, and you're going to give up and get a job working for The Man and referring to us people in startup-land as "legacy micro-ISVs."

That $364 sounds depressing, but it's not, because you'll soon discover the one fatal flaw that's keeping 50% of your potential customers from whipping out their wallets, and then ta-da! you'll be making $728 a month. And then you'll work really hard, and you'll get some publicity, and you'll figure out how to use AdWords effectively, and there will be a story about your company in the local wedding planner newsletter, and ta-da! you'll be making $1,456 a month. And you'll ship version

2.0, with spam filtering and a Common Lisp interpreter built in, and your customers will chat amongst themselves, and ta-da! you'll be making $2,912 a month. And you'll tweak the pricing, add support contracts, ship version 3.0, and get mentioned by Jon Stewart on *The Daily Show*, and ta-da! $5,824 a month.

Now we're cooking with fire. Project out a few years, and if you plug away at it, there's no reason you can't double your revenues every 12–18 months, so no matter how small you start [detailed math formula omitted—*Ed.*], you'll soon be building your own skyscraper in Manhattan with a heliport so you can get to that twenty-acre Southampton spread in thirty minutes flat.

And that, I think, is the real joy of starting a company: creating something, all by yourself, and nurturing it and working on it and investing in it and watching it grow, and watching the investments pay off. It's a hell of a journey, and I wouldn't miss it for the world.

twenty-six

HITTING THE HIGH NOTES

Monday, July 25, 2005

In March, 2000, I launched my site, *Joel on Software*, with the shaky claim that most people are wrong in thinking you need an idea to make a successful software company (`www.joelonsoftware.com/articles/fog0000000074.html`):

> *The common belief is that when you're building a software company, the goal is to find a neat idea that solves some problem which hasn't been solved before, implement it, and make a fortune. We'll call this the build-a-better-mousetrap belief. But the real goal for software companies should be converting capital into software that works.*

For the last five years, I've been testing that theory in the real world. The formula for the company I started with Michael Pryor in September 2000 can be summarized in four steps:

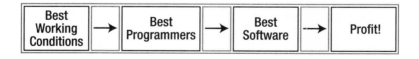

It's a pretty convenient formula, especially since our *real* goal in starting Fog Creek was to create a software company where *we would want to work*. I made the claim, in those days, that good working conditions (or, awkwardly, "building the company where the best software developers in the world would want to work") would *lead* to profits as naturally as chocolate leads to chubbiness or cartoon sex in video games leads to gangland-style shooting sprees.

For today, though, I want to answer just one question, because if this part isn't true, the whole theory falls apart. That question is, does it even make sense to talk about having the "best programmers"? Is there so much variation between programmers that this even matters?

Maybe it's obvious to us, but to many, the assertion still needs to be proven.

Several years ago a larger company was considering buying out Fog Creek, and I knew it would never work as soon as I heard the CEO of that company say that he didn't really agree with my theory of hiring the best programmers. He used a biblical metaphor: you only need one King David, and an army of soldiers who merely had to be able to carry out orders. His company's stock price promptly dropped from $20 to $5, so it's a good thing we didn't take the offer, but it's hard to pin that on the King David fetish.

And in fact, the conventional wisdom in the world of copycat business journalists and large companies who rely on overpaid management consultants to think for them, chew their food, etc., seems to be that the most important thing is reducing the *cost* of programmers.

In some other industries, cheap *is* more important than good. Wal-Mart grew to be the biggest corporation on earth by selling cheap products, not good products. If Wal-Mart tried to sell high-quality goods, their costs would go up, and their whole cheap advantage would be lost. For example, if they tried to sell a tube sock that can withstand the unusual rigors of, say, being washed in a washing machine, they'd have to use all kinds of expensive components, like, say, *cotton,* and the cost for every single sock would go up.

So, why isn't there room in the software industry for a low-cost provider, someone who uses the cheapest programmers available? (Remind me to ask Quark how that whole fire-everybody-and-hire-low-cost-replacements plan is working.)

Here's why: duplication of software is free. That means the cost of programmers is spread out over all the copies of the software you sell. With software, you can improve quality without adding to the incremental cost of each unit sold.

Essentially, *design adds value faster than it adds cost.*

Or, roughly speaking, if you try to skimp on programmers, you'll make crappy software, and you won't even save that much money.

The same thing applies to the entertainment industry. It's worth hiring Brad Pitt for your latest blockbuster movie, even though he demands a high salary, because that salary can be divided by all the millions of people who see the movie solely because Brad is so damn *hot*.

Or, to put it another way, it's worth hiring Angelina Jolie for your latest blockbuster movie, even though she demands a high salary, because that salary can be divided by all the millions of people who see the movie solely because Angelina is so damn *hot*.

But I still haven't proven anything. What does it mean to be "the best programmer," and are there really such major variations between the quality of software produced by different programmers?

Let's start with plain old productivity. It's rather hard to measure programmer productivity; almost any metric you can come up with (lines of debugged code, function points, number of command-line arguments) is trivial to game, and it's very hard to get concrete data on large projects because it's very rare for two programmers to be told to do the same thing.

The data I rely upon comes from Professor Stanley Eisenstat at Yale. Each year he teaches a programming-intensive course, CS 323, where a large proportion of the work consists of about five programming assignments, each of which takes about two weeks. The assignments are very serious for a college class: implement a Unix command-line shell, implement a ZLW file compressor, etc.

There was so much griping among the students about how much work was required for this class that Professor Eisenstat started asking the students to report back on how much time they spent on each assignment. He has collected this data carefully for several years.

I spent some time crunching his numbers; it's the only data set I know of that measures dozens of students working on identical assignments using the same technology at the same time. It's pretty darn controlled, as experiments go.

The first thing I did with this data was to calculate the average, minimum, maximum, and standard deviation of hours spent on each of twelve assignments. The results:

Project	Avg Hrs	Min Hrs	Max Hrs	StDev Hrs
CMDLINE99	14.84	4.67	29.25	5.82
COMPRESS00	33.83	11.58	77.00	14.51
COMPRESS01	25.78	10.00	48.00	9.96
COMPRESS99	27.47	6.67	69.50	13.62
LEXHIST01	17.39	5.50	39.25	7.39
MAKE01	22.03	8.25	51.50	8.91
MAKE99	22.12	6.77	52.75	10.72
SHELL00	22.98	10.00	38.68	7.17
SHELL01	17.95	6.00	45.00	7.66
SHELL99	20.38	4.50	41.77	7.03
TAR00	12.39	4.00	69.00	10.57
TEX00	21.22	6.00	75.00	12.11
ALL PROJECTS	21.44	4.00	77.00	11.16

The most obvious thing you notice here is the huge variations. The fastest students were finishing three or four times faster than the average students and as much as ten times faster than the slowest students. The standard deviation is outrageous. So then I thought, hmm, maybe some of these students are doing a terrible job. I didn't want to include students who spent four hours on the assignment without producing a working program. So I narrowed the data down and only included the data from students who were in the top quartile of grades . . . the top 25% in terms of the quality of the code. I should mention that grades in Professor Eisenstat's class are *completely* objective: they're calculated formulaically based on how many automated tests the code passes and nothing else. No points are deducted for bad style or lateness.

Anyway, here are the results for the top quartile:

Project	Avg Hrs	Min Hrs	Max Hrs	StdDev Hrs
CMDLINE99	13.89	8.68	29.25	6.55
COMPRESS00	37.40	23.25	77.00	16.14
COMPRESS01	23.76	15.00	48.00	11.14

Project	Avg Hrs	Min Hrs	Max Hrs	StdDev Hrs
COMPRESS99	20.95	6.67	39.17	9.70
LEXHIST01	14.32	7.75	22.00	4.39
MAKE01	22.02	14.50	36.00	6.87
MAKE99	22.54	8.00	50.75	14.80
SHELL00	23.13	18.00	30.50	4.27
SHELL01	16.20	6.00	34.00	8.67
SHELL99	20.98	13.15	32.00	5.77
TAR00	11.96	6.35	18.00	4.09
TEX00	16.58	6.92	30.50	7.32
ALL PROJECTS	**20.49**	**6.00**	**77.00**	**10.93**

Not much difference! The standard deviation is almost exactly the same for the top quartile. In fact, when you look closely at the data, it's pretty clear there's *no discernable correlation between the time and score.* Here's a typical scatter plot of one of the assignments . . . I chose the assignment COMPRESS01, an implementation of Ziv-Lempel-Welch compression assigned to students in 2001, because the standard deviation there is close to the overall standard deviation.

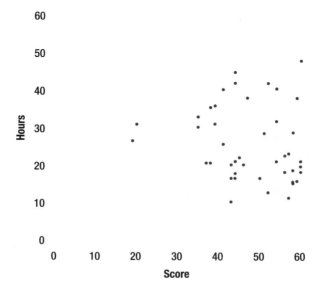

There's just nothing to see here, and that's the point. *The quality of the work and the amount of time spent are simply uncorrelated.*

I asked Professor Eisenstat about this, and he pointed out one more thing: because assignments are due at a fixed time (usually midnight) and the penalties for being late are significant, a lot of students stop before the project is done. In other words, the maximum time spent on these assignments is as low as it is partially because there just aren't enough hours between the time the assignment is handed out and the time it is due. If students had unlimited time to work on the projects (which would correspond a little better to the working world), the spread could only be *higher.*

This data is not completely scientific. There's probably some cheating. Some students may overreport the time spent on assignments in hopes of gaining some sympathy and getting easier assignments the next time. (Good luck! The assignments in CS 323 are the same today as they were when I took the class in the 1980s.) Other students may underreport because they lost track of time. Still, I don't think it's a stretch to believe this data shows 5:1 or 10:1 productivity differences between programmers.

~

But wait, there's more!

If the only difference between programmers were productivity, you might think that you could substitute five mediocre programmers for one really good programmer. That obviously doesn't work. Brooks' Law, "Adding manpower to a late software project makes it later," is why (Fredrick Brooks, *The Mythical Man-Month: Essays on Software Engineering*, Addison-Wesley, 1975). A single good programmer working on a single task has no coordination or communication overhead. Five programmers working on the same task must coordinate and communicate. That takes a lot of time. There are added benefits to using the smallest team possible; the man-month really is mythical.

~

But wait, there's even more!

The real trouble with using a lot of mediocre programmers instead of a couple of good ones is that no matter how long they work, they never produce something as good as what the great programmers can produce.

Five Antonio Salieris won't produce Mozart's *Requiem*. Ever. Not if they work for 100 years.

Five Jim Davises—creator of that unfunny cartoon cat, where 20% of the jokes are about how Monday sucks and the rest are about how much the cat likes lasagna (and those are the *punchlines!*) . . . five Jim Davises could spend the rest of their *lives* writing comedy and never, ever produce the "Soup Nazi" episode of *Seinfeld*.

The Creative Zen team could spend years refining their ugly iPod knockoffs and never produce as beautiful, satisfying, and elegant a player as the Apple iPod. And they're not going to make a dent in Apple's market share because the magical design talent is just *not there*. They *don't have it*.

The mediocre talent just *never hits the high notes* that the top talent hits all the time. The number of divas who can hit the F6 in Mozart's "Queen of the Night" is vanishingly small, and you just can't perform "Queen of the Night" without that famous F6.

Is software really about artistic high notes? "Maybe some stuff is," you say, "but I work on accounts receivable user interfaces for the medical waste industry." Fair enough. My focus is on product companies, where success or failure depends on the quality of the product. If you're only using software internally to support your operations, you probably only need software to be good enough.

And we've seen plenty of examples of great software, the really high notes, in the past few years: stuff that mediocre software developers just *could not* have developed.

Back in 2003, Nullsoft shipped a new version of Winamp, with the following notice on their web site:

- Snazzy new look!
- Groovy new features!
- Most things actually work!

It's the last part—the "Most things actually work!"—that makes everyone laugh. And then they're happy, and so they get excited about Winamp, and they use it, and tell their friends, and they think Winamp is awesome, all because they actually wrote on their web site, "Most things actually work!" How cool is that?

If you threw a bunch of extra programmers onto the Windows Media Player team, would they ever hit that high note? Never in a thousand years. Because the more people you added to that team, the more likely they would be to have one real grump who thought it was unprofessional and immature to write "Most things actually work!" on your web site.

Not to mention the comment, "Winamp 3: Almost as new as Winamp 2!"

That kind of stuff is what made us love Winamp.

By the time AOL Time Warner Corporate Weenieheads got their hands on that thing, the funny stuff from the web site was gone. You can just see them, fuming and festering and snivelling like Salieri in the movie *Amadeus*, trying to beat down all signs of creativity that might scare one old lady in Minnesota, at the cost of wiping out anything that might have made people *like* the product.

Or look at the iPod. *You can't change the battery*. So when the battery dies, *too bad. Get a new iPod*. Actually, Apple will replace it if you send it back to the factory, but that costs $65.95. Wowza.

Why can't you change the battery?

My theory is that it's because Apple didn't want to mar the otherwise perfectly smooth, seamless surface of their beautiful, sexy iPod with one of those ghastly battery covers you see on other cheapo consumer crap, with the little latches that are always breaking and the seams that fill up with pocket lint and all that general yuckiness. The iPod is the most seamless piece of consumer electronics I have ever seen. It's beautiful. It *feels* beautiful, like a smooth river stone. One battery latch can blow the whole river stone effect.

Apple made a decision based on *style*; in fact, iPod is full of decisions that are based on style. And style is not something that 100 programmers at Microsoft or 200 industrial designers at the inaptly named Creative are going to be able to achieve, because they don't have Jonathan Ive, and there aren't a heck of a lot of Jonathan Ives floating around.

I'm sorry, I can't stop talking about the iPod. That beautiful thumbwheel with its little clicky sounds . . . Apple spent *extra money* putting a speaker *in the iPod itself* so that the thumbwheel clicky sounds would come from the thumbwheel. They could have saved pennies—*pennies!*—by playing the clicky sounds through the headphones. But the thumbwheel makes you feel like you're in control. People like to feel in control. *It makes people happy to feel in control.* The fact that the thumbwheel responds smoothly, fluently, and *audibly* to your commands makes you *happy*. Not like the other 6,000 pocket-sized consumer electronics bits of junk, which take so long booting up that when you hit the on/off switch you have to wait a minute to find out if anything happened. Are you in control? Who knows? When was the last time you had a cell phone that went on the instant you pressed the on button?

Style.

Happiness.

Emotional appeal.

These are what make the huge hits, in software products, in movies, and in consumer electronics. And if you don't get this stuff right, you may solve the problem, but your product doesn't become the number one hit that makes everybody in the company rich so you can *all* drive stylish, happy, appealing cars like the Ferrari Spider F1 and still have enough money left over to build an ashram in your backyard.

It's not just a matter of "ten times more productive." It's that the "average productive" developer never hits the high notes that make great software.

Sadly, this doesn't really apply in nonproduct software development. Internal, in-house software is rarely important enough to justify hiring rock stars. Nobody hires Dolly Parton to sing at weddings. That's why the most satisfying careers, if you're a software developer, are at actual software companies, not doing IT for some bank.

The software marketplace, these days, is something of a winner-take-all system. Nobody else is making money on MP3 players other than

Apple. Nobody else makes money on spreadsheets and word processors other than Microsoft, and, yes, I know, they did anticompetitive things to get into that position, but that doesn't change the fact that it's a winner-take-all system.

You can't afford to be number two or to have a "good enough" product. It has to be remarkably good, by which I mean, so good that people remark about it. The lagniappe that you get from the really, really, really talented software developers is your only hope for remarkableness. It's all in the plan:

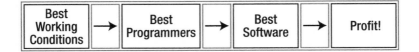

part seven

Running a Software Business

twenty-seven

BIONIC OFFICE

WEDNESDAY, SEPTEMBER 24, 2003

Well.

That took *rather* longer than expected.

We have, *finally*, moved into the new Fog Creek office at 535 8th Avenue, officially ten months after I started pounding the pavement looking for a replacement for my grandmother's old brownstone where we spent our first few years, working from bedrooms and the garden.

Most software managers know what good office space would be like, and they know they don't have it and can't have it. Office space seems to be the one thing that nobody can get right and nobody can do anything about. There's a ten-year lease, and whenever the company moves, the *last* person anybody asks about how to design the space is the manager of the software team, who finds out what his new veal-fattening pens, uh, cubicle farm is going to be like for the first time on the Monday after the move-in.

Well, it's my own damn company and I can do something about it, so I did.

Maybe I'm just an architecture queen. I probably pay more attention to my physical surroundings than the average software developer. I might take it *too* seriously. But there are three reasons I take it so seriously:

- There's a lot of evidence that the right kind of office space can improve programmer productivity, especially private offices.

- Having drop-dead gorgeous, private, windowed offices makes it a lot easier to recruit the kinds of superstars that produce ten times as much as the merely brilliant software developers. If I have to compete at New York salaries against Bangalore salaries, I'm going to need those superstars, so when people come in for an interview, I need to see jaws on the floor. It's about *drama*.

- Hey, this is my *job*; this is where I spend my *days*; it's my time away from my friends and family. It *better* be nice.

Working with architect Roy Leone, a lot of space (425 rsf per employee), and an enlightened CEO, I set out to create the ultimate software development environment.

Architects use the term "brief" for what we software developers call "system requirements." Here was the brief I gave Roy:

1. Private offices with doors that close were absolutely required and not open to negotiation.

2. Programmers need lots of power outlets. They should be able to plug new gizmos in at desk height without crawling on the floor.

3. We need to be able to rewire any data lines (phone, LAN, cable TV, alarms, etc.) easily without opening any walls, ever.

4. It should be possible to do pair programming.

5. When you're working with a monitor all day, you need to rest your eyes by looking at something far away, so monitors should not be up against walls.

6. The office should be a hangout: a pleasant place to spend time. If you're meeting your friends for dinner after work, you should *want* to meet at the office. As Philip Greenspun bluntly puts it (ccm.redhat.com/asj/managing-software-engineers/): "Your business success will depend on the extent to which programmers essentially live at your office. For this to be a common choice, your office had better be nicer than the average programmer's home. There are two ways to achieve this result. One is to hire programmers who live in extremely shabby apartments. The other is to create a nice office."

Roy did a great job. This is what you pay an architect for. I predict he will become something of a world expert on designing offices for software teams. Here's how he translated my brief into three-dimensional space:

Private offices. Not only did we get spacious, windowed private offices, but even the common area workstations (for nondevelopers) are hidden in clever angular alcoves, so everyone gets their own private space without line of sight to anyone else.

The walls between the offices and the workstations are made of high-tech, translucent acrylic that glows softly and provides natural light to the interior without reducing privacy.

Power. Every desk has twenty, that's right, twenty outlets. Four of them are colored orange and have uninterruptible power coming off of a UPS in the server closet, so you don't need a UPS in every office.

The outlets are right below desk level in a special trough that runs the entire length of the desk, about six inches deep and six inches wide. The trough is a place to hide all your cables neatly and has a handy cover that blends in with the desk.

Wiring. There is a Snake Tray system running near the ceiling from the server room and throughout the office, running through every room. It is completely accessible, so if you want to run any kind of (low-voltage) cable from point A to point B, you can do this neatly. We only moved in Friday, and we've already redone the intraoffice LAN wiring, in a project that took about half an hour, so the Snake Tray has already proven itself. Every office has its own eight-port network switch, so you can plug in your laptop *and* your desktop *and* your Macintosh *and* that old computer you keep around to read *Joel on Software* when your main computer is rebooting to install today's Windows Update, and *still* have three ports left over. (Attention math geniuses: no need to e-mail. One port is the uplink.) I sneer at silly building managers who still think that one LAN port per office is about right. For lawyers, maybe.

Pair programming. When you make typical L-shaped desks, many developers set themselves up in the corner. When they need to collaborate temporarily, or pair program, or even just show something to someone on their screen, the second person has to either lean all the way across the desk or look over the first person's shoulder. To avoid this, we designed all the desks to be long and straight so that wherever a software developer sits, there's always room for another person to pull up a chair and sit next to them.

Resting eyes. Although the desks are up against the walls, there is an interior window in that wall, which cleverly looks across the corner of the next developer's office and through *his* window. Due to the rather brilliant layout, this doesn't reduce privacy, because even though you have a window onto the next office, it is angled so that from most positions you really only look across a small corner of that room and out its exterior window. The net result is that every office has windows on three sides, two of which look outside, creating the architectural pattern Light on Two Sides of Every Room. This is quite an accomplishment: *you* try coming up with a scheme to give everyone a corner office in a conventional building. Another reason hiring a great architect was well worth the money.

Hang out. We furnished the office with a kitchenette and a lounge area with sofas and a huge HDTV plasma screen with DVD player. We're planning a pool table and game console. Private offices means you can listen to music at reasonable volumes without headphones and nobody will care.

Bottom line it for me

The monthly rent for our offices, when fully occupied, will run about $700 per employee. The build-out was done on budget and paid for almost entirely by the landlord. I suspect that $700 per person is on the high side for software developers throughout the world, but if it means we can hire from the 99.9 percentile instead of the 99 percentile, it'll be worth it.

twenty-eight

UP THE TATA WITHOUT
A TUTU

Until yesterday, the FogBugz license said that you couldn't reverse engi-neer the program, attempt to look at the source code, or modify it in any way. Various honest people have asked how much we charge for a source license so that they could customize a few things.

Hmmm. Why *does* the license say you can't change the source code? I couldn't think of a single reason. In fact, I thought of a lot of counter-reasons, and immediately changed the license agreement. So now you're going to have to sit through one of those old-fuddy-duddy stories from my past.

Way back in 1995, I was working at Viacom, where a small group of us hardy pioneers were building web sites for various Viacom properties.

In those days, there were no application servers. Sybase was so clueless that if you wanted to use their database on the Internet, they told you that you needed to buy a $150 client license for *every user that connects to your web site*. Netscape's web server was up to version 1.0.

A brave company called Illustra started telling people that their data-base management system was *perfect* for the Web. You see, Illustra was designed to make it easy to add new data types by writing some C code and linking it in with their DBMS. (Any programmer who's used a DBMS will tell you that this is already sounding a bit too dangerous. C code? Linked in? Oy.) This was originally intended for exciting data types like latitude/longitude, time series, and so on. But then the Web happened. Illustra wrote something they called a Web Blade and linked it in. The Web Blade was a sort of half-baked system that allegedly made it possible to extract data from the database and create dynamic web pages on the fly, which was the biggest problem everybody had in 1995.

A colleague of mine at Viacom was put in charge of building an e-commerce site so that Blockbuster could sell, I kid you not, *CDs* on the Web. (Because that's what people think of when they think of Blockbuster, right?) Anyway, he thought that Illustra would be *perfect* for the job. Now, Illustra cost something like $125,000, and shaking that much money loose from the Viacom Tree is like herding cats, so it took a while. My colleague taped a paper cup to his cube labeled "Illustra Fund" and collected a few dollars that way. The CTO negotiated hard and long hours with Illustra, and eventually a deal was struck. We installed Illustra and got to work.

Unfortunately, disaster struck. Illustra's Web Blade was barely half-baked and completely not up to the task. It crashed every few minutes. When it did run, it proved to have the only programming language I've ever seen that *wasn't* Turing-equivalent, if you can imagine that. The license manager kept deciding to shut you off, and your site would die. Building a site with it was terrible, my colleague's annus horribilis. So when they came to me and said, "Joel, you're making a site for MTV," I said, "Uh oh."

"Please can I not use Illustra?" I begged.

"Well, OK, but what are you going to use instead?" There really weren't any other app servers in those days. There was no PHP, no AOLserver with TCL stuff, Perl had to fork, we didn't have penicillin, life was terrible.

And my reputation was on the line. And I decided that the scariest thing about Illustra was that when it crashed, you couldn't do anything about it. At least, if you had the source code, I thought, if Illustra crashes, well, it falls into your lap in the debugger, and you can try to fix the bug. You may have to stay up all night for a week debugging someone else's code, but at least you have a *chance*. Whereas, without the source code, you are up the proverbial tata without a tutu.

And that's where I learned a key lesson in software architecture: for your most important, mission-critical stuff, you have to use a tool that is one level *lower* in abstraction than ideal. For example, if you're writing a cool 3D shoot-em-up game (like Quake, around the same time period) and your key number one differentiator is to have the *coolest* 3D graphics, you do *not* use whatever 3D library you can find. You *write your own*, because it's fundamental to what you do. The people who use 3D libraries like DirectX are using them because they are trying to differentiate their games on something other than 3D performance. (Maybe the story line.)

That's when I decided not to trust anyone else's poxy application server and decided to just write my own, in C++, using Netscape Server's low-level API. Because I knew that at least if anything went wrong, it was in *my code*, and I could eventually fix it.

And this is one of the greatest virtues of open source/free software, even if you could afford Illustra's $125,000 piece of tata: at least if anything goes wrong, you are going to be able to fix it, *somehow*, and you won't get fired, and the nice-if-hyperactive people at MTV won't be all pissed off at you.

When I sit down to architect a system, I have to decide which tools to use. And a good architect only uses tools that can either be trusted or be fixed. "Trusted" doesn't mean that they were made by some big company that you're supposed to trust like IBM, it means that you know in your heart that it's going to work right. I think today most Windows programmers trust Visual C++, for example. They may not trust MFC, but MFC comes with source, and so even though it can't be trusted, it can be *fixed* when you discover how truly atrocious the async socket library is. So it's OK to bet your career on MFC, too.

You can bet your career on the Oracle DBMS, because it just works and everybody knows it. And you can bet your career on Berkeley DB, because if it screws up, you go into the source code and fix it. But you probably don't want to bet your career on a non–open source, not-well-known tool. You can use that for experiments, but it's not a bet-your-career kind of tool.

So I got to thinking about how to make FogBugz a safe bet for smart engineers. Almost by accident, it ships in source code form—because that's how ASP pages work these days. Which doesn't bother me. There are no magical, trade-secret algorithms in bug tracking software. This stuff is not rocket science. (In fact, there are very few magical, trade-secret algorithms in *any* software. The fact that it's fairly easy to disassemble an executable and figure out how it works just doesn't matter as much as intellectual property lawyers think it should.) It doesn't matter to me that people look at the code or modify the code for their own use.

There's another risk when you modify source code that you bought from a vendor: when the vendor upgrades the code, you are going to have a heck of a time migrating your changes to their new version. There's something I can do to ameliorate that, too: if you find a bug in FogBugz and fix it, and send me the fix, I'll incorporate it into the next version. This is intended to make people feel a little bit more comfortable that (a) FogBugz works, and (b) if it doesn't work, in some mission-critical way, they can fix it rather than get fired, and (c) if they do have to fix it, and their fix makes sense, it will get back into the source tree so that the next version will incorporate their fixes, and life will be less brutish.

By now I can hear the open source and free software advocates practically screaming, "You silly goose! Just make it open source and be done with it! Open source doesn't have any of these problems!" And that's nice. But my wee company with three programmers costs $40,000 a month to operate. So we just charge for our software, and we don't apologize, because it's worth the money. We don't claim to be open source, but we can make sure that FogBugz is a safe decision to make, by adopting two or three nice features from the open source world.

twenty-nine

SIMPLICITY

SATURDAY, DECEMBER 9, 2006

Donald Norman concludes that simplicity is overrated (www.jnd.org/dn.mss/simplicity_is_highly.html): "But when it came time for the journalists to review the simple products they had gathered together, they complained that they lacked what they considered to be 'critical' features. So, what do people mean when they ask for simplicity? One-button operation, of course, but with all of their favorite features."

A long time ago, I wrote the following (*Joel on Software*, Apress, 2004):

A lot of software developers are seduced by the old "80/20" rule. It seems to make a lot of sense: 80% of the people use 20% of the features. So you convince yourself that you only need to implement 20% of the features, and you can still sell 80% as many copies.

Unfortunately, it's never the same 20%. Everybody uses a different set of features. In the last 10 years, I have probably heard of dozens of companies who, determined not to learn from each other, tried to release "lite" word processors that only implement 20% of the features. This story is as old as the PC. Most of the time, what happens is that they give their program to a journalist to review, and the journalist reviews it by writing their review using the new word processor, and then the journalist tries to find the "word count" feature, which they need because most journalists have precise word count requirements, and it's not there, because it's in the "80% that nobody uses," and the journalist ends up writing a

*story that attempts to claim simultaneously that lite programs are
good, bloat is bad, and I can't use this damn thing 'cause it won't
count my words.*

Making simple, 20% products is an excellent bootstrapping strategy
because you can create them with limited resources and build an audience. It's a judo strategy, using your weakness as a strength, like the way
The Blair Witch Project, filmed by kids with no money at all, used the
only camera they could afford, a handheld video camera, but they
invented a plot in which that was actually a virtue. So you sell "simple"
as if it were this wonderful thing, when, coincidentally, it's the only thing
you have the resources to produce. Happy coincidence, that's all, but it
really is wonderful!

What works for bootstrapping, I believe, will not work as a good
long-term strategy, because there's very little to prevent the next two-
person startup from cloning your simple app, and because eventually
you can't fight human nature: "The people want the features," says
Norman. Just because handheld video was perfect for *The Blair Witch
Project* doesn't mean every Hollywood blockbuster will use it.

Devotees of simplicity will bring up 37signals and the Apple iPod as
anecdotal proof that Simple Sells. I would argue that in both of these
cases, success is a result of a combination of things: building an audience, evangelism, clean and spare design, emotional appeal, aesthetics,
fast response time, direct and instant user feedback, program models
that correspond to the user model, resulting in high usability, and putting the user in control, all of which are *features* of one sort, in the sense
that they are benefits that customers like and pay for, but none of which
can really be described as "simplicity." For example, the iPod has the
feature of being beautiful, which the Creative Zen Ultra Nomad
Jukebox doesn't have, so I'll take an iPod, please. In the case of the iPod,
the way beauty is provided happens to be through a clean and simple
design, but it doesn't have to be. The Hummer is aesthetically appealing
precisely because it's ugly and complicated.

I think it is a misattribution to say, for example, that the iPod is successful *because it lacks features*. If you start to believe that, you'll
believe, among other things, that you should *take out* features to
increase your product's success. With six years of experience running
my own software company, I can tell you that *nothing* we have *ever*

done at Fog Creek has increased our revenue more than releasing a new version with more features. Nothing. The flow to our bottom line from new versions with new features is absolutely undeniable. It's like gravity. When we tried Google ads, when we implemented various affiliate schemes, or when an article about FogBugz appears in the press, we could barely see the effect on the bottom line. When a new version comes out with new features, we see a sudden, undeniable, substantial, and permanent increase in revenue.

If you're using the term "simplicity" to refer to a product in which the user model corresponds closely to the program model so the product is easy to use, fine, more power to ya. If you're using the term "simplicity" to refer to a product with a spare, clean visual appearance, so the term is nothing more than an aesthetic description much in the same way you might describe Ralph Lauren clothes as "Southampton WASP," fine, more power to ya. Minimalist aesthetics are quite hip these days. But if you think simplicity means "not very many features" or "does one thing and does it well," then I applaud your integrity, but you can't go that far with a product that deliberately leaves features out. Even the iPod has a gratuitous Solitaire game. Even Ta-da List supports RSS.

Anyway, I gotta go . . . it's time to go upgrade my cellphone to one that includes high-speed Internet access, e-mail, a podcast catcher, and an MP3 player.

thirty

RUB A DUB DUB

Wednesday, January 23, 2002

One reason people are tempted to rewrite their entire code base from scratch is that the original code base wasn't designed for what it's doing. It was designed as a prototype, an experiment, a learning exercise, a way to go from zero to IPO in nine months, or a one-off demo. And now it has grown into a big mess that's fragile and impossible to add code to, and everybody's whiny, and the old programmers quit in despair, and the new ones that are brought in can't make head or tail of the code, so they somehow convince management to give up and start over while Microsoft takes over their business. Today let me tell you a story about what they could have done instead.

FogBugz started out six years ago as an experiment to teach myself ASP programming. Pretty soon it became an in-house bug tracking system. It got embellished almost daily with features that people needed until it was *good enough* that it no longer justified any more work.

Various friends asked me if they could use FogBugz at *their* companies. The trouble was, it had too many hard-coded things that made it a pain to run anywhere other than on the original computer where it was deployed. I had used a bunch of SQL Server stored procedures, which meant that you needed SQL Server to run FogBugz, which was expensive and overkill for some of the two-person teams that wanted to run it. And so on. So I would tell my friends, "Gosh, for $5,000 in consulting fees, I'll spend a couple of days and clean up the code so you can run it on your server using Access instead of SQL Server." Generally, my friends thought this was too expensive.

After this happened a few times I had a revelation—if I could sell the same program to, say, three people, I could charge $2,000 and come out

236 MORE FROM JOEL ON SOFTWARE

ahead. Or thirty people for $200. Software is neat like that. So in late 2000, Michael sat down, ported the code so that it worked on Access or SQL Server, pulled all the site-specific stuff out into a header file, and we started selling the thing. I didn't really expect much to come of it.

In those days, I thought, golly, there are zillions of bug tracking packages out there. Every programmer has written a dinky bug tracking package. Why would anyone buy ours? I knew one thing: programmers who start businesses often have the bad habit of thinking everybody *else* is a programmer *just like them* and wants the same stuff as them, and so they have an unhealthy tendency to start businesses that sell programming tools. That's why you see so many scrawny companies hawking source-code-generating geegaws, error-catching and e-mailing geegaws, debugging geegaws, syntax-coloring editing tchotchkes, FTPing baubles, and, ahem, bug tracking packages. All kinds of stuff that only a programmer could love. I had no intention of falling into *that* trap!

Of course, nothing ever works out exactly as planned. FogBugz was popular. Really popular. It accounts for a significant chunk of Fog Creek's revenue, and sales are growing steadily. The People won't stop buying it.

So we did version 2.0. This was an attempt to add some of the most obviously needed features. While David worked on version 2.0, we honestly didn't think it was worth that much effort, so he tended to do things in what you might call an "expedient" fashion rather than, say, an "elegant" fashion. Certain, ahem, *design issues* in the original code were allowed to fester. There were two complete sets of nearly *identical* code for drawing the main bug-editing page. SQL statements were scattered throughout the HTML hither and yon, to and fro, pho and ton. Our HTML was creaky and designed for those ancient browsers that were so buggy they could crash loading about:blank.

Yeah, it worked brilliantly, we've been at zero known bugs for a while now. But inside, the code was, to use the technical term, a "big mess." Adding new features was a hemorrhoid. To add one field to the central bug table would probably require fifty modifications, and you'd still be finding places you forgot to modify long after you bought your first family carplane for those weekend trips to your beach house on Mars.

A lesser company, perhaps one run by an executive from the express-package-delivery business, might have decided to scrap the code and start over.

Did I mention that I don't believe in starting from scratch? I guess I talk about that a lot.

Anyway, instead of starting from scratch, I decided it was worth three weeks of my life to completely scrub the code. Rub a dub dub. In the spirit of refactoring, I set out a few rules for this exercise:

1. No New Features, not even small ones, would be added.

2. At any time, with any check in, the code would still work perfectly.

3. All I would do is logical transformations—the kinds of things that are almost mechanical and that you can convince yourself immediately will not change the behavior of the code.

I went through each source file, one at a time, top to bottom, looking at code, thinking about how it could be better structured, and making simple changes. Here are some of the kinds of things I did during these three weeks:

- Changed all HTML to XHTML. For example, <BR> became <br />, all attributes were quoted, all nested tags were matched up, and all pages were validated.

- Removed all formatting (<FONT> tags, etc.) and put everything in a CSS style sheet.

- Removed all SQL statements from the presentation code and indeed all program logic (what the marketing types like to call business rules). This stuff went into classes that were not really designed—I simply added methods lazily as I discovered a need for them. (Somewhere, someone with a big stack of 4×6 cards is sharpening their pencil to poke my eyes out. What do you mean you didn't design your classes?)

- Found repeated blocks of code and created classes, functions, or methods to eliminate the repetition. Broke up large functions into multiple smaller ones.

- Removed all remaining English language text from the main code and isolated that in a single file for easy internationalization.

- Restructured the ASP site so there is a single entry point instead of lots of different files. This makes it very easy to do things that used to be hard; for example, now we can display input error messages in the very form where the invalid input occurred, something that *should* be easy if you lay things out right, but I hadn't laid things out right when I was learning ASP programming way back when.

Over three weeks, the code got better and better internally. To the end user, not too much changed. Some fonts are a little nicer thanks to CSS. I could have stopped at any point, because at any given time I had 100% working code (and I uploaded every check-in to our live internal FogBugz server to make sure). And in fact I never really had to think very hard, and I never had to design a thing, because all I was doing was simple, logical transformations. Occasionally, I would encounter a weird nugget in the code. These nuggets were usually bug fixes that had been implemented over the years. Luckily, I could keep the bug fix intact. In many of these cases, I realized that had I started from scratch, I would have made the same bug all over again, and may not have noticed it for months or years.

I'm basically done now. It took, as planned, three weeks. *Almost every line of code is different now.* Yep, I looked at every line of code, and changed *most* of them. The structure is completely different. All the bug tracking functionality is completely separate from the HTML UI functionality.

Here are all the good things about my code-scrubbing activity:

- It took vastly less time than a complete rewrite. Let's assume (based on how long it took us to get this far with FogBugz) that a complete rewrite would have taken a year. Well, that means I saved forty-nine weeks of work. Those forty-nine weeks represent knowledge in the *design* of the code that I preserved intact. I never had to think, "Oh, I need a new line here." I just had to change <BR> to <br /> mindlessly and move on. I didn't have to figure out how to get multipart working for file uploads. It works. Just tidy it up a bit.

- I didn't introduce any new bugs. A couple of tiny ones, of course, probably got through. But I was never doing the types of things that cause bugs.

- I could have stopped and shipped at any time if necessary.

- The schedule was entirely predictable. After a week of this, you can calculate exactly how many lines of code you clean in an hour, and get a darn good estimate for the rest of the project. Try that, Mozilla river-drawing people.

- The code is now much more amenable to new features. We'll probably earn back the three weeks with the first new major feature we implement.

Much of the literature on refactoring is attributable to Martin Fowler, although of course the principles of code cleanups have been well known to programmers for years. An interesting new area is refactoring tools, which is just a fancy word for programs that do some of this stuff automatically. We're a long way from having all the good tools we need—in most programming environments, you can't even do a simple transformation like changing the name of a variable (and having all the references to it change automatically). But it's getting better, and if you want to start one of those scrawny companies hawking programming tool geegaws or make a useful contribution to open source, the field is wide open.

thirty-one

TOP TWELVE TIPS FOR RUNNING A BETA TEST

Tuesday, March 2, 2004

Here are a few tips for running a beta test of a software product intended for large audiences—what I call "shrink-wrap." These apply for commercial or open source projects; I don't care whether you get paid in cash, eyeballs, or peer recognition, but I'm focused on products for lots of users, *not* internal IT projects.

1. Open betas don't work. You either get too many testers (think Netscape), in which case you can't get good data from the testers, or you get too few reports from the existing testers.

2. The best way to get a beta tester to send you feedback is to appeal to their psychological need to be *consistent*. You need to get them to *say* that they will send you feedback, or, even better, *apply* to be in the beta testing program. Once they have taken some positive action such as filling out an application and checking the box that says "I agree to send feedback and bug reports promptly," many more people will do so in order to be consistent.

3. Don't think you can get through a full beta cycle in less than eight to ten weeks. I've tried; lord help me, it just can't be done.

4. Don't expect to release new builds to beta testers more than once every two weeks. I've tried; lord help me, it just can't be done.

5. Don't plan a beta with fewer than four releases. I haven't tried that because it was so obviously not going to work!

6. If you add a feature, even a small one, during the beta process, the clock goes back to the beginning of the eight weeks, and you need another three or four releases. One of the biggest mistakes I ever made was adding some whitespace-preserving code to CityDesk 2.0 toward the end of the beta cycle, which had some, shall we say, unexpected side effects that a longer beta would have fleshed out.

7. Even if you have an application process, only about one-in-five people will send you feedback anyway.

8. We have a policy of giving a free copy of the software to anyone who sends *any* feedback, positive, negative, whatever. But people who don't send us anything don't get a free copy at the end of the beta.

9. The minimum number of *serious* testers you need (i.e., people who send you three page summaries of their experience) is probably about 100. If you're a one-person shop, that's all the feedback you can handle. If you have a team of testers or beta managers, try to get 100 serious testers for every employee who is available to handle feedback.

10. Even if you have an application process, only one out of five testers is really going to try the product and send you feedback. So, for example, if you have a QA department with three testers, you should approve 1,500 beta applications to get 300 serious testers. Fewer than this, and you won't hear everything. More than this, and you'll be deluged with repeated feedback.

11. Most beta testers will try out the program when they first get it and then lose interest. They are not going to be interested in retesting it every time you drop them another build unless they really start using the program every day, which is unlikely for most people. Therefore, stagger the releases. Split your beta population into four groups, and with each new release, add another group that gets the software, so there are new beta testers for each milestone.

12. Don't confuse a technical beta with a marketing beta. I've been talking about technical betas here, in which the goal is to find bugs and get last-minute feedback. Marketing betas are pre-release versions of the software given to the press, to big customers, and to the guy who is going to write the *Dummies* book that has to appear on the same day as the product. With marketing betas, you don't expect to get feedback (although the people who write the books are likely to give you *copious* feedback no matter what you do, and if you ignore it, it will be cut and pasted into their book).

thirty-two

SEVEN STEPS TO REMARKABLE CUSTOMER SERVICE

Monday, February 19, 2007

As a bootstrapped software company, Fog Creek couldn't afford to hire customer service people for the first couple of years, so Michael and I did it ourselves. The time we spent helping customers took away from improving our software, but we learned a lot, and now we have a much better customer service operation.

Here are seven things we learned about providing remarkable customer service. I'm using the word *remarkable* literally—the goal is to provide customer service so good that people *remark*.

~

1. Fix everything two ways

Almost every tech support problem has two solutions. The superficial and immediate solution is just to solve the customer's problem. But when you think a little harder, you can usually find a deeper solution: a way to prevent this particular problem from ever happening again.

Sometimes that means adding more intelligence to the software or the Setup program; by now, our Setup program is loaded with special case checks. Sometimes you just need to improve the wording of an error message. Sometimes the best you can come up with is a knowledge base article.

We treat each tech support call like the NTSB treats airliner crashes. Every time a plane crashes, the NTSB sends out investigators, figures out what happened, and then figures out a new policy to prevent that particular problem from ever happening again. It's worked so well for aviation safety that the very, very rare airliner crashes we still get in the US are always very unusual, one-off situations.

This has two implications.

One: it's crucial that tech support staff have access to the development team. This means that you can't outsource tech support: they have to be right there at the same street address as the developers, with a way to get things fixed. Many software companies still think that it's "economical" to run tech support in Bangalore or the Philippines, or to outsource it to another company altogether. Yes, the cost of a single incident might be $10 instead of $50, but you're going to have to pay $10 again and again.

When we handle a tech support incident with a well-qualified person here in New York, chances are that's the *last time* we're ever going to see that particular incident. So with one $50 incident, we've eliminated an entire class of problems.

Somehow, the phone companies and the cable companies and the ISPs just don't understand this equation. They outsource their tech support to the cheapest possible provider and end up paying $10 again and again and again fixing the same problem again and again and again instead of fixing it once and for all in the source code. The cheap call centers have no mechanism for getting problems fixed; indeed, they have no *incentive* to get problems fixed because their income depends on repeat business, and there's nothing they like better than being able to give the same answer to the same question again and again.

The second implication of fixing everything two ways is that eventually, all the common and simple problems are solved, and what you're left with is very weird uncommon problems. That's fine, because there are far fewer of them, and you're saving a fortune not doing any rote tech support, but the downside is that there's no rote tech support left: only serious debugging and problem solving. You can't just teach new support people ten common solutions: you have to teach them to debug.

For us, the "fix everything two ways" religion has really paid off. We were able to increase our sales *tenfold* while only doubling the cost of providing tech support.

∼

2. Suggest blowing out the dust

Microsoft's Raymond Chen tells the story of a customer who complains that the keyboard isn't working (blogs.msdn.com/oldnewthing/archive/2004/03/03/83244.aspx). Of course, it's unplugged. If you try asking them if it's plugged in, "they will get all insulted and say indignantly, 'Of course it is! Do I look like an idiot?' without actually checking."

"Instead," Chen suggests, "say 'OK, sometimes the connection gets a little dusty and the connection gets weak. Could you unplug the connector, blow into it to get the dust out, then plug it back in?'

"They will then crawl under the desk, find that they forgot to plug it in (or plugged it into the wrong port), blow out the dust, plug it in, and reply, 'Um, yeah, that fixed it, thanks.'"

Many requests for a customer to check something can be phrased this way. Instead of telling them to check a setting, tell them to change the setting and then change it back "just to make sure that the software writes out its settings."

∼

3. Make customers into fans

Every time we need to buy logo gear here at Fog Creek, I get it from Lands' End.

Why?

Let me tell you a story. We needed some shirts for a trade show. I called up Lands' End and ordered two dozen, using the same logo design we had used for some knapsacks we bought earlier.

When the shirts arrived, to our dismay, we couldn't read the logo.

It turns out that the knapsacks were brighter than the polo shirts. The thread color that looked good on the knapsacks was too dark to read on the shirts.

I called up Lands' End. As usual, a human answered the phone *even before it started ringing*. I'm pretty sure that they have a system where the next agent in the queue is told to stand by, *so customers don't even have to wait one ringy-dingy before they're talking to a human.*

I explained that I screwed up.

They said, "Don't worry. You can return those for a full credit, and we'll redo the shirts with a different color thread."

I said, "The trade show is in two days."

They said they would FedEx me a new box of shirts, and I'd have it tomorrow. I could return the old shirts at my convenience.

They paid shipping both ways. I wasn't out a cent. Even though they had no possible use for a bunch of Fog Creek logo shirts with an illegible logo, they ate the cost.

And now I tell this story to everyone who needs swag. In fact, I tell this story every time we're talking about telephone menu systems. Or customer service. By providing remarkable customer service, they've gotten me to remark about it.

When customers have a problem *and you fix it,* they're actually going to be even more satisfied than if they never had a problem in the first place.

It has to do with expectations. Most people's experience with tech support and customer service comes from airlines, telephone companies, cable companies, and ISPs, all of whom provide generally *awful* customer service. It's so bad you don't even bother calling any more, do you? So when someone calls Fog Creek, and immediately gets through to a human, with no voice mail or phone menus, and that person turns out to be nice and friendly and actually *solves their problem,* they're apt to think even more highly of us than someone who never had the opportunity to interact with us and just assumes that we're average.

Now, I wouldn't go so far as to actually *make* something go wrong, just so we have a chance to demonstrate our superior customer service. Many customers just won't call; they'll fume quietly.

But when someone does call, look at it as a great opportunity to create a *fanatically devoted* customer, one who will prattle on and on about what a great job you did.

~

4. Take the blame

One morning I needed an extra set of keys to my apartment, so on the way to work, I went to the locksmith around the corner.

Thirteen years living in an apartment in New York City has taught me never to trust a locksmith; half of the time their copies don't work. So I went home to test the new keys, and, lo and behold, one didn't work.

I took it back to the locksmith.

He made it again.

I went back home and tested the new copy.

It *still* didn't work.

Now I was fuming. Squiggly lines were coming up out of my head. I was a half hour late to work and had to go to the locksmith for a *third* time. I was tempted just to give up on him. But I decided to give this loser one more chance.

I stomped into the store, ready to unleash my fury.

"It *still* doesn't work?" he asked. "Let me see."

He looked at it.

I was sputtering, trying to figure out how best to express my rage at being forced to spend the morning going back and forth.

"Ah. It's my fault," he said.

And suddenly, I wasn't mad at all.

Mysteriously, the words "It's my fault" completely defused me. That was all it took.

He made the key a third time. I wasn't mad any more. The key worked.

And, here I was, on this planet for forty years, and I couldn't believe how much the three words "It's my fault" had completely changed my emotions in a matter of seconds.

Most locksmiths in New York are not the kinds of guys to admit that they're wrong. Saying "It's my fault" was completely out of character. But he did it anyway.

~

5. Memorize awkward phrases

I figured, OK, since the morning is shot anyway, I might as well go to the diner for some breakfast.

It's one of those classic New York diners, like the one on *Seinfeld*. There's a thirty-page menu and a kitchen the size of a phone booth. It doesn't make sense. They must have *Star Trek* technology to get all those ingredients into such a small space. Maybe they rearrange atoms on the spot.

I was sitting by the cash register.

An older woman came up to pay her check. As she was paying, she said to the owner, "You know, I've been coming here for years and years, and that waiter was really rather rude to me."

The owner was furious.

"What do you mean? No he wasn't! He's a good waiter! I never had a complaint!"

The customer couldn't believe it. Here she was, a loyal customer, and she wanted to help out the owner by letting him know that one of his waiters needed a little bit of help in the manners department, but the owner was arguing with her!

"Well, that's fine, but I've been coming here for years, and everybody is always very nice to me, but that guy was rude to me," she explained, patiently.

"I don't care if you've been coming here forever. My waiters are not rude." The owner proceeded to yell at her. "I never had no problems. Why are you making problems?"

"Look, if you're going to treat me this way, I won't come back."

"I don't care!" said the owner. One of the great things about owning a diner in New York is that there are so many people in the city that you can offend *every single customer* who *ever comes into your diner* and you'll still have a lot of customers. "Don't come back! I don't want you as a customer!"

Good for you, I thought. Here's a sixty-something-year-old man, owner of a diner, and you won some big moral victory against a little old lady. Are you proud of yourself? How macho do you have to be? Does the moral victory make you feel better? Did you really have to lose a repeat customer?

Would it have made you feel totally emasculated to say, "I'm so sorry. I'll have a word with him"?

It's easy to get caught up in the emotional heat of the moment when someone is complaining.

The solution is to memorize some key phrases and *practice saying them*, so that when you need to say them, you can forget your testosterone and make a customer happy.

"I'm sorry, it's my fault."

"I'm sorry, I can't accept your money. The meal's on me."

"That's terrible, please tell me what happened so I can make sure it never happens again."

It's completely natural to have trouble saying "It's my fault." That's human. But those three words are going to make your angry customers much happier. So you're going to have to say them. And you're going to have to sound like you mean it.

So start practicing.

Say "It's my fault" a hundred times one morning in the shower, until it starts to sound like syllabic nonsense. Then you'll be able to say it on demand.

One more point. You may think that admitting fault is a strict no-no that can get you sued. This is nonsense. The way to avoid getting sued is *not to have people who are mad at you*. The best way to do this is to admit fault and *fix the damn problem*.

～

6. Practice puppetry

The angry diner owner clearly took things very personally, in a way that the locksmith didn't. When an irate customer is complaining or venting, it's easy to get defensive.

You can never win these arguments, and if you take them personally, it's going to be a million times worse. This is when you start to hear business owners saying, "I don't want an asshole like you for a customer!" They get excited about their Pyrrhic victory. Wow, isn't it great? When you're a small business owner, you get to fire your customers. Charming.

The bottom line is that this is not good for business, and it's not even good for your emotional well-being. When you win a victory with a customer by firing them, you still end up feeling riled up and angry, they'll get their money back from the credit card company anyway, and they'll tell a dozen friends. As Patrick McKenzie writes, "You will never win an argument with your customer" (`kalzumeus.com/2007/02/16/how-to-deal-with-abusive-customers/`).

There is only one way to survive angry customers emotionally: you have to realize that they're not angry at you; they're angry at your business, and you just happen to be a convenient representative of that business.

And since they're treating you like a puppet, an iconic stand-in for the real business, you need to treat yourself as a puppet, too.

Pretend you're a puppeteer. The customer is yelling at the puppet. They're not yelling at you. They're angry with the puppet.

Your job is to figure out, "Gosh, what can I make the puppet say that will make this person a happy customer?"

You're just a puppeteer. You're not a party to the argument. When the customer says, "What the hell is wrong with you people," they're just playing a role (in this case, they're quoting Tom Smykowski in the movie *Office Space*). You, too, get to play a role. "I'm sorry. It's my fault." Figure out what to make the puppet do that will make them happy and stop taking it so dang personally.

~

7. Greed will get you nowhere

Recently, I was talking with the people who have been doing most of the customer service for Fog Creek over the last year, and I asked what methods they found most effective for dealing with angry customers.

"Frankly," they said, "we have pretty nice customers. We haven't really had any angry customers."

Well, OK, we do have nice customers, but it seems rather unusual that in a year of answering the phones, *nobody* was angry. I thought the *nature* of working at a call center was dealing with angry people all day long.

"Nope. Our customers are nice."

Here's what I think. I think that our customers are nice because they're not worried. They're not worried because we have a ridiculously liberal return policy: "We don't want your money if you're not amazingly happy."

Customers know that they have nothing to fear. They have the power in the relationship. So they don't get abusive.

The no-questions-asked 90-day money-back guarantee was one of the best decisions we ever made at Fog Creek. Try this: use Fog Creek Copilot for a full twenty-four hours, call up three months later, and say, "Hey guys, I need $5 for a cup of coffee. Give me back my money from that Copilot day pass," and we'll give it back to you. Try calling on the 91st or 92nd or 203rd day. You'll still get it back. We really don't want your money if you're not satisfied. I'm pretty sure we're running the only job listing service around that will refund your money just because your ad didn't work. This is unheard of, but it means we get a lot more ad listings, because there's nothing to lose.

Over the last six years or so, letting people return software has cost us 2%.

2%.

And you know what? Most customers pay with credit cards, and if we didn't refund their money, a bunch of them would have called their bank. This is called a chargeback. They get their money back, we pay a chargeback fee, and if this happens too often, our processing fees go up.

Know what our chargeback rate is at Fog Creek?

0%.

I'm not kidding.

If we were tougher about offering refunds, the only thing we would possibly have done is piss a few customers off, customers who would have ranted and whined on their blogs. We wouldn't even have kept more of their money.

I know of software companies who are very explicit on their web site that you are not entitled to a refund under any circumstances, but the truth is, if you call them up, they will eventually return your money because they know that if they don't, your credit card company *will*. This is the worst of both worlds. You end up refunding the money anyway, and you don't get to give potential customers the warm and fuzzy feeling of knowing Nothing Can Possibly Go Wrong, so they hesitate before buying. Or they don't buy at all.

~

8. (Bonus!) Give customer service people a career path

The last important lesson we learned here at Fog Creek is that you need very highly qualified people talking to customers. A salesperson at Fog Creek needs to have significant experience with the software development process and needs to be able to explain why FogBugz works the way it does, and why it makes software development teams function better. A tech support person at Fog Creek can't get by on canned answers to common questions, because we've eliminated the common questions by fixing the software, so tech support here has to *actually troubleshoot*, which often means debugging.

Many qualified people get bored with front-line customer service, and I'm OK with that. To compensate for this, I don't hire people into those positions without an explicit career path. Here at Fog Creek, customer support is just the first year of a three-year management training program that includes a master's degree in technology management at Columbia University. This allows us to get ambitious, smart geeks on a terrific career path talking to customers and solving their problems. We end up paying quite a bit more than average for these positions (especially when you consider $25,000 a year in tuition), but we get far more value out of them, too.

part eight

Releasing Software

thirty-three

PICKING A SHIP DATE

One of the best reasons to make a detailed schedule is because it gives you an excuse to cut features. If there's no way to make the ship date *and* implement Bob's Sing-Along MP3 Chat feature, it's easy to cut that feature without making Bob feel bad.

So my basic rules for software release cycles are

1. Set a ship date, which might as well be arbitrary.

2. Make a list of features and sort them out by priority.

3. Cut low-priority features every time you slip so as to make the date.

If you do this well, you'll soon discover that you don't regret the features that you cut. They're usually kind of dumb. If they are so important, you can do them next time. It's like editing. If you ever want to write a brilliant 750-word essay, start by writing a 1,500-word essay and then edit.

One way to screw this up, by the way, is forgetting to do features *in order of priority*. If you aren't careful, your programmers are going to do features in order of fun, and you won't be able to ship *or* cut features because all the programmers were busy writing Karaoke Recalc before they even got the menus to work, and now here it is, six months after the day you wanted to ship, and you have one *hell* of an easter egg but no functionality.

So the obvious question is, how do you pick a ship date?

It's conceivable that you have outside constraints. The stock market is switching from fractions to decimals on such-and-such a date, and if you haven't got the new software ready, your firm will be forced out of business, and you personally will be taken out behind the loading docks and shot in the head. Or maybe a new version of the Linux kernel is coming out soon with yet *another* all-new system to implement packet filtering; all your customers are getting it; and your existing application won't run on it. OK, for those people, your ship date is easy to figure out. You can stop reading this article now. Go cook a nice dinner for your loved ones.

Bye, now!

But how should the rest of us pick a ship date?

There are three approaches you could take:

1. **Frequent small releases.** This is the Extreme Programming approach, and it is most appropriate for small-team projects with a small number of customers, such as in-house IT development.

2. **Every 12 to 18 months.** This is typical of shrink-wrapped software products, desktop applications, etc., where you have larger teams and thousands or millions of customers.

3. **Every 3 to 5 years.** This is typical of huge software systems and platforms that are worlds unto themselves. Operating systems, .NET, Oracle, and for some reason Mozilla fall into this category. They often have thousands of developers (VS .NET had fifty people on the *installer* team) and enormously complex interactions to other shipping software that can't be allowed to break.

Here are some of the things you need to think about when deciding how often to release software.

Short releases get customer feedback fast. Sometimes the best way to work with a customer is to show them code, let them try it out, and immediately incorporate their feedback into a build that you give them the very next day. You won't waste a year developing a complicated system with lots of features that nobody uses, because you'll be so busy doing things that customers are requesting right now. **If you have a small number of customers, prefer frequent small releases.** The size of each release should be the minimum chunk that does something useful.

Several years ago I was assigned to develop a web content management system for MTV. The requirements called for a database-backed system with templates, and a complete workflow system that allowed unpaid MTV stringers at colleges across the country to input information about clubs, record stores, radio stations, and concerts. "How are you building the site now?" I asked.

"Oh, we just do it all manually with BBEdit," they told me. "Sure, there are thousands of pages, but BBEdit has a really good global-find-and-replace function . . . "

I figured the whole system would take six months to deliver. "But let me suggest something else. Let's get the templating stuff working first. I can get you that in three months, and it will save tons of manual work right away. Once that's working, we'll start in on the workflow component; in the meantime, you can continue to do workflow with e-mail."

They agreed. It sounded like a great idea. Guess what? Once I delivered the templating feature, they realized that they didn't really need workflow that much. And the templating turned out to be useful for lots of other web sites that didn't need workflow, either. So we never built workflow, saving three months that I used to enhance the templating feature, which turned out to be more useful.

Some types of customers don't appreciate being "guinea pigs" in this fashion. Generally, people who buy off-the-shelf software don't want to be part of a Grand Development Experiment; they want something that *anticipates* their needs. As a customer, the only thing better than getting feature requests done quickly is getting them *instantaneously* because they're already in the product, because it was designed thoughtfully and extensively usability and beta tested before being inflicted on the world. **If you have (or want) a large number of paying customers, prefer less frequent releases.**

If you ship an anemic commercial program just to get something out the door so you can "start listening to customers," what you'll hear those customers saying is, "It doesn't do very much," which you might think is OK. Hey, it's 1.0. But then if you release 2.0 four months later, everybody's going to think, "*That* feeble program? What, am I supposed to keep evaluating it every four months just to see if it's gotten better yet?!" And in fact, five years down the line, people will still remember their first impression of 1.0, and it will be almost impossible to get them to reevaluate. Think about what happened to poor Marimba. They launched their company with infinite VC in the days of hyper-Java hype, having lured the key developers from the Java team at Sun. They had a

CEO, Kim Polese, who was *brilliant* at public relations; when she was marketing Java, she had Danny Hillis making speeches about how Java was *the next step in human evolution*; George Gilder wrote these breathless articles about how Java was going to completely upturn the very *nature* of human civilization. Compared to Java, we were to believe, monotheism, for example, was just a *wee blip*. Polese is *that good*. So when Marimba Castanet launched, it probably had more unearned hype than any product in history, but the developers had only been working on it for a total of . . . four months. We all downloaded it and discovered that—ta-da!—it was a list box that downloaded software. (What do you expect from four months of development?) Big whoop. The disappointment was so thick you could cut it with butter. And here it is, six years later, ask anybody what Castanet is, and they'll tell you it's a list box that downloads software. Hardly anyone bothered to reevaluate it, and Marimba has had six *years* to write code; I'm sure it's just the coolest thing now but, honestly, who has time to find out? Let me tell you a little secret: our strategy for CityDesk is to avoid massive PR until 2.0 is out. *That's* the version that we want everybody on earth to get their first impressions from. In the meantime, we'll do quiet guerilla marketing, and anybody who finds it will discover that it's a completely spiffy program that solves a lot of problems, but Arnold Toynbee won't have to rewrite anything.

With most commercial software, you'll discover that the process of designing, prototyping, integrating, fixing bugs, running full alpha and beta cycles, creating documentation, and so forth takes six to nine months. In fact, if you try to do a full release every year, you only have time for about three months' worth of new code development. Software that is upgraded annually usually doesn't feel like it has enough new features to justify the upgrade. (Corel Photo-Paint and Intuit QuickBooks are particularly egregious examples of this; they have a new "major" version every year that is rarely worth buying.) As a result, many people have learned by now to skip every other release. You don't want your customers getting in that habit. If you stretch out your schedule to fifteen or eighteen months between releases, you get six months of new features instead of three months' worth, which makes your upgrade a lot more compelling.

OK, if fifteen months is so good, wouldn't twenty-four months be better? Maybe. Some companies can get away with it, if they are major leaders in their category. Photoshop seems to get away with it. But as soon as an application starts to feel old, people stop buying it because they are expecting that new version Any Day Now. This can cause serious cash flow problems for a software business. And of course, you may have competitors nipping at your heels.

For large platform software—operating systems, compilers, web browsers, DBMSs—the hardest part of the development process is maintaining compatibility with thousands or millions of existing applications or hardware. When a new version of Windows comes out, you very rarely hear about backward-compatibility problems. The only way they can achieve this is with insane amounts of testing that make the construction of the Panama Canal seem like a weekend do-it-yourself project. Given the typical three-year cycle between major Windows releases, almost all of that time is spent in the boring integration and testing phase, not writing new features. Releasing new versions any more often than that is just not realistic. And it would drive people crazy. Third-party software and hardware developers would simply revolt if they had to test against lots of little incremental releases of an operating system. **For systems with millions of customers and millions of integration points, prefer rare releases.** You can do it like Apache: one release at the beginning of the Internet Bubble and one release at the end. Perfect.

If you have a lot of validation and unit tests, and if you write your software carefully, you may get to the point where any daily build is *almost* high enough quality to ship. This is certainly something to strive for. Even if you're planning the next release for three years from now, the competitive landscape may suddenly change, and there may be a good reason to do a quick interim release to react to a competitor. When your wife is about to give birth, it's not really a good idea to take apart your car's engine. Instead, build a new one on the side and don't hook it up until it's perfect.

But don't overestimate what you can accomplish by keeping high-quality daily builds. Even if you are permanently at zero bugs, if your software has to run In The Wild, you're never going to find all the compatibility bugs and Windows 95 bugs and It-Doesn't-Work-With-Large-Fonts-Turned-On bugs until you do a few betas, and there is no realistic way to do a beta cycle in less than eight weeks.

One final thought. If your software is delivered as a service over the Web, like eBay or PayPal, theoretically there's nothing to stop you from frequent small releases, but this might not be the best thing to do. Remember the cardinal rule of usability: an application is usable if it behaves the way that the user *expected* it to behave. If you keep changing things around every week, it won't be so predictable, so it won't be so usable. (And don't think you can get around this by having one of those annoying screens with a paragraph of text saying "Warning! The UI has changed!" Nobody reads those.) From a usability perspective, a better approach would probably be less frequent releases that include a bunch of changes all at once, where you make an effort to change the visuals of the whole site so that it all looks weird and users intuit that things have changed a lot and they have to be careful.

thirty-four

CAMELS AND RUBBER DUCKIES

Wednesday, December 15, 2004

You've just released your latest photo-organizing software. Through some mechanism that will be left as an exercise to the reader, you've managed to actually let people know about it. Maybe you have a popular blog or something. Maybe Walt Mossberg wrote a rave review in the *Wall Street Journal*.

One of the biggest questions you're going to be asking now is, "How much should I charge for my software?" When you ask the experts, they don't seem to know. Pricing is a deep, dark mystery, they tell you. The biggest mistake software companies make is charging too little, so they don't get enough income, and they have to go out of business. An even bigger mistake, yes, even bigger than the biggest mistake, is charging too much, so they don't get enough customers, and they have to go out of business. Going out of business is not good because everybody loses their job, and you have to go work at Wal-Mart as a greeter, earning minimum wage and being forced to wear a polyester uniform all day long.

So if you like cotton uniforms, you better get this right.

The answer is really complicated. I'm going to start with a little economic theory, and then I'm going to tear the theory to bits, and when I'm finished, you'll know a lot more about pricing, and you still won't know how much to charge for your software, but that's just the nature of pricing. If you can't be bothered to read this, just charge $0.05 for your software, unless it does bug tracking, in which case charge $30,000,000 for it.

Now. Where was I.

~

Some economic theory

Imagine, for the moment, that your software costs $199. Why $199? Well, because I have to start somewhere. We'll try other numbers real soon now. For now, imagine that you charge $199 and that gets you 250 customers.

Let me plot that:

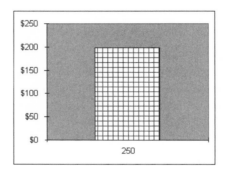

This little chart I made means that if you charge $199, 250 people will buy your software. (As you see, economists are very odd people, and they like to put the quantity sold on the x-axis with the price on the y-axis. If 250 people bought your software, it must mean that you charged $199!)

What would happen if you raised the price to $249?

Some of the people who might have been willing to pay $199 are going to think $249 is too much, so they'll drop out.

Obviously, people who wouldn't even buy it for $199 are *certainly* not going to buy it at the higher price.

If 250 people bought at $199, we must assume that *fewer* than 250 people would buy it at $249. Let's guess, oh, 200:

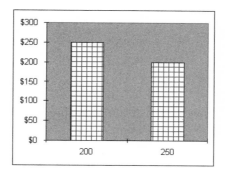

What if we charged *less*? Say, $149? Well, everyone who would buy it for $199 will *certainly* buy it for $149, and there will probably be even more people who think $149 is affordable, so let's say we could sell 325 copies at $149:

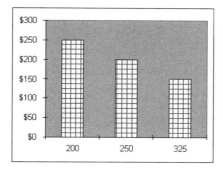

And so on and so forth:

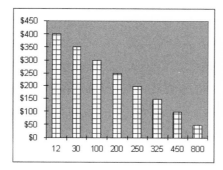

In fact, rather than graphing a few discrete points here, let's draw the complete curve that includes all these points, and while I'm at it, I'll fix the *x*-axis so it's to scale:

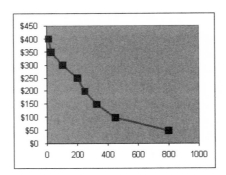

Now you can tell me any price between $50 and $400, and I'll tell you how many people will buy your software at that price. What we have here is a classic *demand curve*, and the demand curve is always downward sloping, because the more you charge, the fewer the people willing to buy your software.

These numbers are not, of course, real. The only thing I'm asking you to believe, so far, is that the demand curve is downward sloping.

(If it's still bothering you that I put the quantity on the *x*-axis and the price on the *y*-axis, when clearly the quantity is a function of the price, not the other way around, please take it up with Augustin Cournot. He probably has a blog by now.)

So how much should you charge?

"Uh, $50, because then I sell the most units!"

No no no. You're not trying to maximize *units*, you're trying to maximize *profits*.

Let's calculate profits.

Assume each unit of software that you sell costs you an **incremental** $35.

Maybe it cost you $250,000 to develop the software in the first place, but that's a sunk cost. We don't care about that anymore, because the $250,000 is the same whether you sell 1,000 units or 0. Sunk. Kiss it goodbye. Set any price you want, the $250,000 is gone and therefore not relevant any more.

At this point, all you can worry about is the incremental cost of selling *each additional* unit. That might include shipping and handling, that might include tech support, bank service charges, CD duplication, and shrink-wrapping, whatever; I'm going to be really hand-wavy here and use $35 as my incremental cost.

Now we can whip out our handy-dandy copy of VisiCalc:

	A	B	C	D	E
1	Quantity	Price	Incr. Cost	Unit Profit	Total Profit
2				(Price - Incr Cost)	(Unit Profit x Quantity)
3	12	$399	$35	$364	$4,368
4	30	$349	$35	$314	$9,420
5	100	$299	$35	$264	$26,400
6	200	$249	$35	$214	$42,800
7	250	$199	$35	$164	$41,000
8	325	$149	$35	$114	$37,050
9	450	$99	$35	$64	$28,800
10	800	$49	$35	$14	$11,200
11					

Here's how to read that spreadsheet. Each row is a scenario. Row 3: *if* we were to charge $399, *then* we would sell 12 copies, making $364 profit *per copy*, for a total profit of $4,368.

NOW WE'RE GETTING SOMEWHERE!

This is really cool. I think we're on the verge of solving the problem of how much to charge for software! I'M SO EXCITED!

The reason I'm so excited is it looks like if you plot price against profit, you get a nice curve with a big hump in the middle! And we all know what humps mean! Humps mean local maxima! Or camels. But here they mean local maxima!

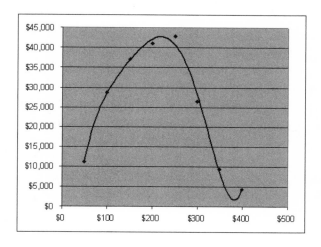

In this chart, the actual data is shown as little diamonds, and I've asked Excel to draw a nice polynomial trendline on top. So now all I have to do is drop a line straight down from the peak of the hump to find out the price I should charge to make a maximal amount of profit:

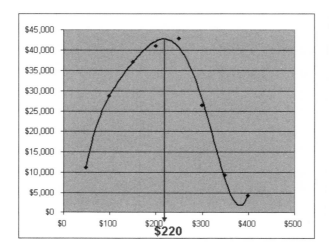

"O frabjous day! Callooh! Callay!" I chortle. We have found the optimum price, $220, and that's how much you should charge for your software. Thanks for your time.

Ahem.

Thank you for your time! Nothing more to see here! Move along now!

You're not leaving.

I see.

Some of the more observant members of my audience have detected that I might have something more to say other than "$220."

Well, maybe. There's just a tiny little loose end I left untied, which I might as well tie up now if you're all still up for it. OK? OK!

You see, by setting the price at $220, we managed to sell, let's say, 233 copies of the software, at a total profit of $43,105, which is all good and fine, but something is distracting me: all those people who were all ready to pay more, like those twelve fine souls who would have paid a full $399, and yet, we're only charging them $220 just like everyone else!

The difference between $399 and $220, i.e., $179, is called *consumer surplus*. It's the extra value that those rich consumers got from their purchase that they would have been perfectly happy to do without.

It's sort of like if you were all set to buy that new merino wool sweater, and you *thought* it was going to cost $70, which is well worth it, and when you got to Banana Republic, it was on sale for only $50! Now you have an extra $20 in found money that you would have been perfectly happy to give to the Banana Republicans!

Yipes!

That bothers good capitalists. Gosh darn it, if you're *willing to do without it*, well, give it to me! I can put it to good use, buying an SUV or a condo or a Mooney or a yacht or one of those other things capitalists buy!

In economist jargon, capitalists want to *capture the consumer surplus*.

Let's do this. Instead of charging $220, let's ask each of our customers if they are rich or if they are poor. If they say they're rich, we'll charge them $349. If they say they're poor, we'll charge them $220.

Now how much do we make? Back to Excel:

	A	B	C	D	E
1	Customers	Price	Qty Sold	Unit Profit	Total Profit
2	Rich	$349	42	$314	$13,188
3	Poor	$220	191	$185	$35,335
4				TOTAL:	$48,523

Notice the quantities: we're still selling the same 233 copies, but the richest forty-two customers, who were all willing to spend $349 or more, are being asked to spend $349. And our profits just went up! From $43K to about $48K! NICE!

Capture me some more of that consumer surplus stuff!

But wait, that's not all. After selling all these 233 copies, I felt kind of bad about the people who were only willing to spend $99. After all, if I could sell a few more copies to those guys at $99, I'd still be making *some* money, since my marginal cost is only $35.

What if we called up all the customers who said, "No thanks" at $220 and offered them the software at $99?

At $99, we have 450 potential customers, but don't forget that 233 of them already paid full price, leaving us with 217 extra customers who just wouldn't go along with the program and pay the full price:

	A	B	C	D	E
1	Customers	Price	Qty Sold	Unit Profit	Total Profit
2	Rich	$349	42	$314	$13,188
3	Poor	$220	191	$185	$35,335
4	Callback & Beg	$99	217	$64	$13,888
5				TOTAL:	$62,411
6					

Babymosesinabasket, I think we just made $62K in profit! All in all, an extra twenty thousand buckeroos, cash spendable money, which goes a loooong way toward a down payment on that fishing boat you've had your eye on. All from the power of **segmentation**: separating your customers into different groups according to how much they are willing to pay, and extracting the maximal consumer surplus from each customer. Holy Segments, Batman, how much money could we make if we ask every customer to *tell us* their maximum willingness to pay and then charge them that?

	A	B	C	D
1	Qty Sold	Price	Unit Profit	Total Profit
2	12	$ 399	364	$ 4,368
3	18	$ 349	314	$ 5,652
4	70	$ 299	264	$ 18,480
5	100	$ 249	214	$ 21,400
6	50	$ 199	164	$ 8,200
7	75	$ 149	114	$ 8,550
8	125	$ 99	64	$ 8,000
9	350	$ 49	14	$ 4,900
10			TOTAL	$ 79,550

Surreal! Almost $80K! That's almost double the profits we made having just one price! Capturing the consumer surplus is clearly quite profitable. Even the 350 annoying people who only want to give me $49 each are making some contribution to the profits. All these customers are happy because we're asking them to pay the amount they were willing to pay already, so it's not like we're ripping anyone off. Kind of.

Here are some examples of segmentation you're probably familiar with:

- Senior citizen discounts, since older people tend to be living on a "fixed income" and are willing to pay less than working-age adults.

- Cheap afternoon movie matinees (useful only to people without jobs).

- Bizarre airfares, where everyone seems to be paying a different price. The secret about airfares is that people who are flying on business get their company to reimburse them, so they couldn't care less how much the ticket costs, while leisure travelers are spending their own money, and they won't go if it costs too much.

  Of course, the airlines can't just *ask* you if you're travelling on business, because pretty quickly everyone would catch on and lie to get the cheaper fares. But business travelers almost always travel on weekdays, and they *hate* spending a weekend away from home. So the airlines instituted policies that if you're staying over a Saturday night, you're probably not travelling on business, and they give you much cheaper fares if you stay over a Saturday night.

There are more subtle ways to segment. You know those grocery coupons you see in the paper? The ones that get you 25 cents off a box of Tide detergent if you clip them out and remember to bring them to the store? Well, the trouble with grocery coupons is that there's so much manual labor involved in clipping them, and sorting them out, and remembering which ones to use, and choosing brands based on which coupons you have, and so on, and the net effect is that if you clip coupons, you're probably working for about $7 an hour.

Now, if you're retired and living off of social security, $7 an hour sounds pretty good, so you do it, but if you're a stock analyst at Merrill Lynch getting paid $12,000,000 a year to say nice things about piece-of-junk Internet companies, working for $7 an hour is a joke, and you're not going to clip coupons. Heck, in one hour you could issue "buy" recommendations on *ten* piece-of-junk Internet companies! So coupons are a way for consumer products companies to charge two different prices and effectively segment their market into two. Mail-in rebates are pretty much the same as coupons, with some other twists like the fact that they reveal your address, so you can be direct-marketed to in the future.

272 More from Joel on Software

There are other ways to segment. You can market your products under different brand names (Old Navy vs. Gap vs. Banana Republic) and hope that the rich people conveniently remember to buy their clothes at the Banana while the po' people go to Old Navy. In case there was any risk of people forgetting and going to the wrong store, the Banana Republic stores are conveniently situated in neighborhoods full of $2,000,000 condos, while the Old Navy store is near the train station where you haul your poor tired ass back to New Jersey after a day of hard manual labor.

In the world of software, you can just make a version of your product called "Professional" and another version called "Home" with some inconsequential differences, and hope that the corporate purchasers (again, the people who are not spending their own money) will be too embarrassed at the thought of using Windows XP Home Edition *at work* and they'll buy the Professional edition. Home Edition at work? Somehow that feels like coming to work in your pajamas! Ick!

Quick trick: if you're going to try to pull the segmenting idea, you're probably going to be better off offering a *discount* to certain users rather than trying to charge some users a *premium*. Nobody likes feeling ripped off: people would rather buy a $199 product for $99 than a $59 product for $79. Theoretically, people should be rational. $79 is less than $99. Realistically, they hate feeling like someone is ripping them off. They'd much rather feel like they're getting a bargain than feel like they're getting gouged.

ANYWAY.

That was the easy part.

The hard part is that everything I just told you is sort of wrong.

Working my way backward, this business about segmenting? It pisses people off. People want to feel they're paying a fair price. They don't want to think they're paying extra just because they're not clever enough to find the magic coupon code. The airline industry got really, really good at segmenting and ended up charging literally a different price to every single person on the plane. As a result, most people felt they weren't getting the best deal, and they didn't like the airlines. When a new alternative arose in the form of low-cost carriers (Southwest, JetBlue, etc.), customers had no loyalty whatsoever to the legacy airlines that had been trying to pick their pockets for all those years.

And God help you if an A-list blogger finds out that your premium printer is identical to the cheap printer, with the speed inhibitor turned off.

So, while segmenting can be a useful tool to "capture consumer surplus," it can have significant negative implications for the long-term image of your product. Many a small software vendor has seen their revenues go up and the amount of customer bickering about price go way down when they eliminated coupons, discounts, deals, multiple versions, and tiers. Somehow, it seems like customers would rather pay $100 when everyone else is paying $100 than pay $79 if they know there's someone out there who got it for $78. Heck, GM made a *whole car company*, Saturn, based on the principle that the offered price is fair and you don't have to bargain.

Even assuming you're willing to deal with a long-term erosion of customer goodwill caused by blatant price discrimination, segmentation is just not that easy to pull off. First of all, as soon as your customers find out you're doing it, they'll lie about who they are:

- Frequent business travelers rearranged their tickets to include dual Saturday-night stays. For example, a consultant living in Pittsburgh and working in Seattle Monday through Thursday would buy a *two-week trip* from Pittsburgh to Seattle and then a weekend trip home in the middle. Both trips included Saturday night stays, it was the same flights they would have taken anyway, just much cheaper.

- Got an academic discount? Everyone who is even *vaguely* related to someone *vaguely* associated with academia will start using it.

- If your customers talk among themselves, they're going to find out about the price you're offering the other people, and you'll find yourself forced to match the lowest prices for everyone. *Especially* the big corporate purchasers who theoretically should have the "maximum willingness to pay" since they represent rich customers. Corporations have full-time purchasing departments staffed with people whose *entire job* is whittling down prices. These people go to *conferences* where they learn how to get the best price. They practice saying "No. Cheaper." *all day long in front of mirrors*. Your sales guy doesn't stand a snowflake's chance in hell.

There are two forms of segmentation that slightly-too-clever software companies engage in that are not such great ideas:

Bad idea #1: Site licenses

The opposite of segmentation, really. I have certain competitors that do this: they charge small customers per-user but then there's an "unlimited" license at a fixed price. This is nutty, because you're giving the biggest price break *precisely* to the largest customers, the ones who would be willing to pay you the *most money*. Do you really want IBM to buy your software for their 400,000 employees and pay you $2,000? Hmm?

As soon as you have an "unlimited" price, you are instantly giving a gigantic gift of consumer surplus to the least price-sensitive customers who should have been the cash cows of your business.

Bad idea #2: "How much money do you have?" pricing

This is the kind used by software startups founded by ex-Oracle salesmen where the price isn't on the web site anywhere. No matter how much you search to find the price, all you get is a form to provide your name, address, phone number, and fax number, for some reason, not that they're ever going to fax you anything.

It's pretty obvious here that the plan is to have a salesman call you up and figure out how much you're worth, and then charge you that much. Perfect segmentation!

This doesn't work so good either. First of all, the low-end buyers are just going to move on. They will assume that if the price isn't listed, they can't afford it. Second, the people who don't like salesmen harassing them will just move on.

Worse, as soon as you send a message that your price is negotiable, you're going to end up *reverse segmenting*. Here's why: the big companies you sell to, the ones who should be willing to give you the most money, are incredibly sophisticated about purchasing. They'll notice that your salesperson is working on commission, and they'll know that the salesperson's got quarterly quotas, and they'll know that both the salesperson and the company are going to be in*cred*ibly desperate to

make a sale at the end of the quarter (the salesperson to get their commission, and the company to avoid getting their knees shot off by their
VCs or Wall Street). So the big customers will always wait until the last
day in the quarter and end up getting a ridiculously good price that
somehow involves weird accounting shenanigans so the company can
book a lot of revenue that they're never really going to get.

So, don't do site licenses, and don't try to make up prices as you go
along.

BUT WAIT!

Do you *really* want to maximize profits? I glossed over something.
You don't necessarily care about maximizing profits this month. You
really care about maximizing all your profits, over time, in the future as
well. Technically, you want to maximize the NPV of the stream of all
future profits (without ever having your cash reserves dip below zero).

Diversion: What's an NPV?

What's worth more, $100 today or $100 in one year?

Obviously $100 today, because you can invest it, say, in bonds, and at the
end of the year you'll have, like, $102.25.

So when you're comparing the value of $100 in one year to $100 today,
you need to *discount* the $100 based on some interest rate. If the interest
rate is 2.25%, for example, that $100 in the future should be discounted to
$97.80, which is called the *net present value* (NPV) of $100 one year in the
future.

Go even further into the future, and you need to discount even more. $100
in five years, at today's interest rates, is worth only $84 today. $84 is the
net present value of $100 in five years.

Which would you rather earn?

Option one: $5,000, $6,000, $7,000 over the next three years

Option two: $4,000, $6,000, $10,000 over the next three years

Option two sounds like a better deal, even after discounting the future earnings. If you take the second option, it's like investing $1,000 in year one and getting $3,000 back two years later, which is a very respectable investment!

The reason I bring this up is because software is priced three ways: free, cheap, and dear:

1. **Free.** Open source, etc. Not relevant to the current discussion. Nothing to see here. Move along.

2. **Cheap.** $10–$1,000, sold to a very large number of people at a low price without a sales force. Most shrink-wrapped consumer and small business software falls into this category.

3. **Dear.** $75,000–$1,000,000, sold to a handful of rich big companies using a team of slick salespeople that do six months of intense PowerPoint just to get one goddamn sale. The Oracle model.

All three methods work fine.

Notice the gap? There's no software priced between $1,000 and $75,000. I'll tell you why. The minute you charge more than $1,000, you need to get *serious* corporate signoffs. You need a line item in their budget. You need purchasing managers and CEO approval and competitive bids and paperwork. So you need to send a salesperson out to the customer to do PowerPoint, with his airfare, golf course memberships, and $19.95 porn movies at the Ritz Carlton. And with all this, the cost of making one successful sale is going to average about $50,000. If you're sending salespeople out to customers and charging less than $75,000, you're losing money.

The joke of it is, big companies protect themselves so well against the risk of buying something expensive that they actually drive up the cost of the expensive stuff, from $1,000 to $75,000, which mostly goes towards the cost of jumping all the hurdles that they set up to ensure that no purchase can possibly go wrong.

Now, a quick glance around the Fog Creek web site reveals that I'm firmly in camp #2. Why? Selling software at a low price means that I can get thousands of customers right away, some small, some large. And all those customers are going to be out there using my software and recommending it to their friends. When those customers grow, they'll buy more licenses. When people working at those customers' companies move to new companies, they'll recommend my software to those new companies. Effectively, I am willing to accept a lower price now in exchange for creating grassroots support. I see the low price of FogBugz as being an investment in advertising that I expect will pay off many times over in the long run. So far, it's working very well: FogBugz sales have grown more than 100% for three years without marketing, solely based on word of mouth and existing customers buying additional licenses.

By comparison, look at BEA. Big company. Big price tag. The price alone means almost nobody has experience with their product. Nobody comes out of college and starts a dot-com using BEA technology, because they couldn't afford BEA technology in college. A lot of other good technologies have doomed themselves with high prices: Apple WebObjects was irrelevant as an application server because it started at $50,000. Who cared how good it was? Nobody ever used it! Anything made by Rational. The only way these products get into the hands of users is with an expensive full-frontal sales pitch. At these prices, the sales pitch is made to the executive, not the techie. The techies may well actively resist bad technology with good sales that the executives force down their throats. We have lots of FogBugz customers who have high-priced Remedy, Rational, or Mercury products sitting on the shelves after investments of well over $100,000, because that software isn't good enough to actually use. Then they buy a couple of thousand dollars worth of FogBugz, and that's the product they really use. The Rational salesperson is laughing at me, because I have $2,000 in the bank and he has $100,000. But I have far more customers than he does, and they're all using my product, and evangelizing it, and spreading it, while Rational customers either (a) don't use it or (b) use it and can't stand it. But he's still laughing at me from his forty-foot yacht while I play with rubber duckies in the bathtub. Like I said, *all three methods work fine.* But cheaper prices is like buying advertising and as such is an investment in the future.

OK.

Where was I.

Oh yeah, before I started frothing at the mouth, I was picking apart the logic of deriving a demand curve. When I walked you through that whole discussion of the demand curve, you were probably asking your-self, "How do I know how much people are willing to pay?"

You're right.

That's a problem.

You *can't* really find out what the demand curve is.

You can have focus groups and ask people, but they'll lie to you. Some people will lie to show off their generosity and wealth. "Heck, yeah, I'd buy a pair of $400 jeans in a New York Minute!" Other people will lie because they really want your thing and they think you'll decide to charge less money if they tell you a low number. "Blogging software? Hmm. I'd pay, at *most*, 38 cents."

Then you ask another focus group the next day, and this time, the first man to speak has a crush on a pretty woman in the group, and he wants to impress her, so he starts talking about how much his car cost and everyone is thinking Big Numbers. And the day after that, you serve Starbucks during the break, and while you're in the john everyone unbe-knownst to you gets into a side conversation about paying $4 for a cup of coffee, and they're in a real frugal mood when you ask them about their willingness to pay.

Then you finally get the focus group to agree that your software is worth $25 a month, and then you ask them how much they would pay for a permanent license and the same people just won't go a penny over $100. People *seriously* can't count.

Or you ask some aircraft designers how much they would pay and they sort of think $99 would be a maximum price, even though aircraft designers regularly use software that costs on the order of $3,000 a month without being aware of it, because someone else does the pur-chasing.

So from day to day, you get radically, and I mean *radically*, different answers when you ask people how much they're willing to pay for some-thing. The truth is, the only way to determine how much someone will pay for something is to put it up for sale, and see how many people actu-ally buy it.

Then you can try twiddling the prices to measure price sensitivity and try to derive the demand curve, but until you have something like 1,000,000 customers and you are absolutely sure that customer A will not find out you are offering a lower price to customer B, you will not get statistically meaningful responses.

There's a real strong tendency to assume that experiments done on large populations of people should work out just like experiments done with chemicals in a high school lab, but everyone who has ever tried to do experiments on people knows that you get wildly variable results that just aren't repeatable, and the only way you can be confident in your results is to carefully avoid ever doing the same experiment twice.

And, in fact, you can't even be sure that the demand curve is downward sloping.

The only reason we assumed that the demand curve is downward sloping is that we assumed things like "If Freddy is willing to buy a pair of sneakers for $130, he is *certainly* willing to buy those same sneakers for $20." Right? Ha! Not if Freddy is an American teenager! American teenagers would not be caught *dead* in $20 sneakers. It's, like, um, the *death penalty*? if you are wearing sneakers? that only cost $20 a pair? in school?

I'm not joking around here: prices send signals. Movies in my town cost, I think, $11. Criminy. There used to be a movie theatre that had movies for $3. Did anyone go there? **I DON'T THINK SO.** It's obviously just a dumping ground for lousy movies. Somebody is now at the bottom of the East River with $20 cement sneakers because they dared to tell the consumer which movies the industry thought were lousy.

You see, people tend to believe that *you get what you pay for*. The last time I needed a lot of hard drive space, I invested in some nice cheap hard drives allegedly designed by Mr. Porsche *himself* that went for about $1 a gigabyte. Within six months, all four had failed. Last week, I replaced them with Seagate Cheetah SCSI hard drives that cost about $4 a gigabyte because I've been running those since I started Fog Creek four years ago without a glitch. Chalk it up to "you get what you pay for."

There are just too many examples where you actually *do* get what you pay for, and the uninformed consumer is generally going to infer that the more expensive product is better. Buying a coffee maker? Want a really *good* coffee maker? You have two choices. Find the right issue of *Consumer Reports* in the library, or go to Williams-Sonoma and get the most expensive coffee maker they have there.

When you're setting a price, you're sending a signal. If your competitor's software ranges in price from about $100 to about $500, and you decide, heck, my product is about in the middle of the road, so I'll sell it for $300, well, what message do you think you're sending to your customers? You're telling them that you think your software is "eh." I have a better idea: charge $1,350. Now your customers will think, "Oh, man, that stuff has to be *the cat's whiskers* since they're charging *mad coin* for it!"

And then they won't buy it because the limit on the corporate AMEX is $500.

Misery.

The more you learn about pricing, the less you seem to know.

I've been nattering on about this topic for well over 5,000 words and I don't really feel like we're getting anywhere, you and I.

Some days it seems like it would be easier to be a taxi driver, with prices set by law. Or to be selling sugar. Plain ol' sugar. Yep. That would be sweet.

Take my advice, offered several pages back: charge $0.05 for your software. Unless it does bug tracking, in which case the correct price is $30,000,000. Thank you for your time, and I apologize for leaving you even less able to price software than you were when you started reading this.

part nine

Revising Software

thirty-five

FIVE WHYS

At 3:30 in the morning of January 10, 2008, a shrill chirping woke up our system administrator, Michael Gorsuch, asleep at home in Brooklyn. It was a text message from Nagios, our network monitoring software, warning him that something was wrong.

He swung out of bed, accidentally knocking over (and waking up) the dog, sleeping soundly in her dog bed, who, angrily, staggered out to the hallway, peed on the floor, and then returned to bed. Meanwhile Michael logged on to his computer in the other room and discovered that one of the three data centers he runs, in downtown Manhattan, was unreachable from the Internet.

This particular data center is in a secure building in downtown Manhattan, in a large facility operated by PEER 1. It has backup generators, several days of diesel fuel, and racks and racks of batteries to keep the whole thing running for a few minutes while the generators can be started. It has massive amounts of air conditioning, multiple high-speed connections to the Internet, and the kind of "right stuff" down-to-earth engineers who always do things the boring, plodding, methodical way instead of the flashy, cool, trendy way, so everything is pretty reliable.

Internet providers like PEER 1 like to guarantee the uptime of their services in terms of a Service Level Agreement, otherwise known as an SLA. A typical SLA might state something like "99.99% uptime." When you do the math, let's see, there are 525,949 minutes in a year (or 525,600 if you are in the cast of *Rent*), so that allows them 52.59 minutes of downtime per year. If they have any more downtime than that, the SLA usually provides for some kind of penalty, but honestly, it's often rather trivial . . . like, you get your money back for the minutes they were down.

I remember once getting something like $10 off the bill from a T1 provider because of a two-day outage that cost us thousands of dollars. SLAs can be a little bit meaningless that way, and given how low the penalties are, a lot of network providers just started advertising 100% uptime.

Within ten minutes, everything seemed to be back to normal, and Michael went back to sleep.

Until about 5:00 a.m. This time Michael called the PEER 1 Network Operations Center (NOC) in Vancouver. They ran some tests, started investigating, couldn't find anything wrong, and by 5:30 a.m., things seemed to be back to normal, but by this point, Michael was as nervous as a porcupine in a balloon factory.

At 6:15 a.m., the New York site lost all connectivity. PEER 1 couldn't find anything wrong on their end. Michael got dressed and took the subway into Manhattan. The server seemed to be up. The PEER 1 network connection was fine. The problem was something with the network switch. Michael temporarily took the switch out of the loop, connecting our router directly to PEER 1's router, and lo and behold, we were back on the Internet.

By the time most of our American customers got to work in the morning, everything was fine. Our European customers had already started e-mailing us to complain. Michael spent some time doing a postmortem and discovered that the problem was a simple configuration problem on the switch. There are several possible speeds that a switch can use to communicate (10, 100, or 1,000 megabits/second). You can either set the speed manually or let the switch automatically negotiate the highest speed that both sides can work with. The switch that failed had been set to autonegotiate. This usually works, but not always, and on the morning of January 10, it didn't.

Michael knew this could be a problem, but when he installed the switch, he had forgotten to set the speed, so the switch was still in the factory-default autonegotiate mode, which seemed to work fine. Until it didn't.

Michael wasn't happy. He sent me an e-mail:

I know that we don't officially have an SLA for On Demand, but I would like us to define one for internal purposes (at least). It's one way that I can measure if myself and the (eventual) sysadmin team are meeting the general goals for the business. I was in the slow process of writing up a plan for this, but want to expedite in light of this morning's mayhem.

An SLA is generally defined in terms of "uptime," so we need to define what "uptime" is in the context of On Demand. Once that is made clear, it'll get translated into policy, which will then be translated into a set of monitoring/reporting scripts, and will be reviewed on a regular interval to see if we are "doing what we say."

Good idea!

But there are some problems with SLAs. The biggest one is the lack of statistical meaningfulness when outages are so rare. We've had, if I remember correctly, two unplanned outages, including this one, since going live with FogBugz On Demand six months ago. Only one was our fault. Most well-run online services will have two, maybe three outages a year. With so few data points, the length of the outage starts to become really significant, and that's one of those things that's wildly variable. Suddenly, you're talking about how long it takes a human to get to the equipment and swap out a broken part. To get really high uptime, you can't wait for a human to switch out failed parts. You can't even wait for a human to figure out what went wrong: you have to have previously thought of every possible thing that can possibly go wrong, which is vanishingly improbable. It's the unexpected unexpecteds, not the expected unexpecteds, that kill you.

Really high availability becomes extremely costly. The proverbial "six nines" availability (99.9999% uptime) means no more than thirty seconds downtime per year. That's really kind of ridiculous. Even the people who claim that they have built some big multimillion dollar superduper ultra-redundant six nines system are gonna wake up one day, I don't know when, but they will, and something completely unusual will have gone wrong in a completely unexpected way, three EMP bombs, one at each data center, and they'll smack their heads and have fourteen days of outage.

Think of it this way: if your six nines system goes down mysteriously *just once*, and it takes you an hour to figure out the cause and fix it, well, you've just blown your downtime budget for the next *century*. Even the most notoriously reliable systems, like AT&T's long distance service, have had long outages (six hours in 1991) that put them at a rather embarrassing three nines . . . and AT&T's long distance service is considered "carrier grade," the gold standard for uptime.

Keeping Internet services online suffers from the problem of *black swans*. Nassim Taleb, who invented the term, defines it thus (www.edge. org/3rd_culture/taleb04/taleb_indexx.html): "A black swan is an outlier, an event that lies beyond the realm of normal expectations." Almost all Internet outages are unexpected unexpecteds: extremely low-probability outlying surprises. They're the kind of things that happen so rarely it doesn't even make sense to use normal statistical methods like "mean time between failure." What's the "mean time between catastrophic floods in New Orleans?"

Measuring the number of minutes of downtime per year does not predict the number of minutes of downtime you'll have the next year. It reminds me of commercial aviation today: the NTSB has done such a great job of eliminating all the common causes of crashes that nowadays, each commercial crash they investigate seems to be a crazy, one-off, black-swan outlier.

Somewhere between the "extremely unreliable" level of service, where it feels like stupid outages occur again and again and again, and the "extremely reliable" level of service, where you spend millions and millions of dollars getting an extra minute of uptime a year, there's a sweet spot, where all the expected unexpecteds have been taken care of. A single hard drive failure, which is expected, doesn't take you down. A single DNS server failure, which is expected, doesn't take you down. But the unexpected unexpecteds might. That's really the best we can hope for.

To reach this sweet spot, we borrowed an idea from Sakichi Toyoda, the founder of Toyota. He calls it *Five Whys*. When something goes wrong, you ask why, again and again, until you ferret out the root cause. Then you fix the root cause, not the symptoms.

Since this fit well with our idea of fixing everything two ways, we decided to start using five whys ourselves. Here's what Michael came up with:

Our link to PEER 1 NY went down.

- Why?—Our switch appears to have put the port in a failed state.
- Why?—After some discussion with the PEER 1 NOC, we speculate that it was quite possibly caused by an Ethernet speed/duplex mismatch.
- Why?—The switch interface was set to autonegotiate instead of being manually configured.
- Why?—We were fully aware of problems like this and have been for many years. But we do not have a written standard and verification process for production switch configurations.
- Why?—Documentation is often thought of as an aid for when the sysadmin isn't around or for other members of the operations team, whereas it should really be thought of as a checklist.

"Had we produced a written standard prior to deploying the switch and subsequently reviewed our work to match the standard, this outage would not have occurred," Michael wrote. "Or, it would occur once, and the standard would get updated as appropriate."

After some internal discussion, we all agreed that rather than imposing a statistically meaningless measurement and hoping that the mere measurement of something meaningless would cause it to get better, what we really needed was a process of continuous improvement. Instead of setting up an SLA for our customers, we set up a blog where we would document every outage in real time, provide complete post-mortems, ask the five whys, get to the root cause, and tell our customers what we're doing to prevent that problem in the future. In this case, the change is that our internal documentation will include detailed checklists for all operational procedures in the live environment.

Our customers can look at the blog to see what caused the problems and what we're doing to make things better, and, hopefully, they can see evidence of steadily improving quality.

In the meantime, our customer service folks have the authority to credit customers' accounts if they feel like they were affected by an outage. We let the customer decide how much they want to be credited, up to a whole month, because not every customer is even going to notice the outage, let alone suffer from it. I hope this system will improve our reliability to the point where the only outages we suffer are really the extremely unexpected black swans.

P.S. Yes, we want to hire another system administrator so Michael doesn't have to be the only one to wake up in the middle of the night.

thirty-six

SET YOUR PRIORITIES

WEDNESDAY, OCTOBER 12, 2005

It was getting time to stop futzing around with FogBugz 4.0 and start working on 5.0. We just shipped a big service pack, fixing a zillion tiny little bugs that nobody would ever come across (and introducing a couple of new tiny little bugs that nobody will ever come across), and it was time to start adding some gen-yoo-ine new features.

By the time we were ready to start development, we had enough ideas for improvement to occupy 1,700 programmers for a few decades. Unfortunately, all we have is three programmers, and we wanted to be shipping next fall, so there had to be some prioritization.

Before I tell you how we prioritized our list of features, let me tell you two ways *not* to do it.

Number one: if you ever find yourself implementing a feature simply because it has been promised to one customer, RED DANGER LIGHTS should be going off in your head. If you're doing things for one customer, either you've got a loose cannon salesperson or you're slipping dangerously down the slope towards consultingware. And there's nothing wrong with consultingware; it's a very comfortable slope to slip down, but it's just not as profitable as shrink-wrap software.

Shrink-wrap is the take-it-or-leave it model of software development. You develop software, wrap it in plastic, and customers either buy it or don't. They don't offer to buy it if you implement just one more feature. They don't call you up and negotiate features. You can't call up Microsoft and tell them, "Hey, I love that BAHTTEXT function you have in Excel for spelling out numbers in Thai, but I could really use an equivalent function for English. I'll buy Excel if you implement that function." Because if you did call up Microsoft, here is what they would say to you:

"Thank you for calling Microsoft. If you are calling with a designated four-digit advertisement code, press 1. For technical support on all Microsoft products, press 2. For Microsoft presales product licensing or program information, press 3. If you know the person at Microsoft you wish to speak to, press 4. To repeat, press star."

Notice? None of the choices was, "To negotiate what features need to be added to our products before you'll buy them, press 5."

Custom development is that murky world where a customer tells you what to build, and you say, "Are you sure?" and they say yes, and you make an absolutely beautiful spec and say, "Is this what you want?" and they say yes, and you make them sign the spec in indelible ink, nay, *blood*, and they do, and then you build that thing they signed off on, promptly, precisely, and exactly, and they see it and they are horrified and shocked, and you spend the rest of the week reading up on whether your E&O insurance is going to cover the legal fees for the lawsuit you've gotten yourself into or merely the settlement cost. Or, if you're really lucky, the customer will smile wanly and put your code in a drawer and never use it again and never call you back.

Somewhere in the middle is consultingware, where you pretend to be doing shrink-wrap while really doing custom development. Here's how consultingware works:

1. You're working as a wage slave writing code for a shoe company, and

2. The company needs shoe-shining software, so

3. You develop shoe-shining software in VB 3.0 using bits and pieces of JavaScript, Franz Lisp, and a FileMaker database running on an old Mac connected over the network using AppleScript, then

4. Everyone thinks it's the cat's whiskers, so, always having dreamed of starting your own software company and maybe being Bill Gates or perhaps even just Larry Ellison

5. You buy the rights to ShoeShiner 1.0 from your old company and get VC to start your own company, ShoeShiner LLC, marketing shoe-shining software, but

6. None of your beta testers can get it to work because of the obscure dependencies on AppleScript and the hard-coded IP addresses in the source code, so it takes a month to install at each client site, and

7. You have trouble getting clients, because your product is so expensive because of all the installation costs, including the vintage Macintosh IIci running System 7, which they have to buy on eBay from computer museums, so your VCs start to get really nervous,

8. Putting pressure on the sales guy,

9. Who finds out that one of your potential customers doesn't need a shoe-shining thing but he could really use trousers-pressing software, and

10. The sales guy, being a sales guy, sells him $100K worth of trousers-pressing software,

11. And now you spend six months writing a one-off "trousers-pressing module" for this client, which

12. No other client will ever need, thus, effectively,

13. For all intents and purposes, you've just spent a year raising VC so that you could work as a wage slave writing code for a trouser company; GOTO 1.

Sparky, I'm gonna have to strongly recommend clinging as strongly as possible to the shrink-wrap side of the equation. That's because shrink-wrap has no marginal costs for each additional customer, so you can essentially sell the same thing over and over again and make a lot more profit. Not only that, but you can lower the price, because you can spread your development costs out over a lot more customers, and lowering the price *gets you more customers* because more people will suddenly find your now-cheaper software worthwhile, and life is good and all is sweet.

Thus, if you ever find yourself implementing a feature simply because it has been promised to a customer, you're drifting over to the land of consultingware and custom development, which is a fine world to operate in if that's what you like, but it just doesn't have the profit potential of off-the-shelf commercial software.

Now, I'm not saying you shouldn't listen to your customers. I for one think that it's about time Microsoft actually implemented a version of the BAHTTEXT function for those of us who haven't yet joined the global economy and learned Thai and who still write checks using other currencies. And in fact, if you want to tell yourself that the best way to allocate your development resources is effectively to let your biggest customers "bid" on features, well, you can do that too, although you'll soon find that the kind of features that big, rich customers want are not the same as the kind of features that the mass market wants, and that feature you put in to handle Baht currency is not really helping you sell Excel to health spas in Scottsdale, Arizona, and in fact what you're really doing is letting your sales force pimp out your developers with the sole goal of maximizing their personal commissions.

The path to being Bill Gates, this is not.

Now, let me tell you the second way *not* to decide what features to implement. Don't do things just because they're inevitable. Inevitability is not a high enough bar. Let me explain.

Sometime during the first year of Fog Creek's operations, I was filing away some papers, and realized that I was all out of blue folders.

Now, I have a system. Blue folders are for clients. Manila folders are for employees. Red folders are receipts. Everything else is yellow. I needed a blue folder and had run out.

So I said to myself, "What the heck, I'm going to need a blue folder eventually anyway, I might as well go to Staples and buy some now."

Which was, of course, a waste of time.

In fact, when I thought about this later, I realized that for a long time, I had been doing dumb shit (that's a technical term) simply because I figured that eventually it would have to get done, so I might as well do it now.

I used this excuse to weed the garden, patch holes in the walls, sort out MSDN disks (by color, language, and number), etc., etc., when I should have been writing code or selling code, the only two things a startup really needs to do.

In other words, I found myself pretending that all nonoptional tasks were equally important, and therefore, since they were inevitable anyway, they could be done in any order! Ta-da!

But to be honest, I was just procrastinating.

What should I have done? Well, for starters, I could get over my fetish for having file folders all be the right color. It just doesn't make any difference. You don't have to color-code your files.

Oh, and those MSDN CD-ROMs? Toss them in a big box. PER-fect.

More importantly, I should have realized that "important" is not a binary thing, it's an analog thing. There are all kinds of different shades of important, and if you try to do everything, you'll never get anything done.

So if you want to get things done, you positively have to understand at any given point in time what is the most important thing to get done *right now* and if you're not doing it, you're not making progress at the fastest possible rate.

Slowly, I'm weaning myself off of my tendency to procrastinate. I'm doing this by letting less important things go undone. There's some nice lady from the insurance company who has been pestering me for two months to get some data she needs to renew our policy, and I didn't actually get her the data until she asked about the fiftieth time, along with a stern warning that our insurance is going to expire in three days. And this is a good thing, I think. I've grown to think that keeping your desk clean is actually probably a sign that you're not being effective.

How's *that* for a mortifying thought!

So don't do features based on what the sales force has inadvertently promised a single customer, and don't do unimportant-slash-fun features first because "you're going to have to do them eventually anyway."

Anyway, back on the topic of choosing features for FogBugz 5.0. Here's how we got our initial prioritization.

First, I took a stack of 5×8 cards, and wrote a feature on each one. Then I called the team together. In my experience, this works with up to about twenty people, and it's a good idea to get as many different perspectives in the room: programmers, designers, people who talk to customers, sales, management, documentation writers and testers, even (!) customers.

I asked everyone to bring their own list of feature ideas to the meeting, too. The first part of the meeting was going over each feature very, very quickly and making sure we had a very, very rough common understanding of what the feature was, and that each feature had a card.

At this stage, the idea was not to debate any feature on its merits, or to design the feature, or even to discuss the feature: just to have a vague, rough idea of what it was. Some of the features for FogBugz 5.0 were things like

- Personalizable home page
- Painless software schedules
- Track billable time
- Fork a bug
- (Forty-six others . . .)

Very vague stuff. Remember, we didn't need to know at this point how each feature would be implemented, or what it involved, because our only goal was getting a rough prioritization that could be used as the basis to start development. This got us a list of about fifty big features.

In part two, we went through all of the features, and everybody voted on each feature: just a quick "thumbs up" or "thumbs down." No discussion, no nothing: just a real quick thumbs up or thumbs down on each feature. This revealed that about fourteen of the feature ideas didn't have much support. I threw out all the features that only got one or two votes, leaving us with thirty-six potential features.

Next, we assigned costs for each of these features, on a scale of 1 to 10, where 1 was a quicky feature and 10 was a big monster feature. Here it's important to remember that the goal was *not* to schedule the features, just to separate the tiny features from the medium features from the huge features. I just went through each of the features and asked the developers to call out "small," "medium," or "large." Even without knowing how long a feature is going to take, it's easy to see that "forking a bug" is a "small" feature while the big, vague "personalizable home page" feature was large. Based on the consensus estimate of costs and my own judgment, we put down prices on all the features:

	Cost:
Personalizable home page	$10
Painless software schedules	$4
Track billable time	$5
Fork a bug	$1

Once again, it's really messy, it's not exact, and it doesn't matter. You're not making a schedule today: you're just prioritizing. The only thing that you have to get approximately right is the vague idea that you could do two medium features or one large feature or ten small features in about the same amount of time. *It doesn't have to be accurate.*

The next step was making a menu of all thirty-six proposed features and their "costs." Everybody on the team got a copy of the menu and was given $50 to play with. They could allocate their money any way they wanted, but they only had $50 to spend. They could buy half-features, if they wanted, or buy double features. Someone who really liked that "track billable time" feature could spend $10 or $15 on it; someone who liked it a little might only spend $1 and hope that enough other people funded it.

Next, we added up how much everyone spent on each feature:

	Cost:	Spent:
Personalizable home page	$10	$12
Painless software schedules	$4	$6
Track billable time	$5	$5
Fork a bug	$1	$3

Finally I divided the amount spent by the cost:

	Cost:	Spent:	
Personalizable home page	$10	$12	1.2
Painless software schedules	$4	$6	1.5
Track billable time	$5	$5	1.0
Fork a bug	$1	$3	3.0

And then sorted by this number to find the most popular features:

	Cost:	Spent:	
Fork a bug	$1	$3	3.0
Painless software schedules	$4	$6	1.5
Personalizable home page	$10	$12	1.2
Track billable time	$5	$5	1.0

Ta-da! A list of all the features you might want to do, in rough order of everyone's best idea of which features are the most important.

And now you can start to refine. You can clump together features that naturally belong together, for example, doing software schedules makes billable time easier, so maybe we should either do both or neither. And sometimes looking down the prioritized list, it's just real obvious that something is messed up. So, you change it! Nothing is carved in stone. You can even change the prioritization as you go through development.

But what surprised me the most is that the final list we produced was really a very good prioritization for FogBugz 5.0 and really did reflect our collective consensus about the relative priorities of various features.

Priority list in hand, we set out to more or less work down the list in order until about March, when we plan to stop adding new features and start the integration and testing phase. We'll write specs for each (nonobvious) feature right before implementing that feature.

(The nattering scorekeepers of the BDUF/Agile beauty contest are now thoroughly confused. "Was that a vote for BDUF? Or Agile? What does he *want? Can't he just take* sides *for once*?!")

The whole planning process took three hours.

If you're lucky enough to have the ability to release software more frequently than we do, (see Chapter 34), you still need to work down the list in order, but you can just stop and do releases more often. The good thing about frequent releases is that you can reprioritize the list regularly based on actual customer feedback, but not every product has this luxury.

Mike Conte taught me this system during the planning of Excel 5, where it only took a couple of hours even with a couple of dozen people in a conference room. The cool thing was that roughly 50% of the features that we didn't have time to do were really stupid features, and Excel was better because it didn't have them.

It's not perfect, but it's better than going to Staples to get blue folders, I'll tell ya that.

INDEX

You Need the Companion eBook